Seeking Begumpura

THE SOCIAL VISION OF ANTICASTE INTELLECTUALS

GAIL OMVEDT

navayana

Seeking Begumpura: The Social Vision of Anticaste Intellectuals

First published in 2008. Reprinted 2011, 2016
ISBN 9788189059453

Printed and bound by Sanjiv Palliwal, New Delhi

Published by Navayana Publishing Pvt Ltd
155, Second Floor, Shahpur Jat, New Delhi 110049
www.navayana.org
Follow us on facebook.com/navayana

Contents

Preface

This book is the product of five years of research and writing as a Senior Fellow at the Nehru Memorial Museum and Library (NMML), New Delhi. I owe thanks for his unstinting support to Dr O.J. Kejariwal, who was Director for most of that period, and to Dr Mridula Mukherjee, who became Director towards the very end, to Dr Balakrishnan and to all the fellows and staff of NMML whose cooperation and company made my tenure there enjoyable.

I began my stay in Delhi living with a family in Vasant Kunj, then discovered an old friend, Sunil Sardar, now settled in South Extension and a leader of the 'Truthseekers' (Satyashodhak) movement. Sunil, Shivkumar, Bhaskar and others of the movement provided moral and other kinds of support for my research and writing, introducing me to Kabir and to other crucial figures of North Indian anticaste movements. I would like to thank all of them for their help, as well as Braj Mani for his contributions to the 'debrahmanisation' of history, to the path-breaking work of G. Aloysius on Iyothee Thass and the

Tamil movement, and for exposing the meaning of 'nationalism without a nation' in India. I owe thanks to Mangesh Dahiwale, Priyadarshi and other friends at Vasant Kunj, and elsewhere in Delhi and Pune. I thank especially for his help in translation from the Marathi and his all-around support, my husband Bharat Patankar. Gauri De, Aloysius and Josna Jacob supplied help in translation. I thank S. Anand of Navayana for help in editing and rewriting many sections of the book. For the sections on Tamilnadu, I owe thanks to Ravikumar.

This book is dedicated to my life companion, Bharat Patankar.

22 January 2008
Pune

Introduction
Visions

This is a study of the socioeconomic perspectives of the leading anticaste intellectuals over a period of five centuries, from the 'early modern' period of the fifteenth to seventeenth centuries to the end of colonial rule. It focuses on the framework of their perspectives, their visions, their 'utopias'. In fact, the first formulation of an Indian version of utopia comes not from elite literature, but from one of the anticaste intellectuals with a mass following. The bhakti radical, Sant Ravidas (c. 1450–1520), was the first to formulate an Indian version of utopia in his song "Begumpura". Begumpura, the 'city without sorrow', is a casteless, classless society; a modern society, one without a mention of temples; an urban society as contrasted with Gandhi's village utopia of *Ram Rajya*. "Begumpura" describes a land with no taxes, toil or harassment, where there is no hierarchy but all are equal. Finally, calling himself a 'tanner now set free' he proclaims that he wanders freely with his friends: the right to walk anywhere in a settlement, city or village, is a unique matter for dalits.

During this long period of five centuries covered by this study, India entered the modern era, first on more or less equal terms and in exchange with Europe, then as a colonized and subject country. It was a period of turmoil, of growth, of the formation of new ideas. Elite intellectuals sought to absorb challenges from the class-caste subalterns, developing their vision of India, which took multiple forms: the 'hard *hindutva*' of Savarkar which saw India as basically a Hindu nation, the 'soft hindutva' of Gandhi which looked to an idealized Ram Rajya as a goal, the mild socialism of Nehru, and the harder leftism of the communists. During the same period, the subalterns put forward their vision and their goals, within the framework of a unique utopia first conceived by Ravidas and other radical sants.

We shall look at the development of this utopian vision and the socioeconomic characteristics of the society envisioned through this long period. The first four chapters will cover the leading sants of the radical bhakti movement—Namdev and his contemporary bhakti sants, Chokhamela, Janabai, Nirmala, Soyra, Banka and Gora Kumbhar; Kabir, Ravidas, and finally Tukaram. Then we look at the main theorists of the early colonial period—Jotirao Phule and Pandit Iyothee Thass and other leaders of his 'Sakya Buddhist' movement. Pandita Ramabai is an important transitional figure, one who actually sought to establish a utopian community of women. Finally, we look at Periyar E.V. Ramasamy and Dr B.R. Ambedkar, who brought these visions to a climax in debates with marxism, gandhism and other forms of nationalism.

The Contradictions of Modernity: Class, Caste and Utopias

'India is shining' proclaim its fans. It was a slogan that failed to move the broader sections of the electorate. The fact is that while superhighways begin to link the country's great urban complexes, thousands of farmers are committing suicide in places like Vidarbha, a backward region of the industrialized state of Maharashtra. The 'me generation' celebrates high rises in salaries for well-trained professionals, while the poor of the oppressed castes scrabble for jobs. Airports become too small to hold the burgeoning airlines and flights, cities too crowded to hold the growing number of cars, while bullock carts continue to ply country roads. Huge high-rises hide the slums below. And privileged-caste killers of bargirls, who wait on men of high society, walk away free from the courts, while their rural counterparts get away with cruel atrocities on dalits.

Modernity is riven with contradictions. Class, race and patriarchy underline the brutalities and achievements of capitalist industrialization, and amid the luxuries of advanced production and the mystic of information technology come clashes of ethnic groups, the sound of missiles, and the fear and reality of war. Every country experiences such contradictions, yet India, as it takes its place in the third millennia modern era, seems to have more than its share.

In marxist terms, contradictions are explained by the nature of capitalist modernity as the stage just before socialism. The rapid growth of the forces of production induced by capitalism has done its work; prosperity is seen as achievable, and can hardly be hidden from the producers of society. Here the main contradiction is between the socialized character of productive forces, the tremendous promise of technology, and the reality of private control and unbridled competition. Socialism, the attainment of a collective human control over all of this, will resolve these contradictions. But as Ambedkar remarked in his "Buddha and Karl Marx" (1987, vol. 3, 444), and as is increasingly clear in the twenty-first century, history has been hard on Marx's predictions: the proletariat instead of becoming immiserated and uniting to destroy the old society and usher in the new, is itself drastically divided. Ambedkar's solution was to attack and level, or annihilate, what marxists called the 'superstructure' – the complex edifice of caste oppression in India – as a necessary prelude to achieving a democratic socialist society.

Indian modernity is marked, naxalites would say, with 'semi-feudal and semi-colonial remnants'. In more modern terms, the presence and power of the West, especially the United States, remain a reality, and even more, the presence and power of caste continue. This defines the contradictions—a rapid rate of growth and 'India shining' for some; drought, hunger, farmer suicides and atrocities on dalits and women for others. Men, women and children are attacked and murdered for going ahead of caste Hindus in processions, for claiming humanity, and because of an assumption that they might have killed a cow. The Other Backward Classes (OBCs) continue to remain next to the bottom economically, lacking pride, and beset with their own caste prejudices. With all of this, India remains one of the poorest societies in the world, even with its supposedly luminescent growth rate.

Such contradictions of modernity have not led the exploited and oppressed into acquiescence; rather there has been struggle, marked by a vision of a better society, marked by utopias. Utopias are given birth to by the contradictions of modernity, and they involve both what we may call 'reason' and 'ecstasy'. Ecstasy arises because of the hope and fervent emotion aroused by the possibility of a utopian society, a society of equality and love. Reason defines the road to utopia; it analyzes the current situation of society and shows the strategy needed to realize a better one. Utopias have existed throughout the long centuries of entering into modernity, but with some changes. In the initial period, with the promise of a better society very distant, ecstasy is dominant. But gradually, as the outlines of the situation become clear, reason takes an equal place, and the actors seeking utopia begin to grapple with the actualities of realizing it.

They are utopias, not simply fantasies, because they have a foothold in reality and yet contradict the uglier aspects of reality. They have existed for the centuries in which modernity has been coming into existence, promising a new world that is seen as both possible and necessary: possible because of economic growth and the rise of oppressed classes whose struggles are marked by a new consciousness, a new awareness and education; necessary because of the daily denial of such a consciousness of hope by the brutalities of actual life. Utopias exist because the promise and a partial, fragmented reality of a prosperous society exist in the productive possibilities of the present, promising ecstasies of living in this world—but not allowing them to be realized. In an era where they can only foreshadow a distant future, utopias provide hope and even ecstasy for the masses. Once, however, the realization becomes possible, reason can be used to delineate the path towards the achievement of such utopias. Thus, utopias in the modern age unite reason and ecstasy, giving inspiration and outlining a path for the creation of the new society, achieving the utopian existence in which ecstasy is made real. Both ecstasy and reason will be recurring themes in this monograph.

In India, utopias have been posed for centuries by the radical anticaste intellectuals coming from dalit and bahujan (former untouchable, former sudra) backgrounds. They can be traced from the early modern period of the bhakti movement, when they were only hints of a future, to the more determinate forms guiding the struggles under colonialism. The inchoate or determined forms of utopias have thus depended on the situation of the time; as modern developments increased, the new society seemed to become more and more one to struggle for, one with specific outlines.

This monograph will give a survey of their development as they have been formulated to frame the socioeconomic vision of anticaste intellectuals from the 'early modern' period of the fifteenth to seventeenth centuries to the end of the colonial period.

'Imagining India': Utopias and Indian traditions

Thomas More's *The Best State of a Commonwealth and the New Island of Utopia*, published in several editions supervised by the author between 1516 and 1518, gave its name to a tradition. More's imagining of an ideal society of 'Christian communism' (xv) was an expression of sixteenth century Renaissance humanism which had promised a more balanced modernity – one uniting reason with emotion, universalism with concern for the particular and its diversities – than what actually came to exist after the advent of a more imperialistic and violent Europe. Strikingly, More's Utopia was envisioned as a society of the 'new world', the still-mysterious continent lying to the west of Europe, later to be plundered, but imagined also as full of wealth and noble humanity. This also indicated a non-Orientalist admiration of the non-European 'Other' as a society that could offer hope to a Europe fallen into a morass of corruption, murderous political onslaughts, warfare, and stark inequalities leading to petty crime and brutal punishments, enclosures that threw thousands off the land and into destitution as a prelude to industrialized agriculture. All of these, according to More, were a result of private property, and his Utopia promised both equality and collective ownership.

As Stephen Toulmin (1990) has argued in his fascinating study, More's 'Erasmian' vision of human ability to achieve a just society was cut off by the brutalities of political assassination and war, among the very phenomenon that More had brought to the fore as the antithesis of Utopia. Europe in the end entered a full-fledged modernity under the aegis of imperialism, just as India was later to experience a forced push into modernity as a colonized land. Utopian promises, which had marked the initial hopeful thrust of the global age at the beginning of the 'early modern' period, failed in both continents. Yet *Utopia* and its continual recreations are reminders that they existed.

In the later brutalities of capitalist industrialization, Marx was scornful about 'utopian socialism' for placing communism in the realm of ideas and fantasy, and giving no clear analysis that would ground the fight for socialism. His own 'scientific socialism', he and his followers believed, had in contrast the solid foundation of an inevitable march of history in which the gravedigger of capitalism, the proletariat, was thrown up by the dynamics of capitalism itself. Yet the original Utopia did make a claim to being realizable by positing itself as actually existing, and history has not been so kind to Marx either. The proletariat at a world level and in advanced capitalist societies has remained divided, one large section coopted into an alliance with its own ruling classes under the rubric of nationalism, other sections still bedazzled by religion, yet other sections too impoverished to think beyond survival. In practice marxian communism has also functioned as a utopia, motivating millions throughout the world but with sometimes questionable results, whether in Stalin's Russia or Mao's China or in the smaller brutalities exercised by communists in partial power elsewhere.

Karl Mannheim tried to deal with the ambivalent but necessary role of utopias in *Ideology and Utopia* (1936), written originally in German in 1929 from a marxist sociological perspective. There he argued that while both 'ideologies' and 'utopias' had emerged from a political struggle of different social groups (classes), the difference was that where ideologies reflect the interests of ruling groups and so obscure realities in order to stabilize society, "certain oppressed groups are intellectually so strongly interested in the destruction and transformation of a given condition of society that they unwittingly see only those elements in the society which tend to negate it" (1936, 40). Thus the utopian mentality is also, at some level, unrealistic. The difference is nevertheless important. Utopianism is necessary for action leading to transformation; if utopianism is lost, "man would lose his will to shape history and his ability to understand it" (263). Here, almost in spite of himself, the historical-materialist Mannheim admits the sociological necessity of ideas and the 'ideal interests' that Weber had stressed.

Utopias, the posing of alternatives, remain a crucial aspect of any struggle; they are, in other terms, the part of social movement discourses or frames that inspire people to action by uniting ideals with an analysis that makes a claim to possible realization. They unite ecstasy and reason, projecting a future that is achievable by present action. It is interesting that much of postmodernist theory rejects utopias as part of a presumed modernist arrogance; post-modernism rather celebrates the diversities of fragmentation and its acceptance but in so doing ignores inequalities and injustices, and efforts to move beyond them (see, for instance, Norgaard 1994).

This celebration of diversity and refusal to pose 'absolutes' can be simply a justification for relying on oppressive 'diverse' traditions or the continuation of existing inequalities of capitalist society. As Vasant Kaiwar points out, in an analysis of one of the well-known Indian postmodernists, "All [of Dipesh Chakrabarty's] stock critiques of historicism and metanarratives, of Marx's myopia about difference, the advocacy of fragments, different ways of being-in-the-world are so many codes for rejecting the Utopian imagination and transformative praxis" (2005, 3738). Postmodernism in fact harks back to premodern romanticism in that it locates whatever ecstasy is possible in the present, banning the future and efforts to move forward to it as oppressive grand narratives, making 'Enlightenment reason' into a curse. It is not surprising that Gandhi is appropriated by postmodernists; he was the symbol of the romanticization of the past in India, as we shall see.

Utopias are projected visions, sometimes imagined in the past, sometimes located in a different world, sometimes inscribed in the future possibility. But they all lay a claim to some kind of reality, the reality of being *possible*, and in so doing provide the motivation for efforts at social transformation. The 'heavenly city' or the glorious life projected in religious traditions is brought down to earth, and posed as inspiration for living and possible action before oppressed human beings. They represent a combination of ecstasy and reason – the two pervading themes of this study – because they envision a society of abundance and enjoyment, and at the same time project through the understanding of history and its forces the way to achieve such a society through reason-guided action.

It is a striking fact that in India we can see the emergence of utopias at almost the same time as in Europe. But these are found at a lower level of society (as contrasted with the high intellectual Thomas More, writing in Latin). Utopias were not available in Sanskrit. Rather they are found in the visions of dalit-bahujan intellectuals of the radical bhakti movement of the fifteenth to seventeenth centuries. These are not so elaborated as in Europe, but that is in part due to the lack of documentation of mass activities and the fact that there were very few among the more literate elites who could move beyond the sanskritized and brahmanic perspectives that militated against visions of equality.

Such utopias were presaged in the universalistic religions of Christianity, Islam and Buddhism. These religions envisaged a 'Kingdom of God', a 'heavenly city' placed beyond the world. However, in crucial ways they saw the working out of human destiny within this world, and sought to fashion this world in ways that could correspond to the heavenly vision. This would be achieved through divine intervention, usually a 'last judgment'. Once, however, industrialization and modernity posed the possibilities of a more just and wealthy society, these heavenly visions laid the ground for envisaging utopias that were more secular and achievable on the earth.

Brahmanism offered no such vision of equality or a just society for all; rather, its 'golden age' was the first yuga or era when varnashrama dharma was truly practised, sacrifices took place, and 'pure' men (the brahmans) united with the gods. History fell from this, passing through degenerative periods until the *kaliyuga* or 'dark age' was reached. Brahmanism has envisaged this as the historically existing society, while its historical 'renewal' was seen as only a repetition. Countless, endless cycles are imagined, which humans also go through in the process of reincarnation. 'Salvation' or *mukti* was seen as attainable outside this world of maya or illusion. A monism was postulated; it was said that the individual could attain a realization of his or her unity with the whole, that the individual self or *atman* was equivalent to this whole, or brahman. But this was seen in terms of an abstract, reified self, quite different from the empirical individual. Thus, monism with its universal identity was quite consistent with extreme discrimination and hierarchy at the empirical level because there was no clear linkage between brahman/atman and empirical reality. In the famous dialogues of Yagnavalkya with Maitreyi in the upanishads, there is almost a denial of love for the actual, empirical other (for a discussion, see Omvedt 1994, 40–42). The 'self' or atman is beyond this empirical world.

Buddhism also maintained a cyclical view; but it posited the original 'utopia' as a society of equalitarianism, even communism, and the emphasis was on seeking transformation of the individual; there was constant stress on the efforts of the empirical self. Though human improvement was at first seen on an individualistic level, with Mahayana Buddhism an element of 'collectivity' was added through the vision of the Boddhisatta that allowed the transfer of merit. This in turn led to the vision of a *Sukkavati*, a land of joy in which all were designed to be liberated; Sukkavati was the creation of a Boddhisatta, but like the Christian heavenly city it was available to all through grace. Therefore, like the heavenly Jerusalem, it had some potential for leading to the vision of an earthly Jerusalem.

For example, in an article on Mongolia, Bulag (1997) argues that the development of Buddhism after the sixteenth century in Mongolia was similar to Renaissance initiatives in Europe. The Mongol Khans took an initiative to 'spread the doctrine like the sun' and while this Buddhist Mongolian metanarrative was oppressive (also like the Renaissance) because it suppressed the counter-narratives of the shamans, destroying them physically, its positive feature was the leading to a vision of empirical transformation. This Bulag argues, in terms of the Buddhist notion of time, where "everybody was governed by two notions of time: the so-called cyclical time of karma and linear time. But karma can only be improved in linear time, it is a gradual, cumulative process" (1997, 63). Bulag then describes how the Mongolian reformer Dorjiev, around 1926 (about the time of Ambedkar), was arguing that the Buddhist doctrine is largely compatible with the communist tradition. Here is a striking example of the degree to which 'modernization' was a worldwide process in which similar trends could be seen in different parts of the world. But what was possible with Buddhism was not so possible within brahmanism. Interestingly, Bulag contrasts Buddhism with Confucianism, which played a role in the East Asian world similar to that of brahmanism in India.

Islam played a similar role in India; creating a just society had also been a goal; *darul-ul-islam* was continually sidetracked historically and interpreted in terms of fundamentalism and repressive laws. Nevertheless it functioned at crucial points in providing a vision, as we shall see in the discussion of Pakistan (in chapter 10), which was, in the thinking of its main founders, Jinnah and Iqbal, a modernistic, democratic society.

In this thesis we will deal with intellectual activists and leaders of the subaltern castes, who in some ways all envisioned an earthly utopia, and sought to use reason to achieve it, not just enjoying an ecstasy of religious devotion. In imagining utopias, they drew on nonbrahmanic, nonbrahman traditions, including Buddhism and certain versions of Saivism, rejecting the ritualism and the inequalities of traditional, elite thinking. In the early modern period, for the radical bhakti sants, this utopia was not so fully worked out; however Ravidas envisaged 'Begumpura', the city without sorrow, without taxes or toil, where he could wander freely with his friends—something a dalit could never do in the actual Banaras. Tukaram talked of Pandharpur as the city where even the headman was made to toil, where time and death 'had no entry', where people went dancing to mingle with each other. Kabir sang of Amrapur, the city of immortality, or of Premnagar, the city of love. These were foreseeings; during the early modern period these subaltern intellectuals had no access to a language of reason and analysis, to a study of history; they were forced to work within and subvert the basically brahmanic religious framework that was hegemonic. Their 'ecstasy' of utopia was envisaged in some timeless place.

This was, however, a beginning and a vision that served to inspire many. Later, during the colonial period, such visions were given a more definite embodiment, as ecstasy was (in our terminology) linked to reason. Leaders from Jotirao Phule to Iyothee Thass and Ambedkar analyzed the roots of current exploitation in the past and sought to outline a way to end it. They drew their inspiration from a dissenting religious imagination, rejecting brahmanic Hinduism for Buddhism,

Christianity, a universalistic monotheism, even an atheism as in the case of Periyar. Their imaginings of a new society accepted technological progress as an important basis for prosperity; they rejected the village for the city, just as in the early modern period the radical sants had envisaged a city of love and sorrowlessness. The metaphors they used and the traditions they evoked were in sharp contrast to the gandhian reading which relied on the *Gita* and enscribed a Ram Rajya with its stabilized, harmonic and hierarchical idealized village on the national consciousness, just as the identification with the indigenous 'non-Aryan' inhabitants contrasted with the elite identification as Aryans.

Methodological Issues

This research has broadened in two major ways since its beginning. Earlier I was to focus on the socioeconomic perspectives of the anticaste movement, taking the 'colonial modern' period from roughly the middle of the eighteenth century to independence. This would include figures such as B.R. Ambedkar, Jotirao Phule and Periyar, but I also wanted to examine the development of such thinking among the anticaste movement's activists as a whole.

Two developments made me broaden the focus. As I was beginning to translate Tukaram and engage with bhakti, it was becoming clear to me that there was a strong strain of radicalism here that had been ignored by the more well-known scholars (see for example "Introduction" to Tukaram by Chitre 1991, and More 1996). Tukaram, and later Kabir anticipated 'modern' themes in many respects—above all equalitarianism and an insistence on experience. At the same time, I began to realize that economists and historians (such as Subrahmanyam and Richards) were beginning to talk of an 'early modern' period beginning in the fifteenth century or so. It would be incorrect, in other words, to see 'modernity' as solely a colonially induced phenomenon. There were interesting parallels and interactions between Europe and India much earlier than that, and a shared history. These included fights against priestly dominance, the beginnings of scientific enquiry, political themes of equality and democratic participation—and the expression of utopian imaginings. In India, as in Europe, these themes emerged, expressed in many ways by the radical sants of the bhakti movement, who represented early modern anticaste movements that dated some centuries before colonialism.

My work, therefore, looks at a specific trend of intellectual thought in India; it touches on the salient aspects of the vision and thought of some of the important 'organic intellectuals' emerging from the dalit-bahujan masses over a period of roughly five centuries.

Any study is taken from a particular perspective, with a methodological framework. My methodological premise can be stated simply: there are conflicts and contradictions in society; these conflicts and contradictions have a material foundation in the socioeconomic relations of production; they appear at the ideological and ideational levels also, not simply as a reflection of the 'material base' but with relative independence. However social scientists or historians may define 'society', it cannot be assumed to be a tightly integrated whole. All societies contain elements that are in contradiction with one another, as well as elements that are disparate.

I also hold that these conflicts and contradictions in any social formation are shaped not simply by 'class' or economic factors but also by nonclass factors such as gender, religion, race or other ethnic identities. In South Asia, for 3,500 years the shaping of these conflicts and contradictions has been heavily structured by caste (at the 'material' level of relations of production) and brahmanism (at the ideological level). This social structure of brahmanism/caste has had a complex history in the subcontinent.

Caste was apparently unknown in the earliest civilization in India, the Harappan, and was only foreshadowed in the Vedic period. Brahmanism, defined in terms of *varnashrama dharma*, was comparatively a latecomer. It emerged as a full-fledged ideology around the middle of the first millennium BCE, struggled with Buddhism and other *samanic*[1] ideological systems for over a thousand years, and became hegemonic in the major part of the subcontinent only from about the fifth and sixth centuries of the common era. Brahmanism as ideology and social structure also confronted, from the eighth century onward, Islamic religious and social thought that became a powerful force through almost the entire country. At the same time, the defeated Buddhism survived as a dominated ideological system for much longer, while Christianity was an influence in parts of the subcontinent perhaps from the first century onwards, and certainly from the sixteenth century. Popular religious movements, including radical Saivism and some forms of bhakti, struggled against this brahmanic domination from very early.

From about the time of the broad period of 'modernity' in India – stimulated by Islam and the subaltern, subterranean movements of Buddhism (now mainly in tantric forms), Sufism and radical Saivism – radical bhakti movements can be clearly traced. During the fifteenth to seventeenth centuries, in what social scientists and historians are increasingly describing as an 'early modern' period, these movements flourished in almost every region of India. The late seventeenth and eighteenth centuries can be identified as a period of setback for the movements, for after a long struggle their radical edge was blunted, and the

[1] Samanic is the non-sanskritic spelling for what is corrupted as *shramanic* and *sramanic* in brahmanic literature. Samana refers to the nonbrahman seers and wandering ascetics of the Jain, Buddhist and Ajivaka religions. While *sramana* in Sanskrit means "one who exerts himself and performs religious austerities," Buddhist commentaries associate the word *samana* with the 'quieting' (*samita*) of evil (*papa*). According to *Dhammapada* (verse 265), "someone who has pacified evil is called *samana*."

processes of brahmanic cooptation became dominant. This was precisely the time when the formation of new 'nationalities' – or patriotisms, as Bayly (1998) would have it – replaced the 'imperial' claims of the Mughals. Thus, for example, the rising Maratha powers and their regional expressions (those states that grew under the sardars of the Peshwas) were thoroughly brahmanic; while even the new Sikh power under Ranjit Singh saw the consolidation of a conservative form of Sikhism that allowed untouchability to continue.

The colonial period saw even more complex processes. Up to perhaps the late eighteenth century, the varying regions of India had been more or less at an equal level with Europe; but colonialism meant that the decisive entry into full modernity was made under the domination of an alien power. This did not mean that Indians lacked agency in the shaping of the new world; as scholars are increasingly emphasizing, not only did they participate in the formation of what we know today as 'Hindu' culture, the experience of colonialism influenced Britain too (see, for instance, Pennington 2005). However, it warped intellectual as well as economic development. In many ways colonialism helped the brahmanic elite to consolidate itself even as it gave new scope – through education – to subaltern groups. This elite responded to colonialism with the updating of brahmanism, now known as 'Hinduism'; and with its inscription into nationalism, 'Hindu nationalism' was born. At the same time, the response of the subalterns took on new and modern forms.

Thus the framework used in this monograph approaches what many in Maharashtra are calling a 'Marx-Phule-Ambedkarite' methodological perspective. Sociologically, it is broadly speaking a weberian framework. Weber had argued, in a classic formulation, that while economic (material) forces were crucial, ideologies also exerted influence, especially at certain crucial periods of history in determining the future of society (Weber 1904–05, 1996 edition). This is thus a study in 'subaltern' social thought, but it needs to be stressed that 'subalterns' in India have to be defined not simply in 'class' or economic terms, but also in caste terms. Thus, in the conflict against the dominant brahmanic ideologies, we can identify the intellectuals from the subordinated masses primarily in caste terms—they are identified in the literature primarily in this way. While a few members of these subordinated groups may have been relatively more upwardly mobile in economic terms – Tukaram was a mahajan, a moneylender as well as a farmer; Phule was a contractor, a position he shared with many from privileged castes; Ambedkar became a relatively successful lawyer and was no 'ordinary' untouchable – their lives were still marked by the experiences of caste discrimination, and they very often either started from or remained much more subordinated in 'class' terms than most *dwija* castes.

Anticaste: Radical *Bhakti* and Nonbrahman Movements

This study, then, looks at the socioeconomic thinking of leaders of anticaste movements over a period of five centuries, from about the fifteenth century to 1956. It analyzes the movements in two main stages. The first was the early modern period from about 1500 to 1750, when radical sants pioneered a strong form of a devotional movement with a vision of equality, an emphasis on empirical thinking, and access to ecstasy for all. The second phase began with colonialism, when full-fledged modernity came to India and anticaste intellectuals had to form their own vision in confrontation with the developing 'Hindu nationalism' of the elite. This, in turn, had two phases, the first up to about 1920 when the focus was on analysis of historical and current subjugation, and the second from the 1920s onward when leaders like Periyar and Ambedkar focused on the coming of a new independence, and in dealing with marxism, gandhism and the developing movement for Pakistan among Muslims.

The study of anticaste movements (the nonbrahman movement, the dalit movement) as social movements is now well established in India. What is not so clear is why what I call 'radical bhakti' should be considered a social movement. Most social movement theory takes it for granted that social movements are the phenomenon of 'modernity', but without giving much justification for this and without clearly defining the periodization of 'modernity'. At the same time, studies of bhakti often refer to them as social movements, for instance, Krishna Sharma, *Bhakti and the Bhakti Movement* (1987) – which ascribes a singular form to this – and the even more influential David Lorenzen's edited collection, *Religious Movements in South Asia 600–1800* (2004). These studies see one or more 'movements' in the premodern period, without bothering to define 'movements'. In fact, by the broad definition given of social movements – for example, by Oberschall (1993) and McAdam, McCarty and Zald (1996) – there is no reason to exclude such movements.

However, the question, what constitutes a 'movement', remains. That is, when should we speak of 'one' bhakti movement or 'many' and over what territory and time span? Social movements are, after all, delimited phenomena including action, and not simply expressions of a timeless essence. Among other criteria, they assume some kind of interaction between the various agents involved.

I would argue that such a process of interaction existed for the movement of 'radical bhakti' I am referring to, covering an area ranging from Maharashtra (the Varkaris) to northern India. This was one of many such movements in the same period; others included, for example, the Virasaivas in what is now Karnataka and Andhra, Sikhism which came to centre in the northwest, Vaishnavite movements in eastern India (the

Oriya and Bengali-speaking areas) and so on.[2] The sants of the western and northern circuit knew of each other, yet were cut off from similar movements in south India. This particular bhakti movement, which has its beginnings in the thirteenth and fourteenth centuries, can be said to be the first phase of the broad anticaste movement of 'modern' times in India. From this period, I discuss here Namdev, Janabai, Kabir and Tukaram.

The second phase took place in the early 'colonial yuga' (1850–1930). Here I discuss Phule, Iyothee Thass and (Pandita) Ramabai. They undertook a search for the historical origins of caste inequality and brahmanic dominance; the intellectuals of the movement asked most strongly 'Where do we come from?' With the new input from European intellectuals – missionaries, besides rationalists and scientists of various kinds, being most important – this question could be and was asked. It was often answered in terms derived from the discourse of Europeans (for instance, the Aryan theory) but the anticaste intellectuals used these in their own way.

The third phase begins in the 1920s, and took place in the context not only of a strong Indian nationalist movement under the hegemony of Gandhi, but also, perhaps even more importantly, of grappling with marxism. Marxist and socialist ideology was making its entrance in a big way and had a major intellectual influence on Indian intellectuals far beyond the limited reach of communists and socialists—simply because it posed in its terms utopia as an earthly utopia (the communist society, following on the original 'primitive communism' and intervening period of suffering

---

[2] I am not discussing here the earliest 'bhakti' movement in Tamilnadu, dating from the seventh to eighth century CE. The historical context was very different – the movement was associated with the persecution Jains and Buddhists – and the equalitarianism was perhaps more questionable. There is no historical evidence to back up the thesis that all bhakti movements originated from this one.

and exploitation through slavery, feudalism and capitalism). As anticaste intellectuals grappled with these issues – thrown up by marxists, nationalists who borrowed mostly the Hindu/ hindutva identity, and Muslims who were increasingly seen as constituting a separate 'community', 'samaj'or 'nation' – they formulated anew their own utopia, which differed from that of the marxists primarily in emphasizing that the end of caste oppression and exploitation must go along with the end of class oppression and exploitation.

It has long been my thesis that the nonbrahman/anticaste movement represented the true Enlightenment in India, that it expressed most strongly the values of democracy, equality, the use of rationality/reason, the notion of progress (see Omvedt, 2005; also Meera Nanda (2002, 2004)). In this work I shall show that visions of utopia provided a motivating power for the anticaste movement from the time of Namdev and Kabir through Ambedkar's version of Buddhism as 'reconstructing the world'. In the period of the radical bhakti movement the vision lacked an earthly grounding, but from the eighteenth century onwards, which was the colonial period in India (a period of 'modernization' throughout the world), old religious utopias of bhakti, Christianity, Islam, etc, were brought down to earth and given a historical embodiment. As utopias, they shared a vision with marxism – in spite of marxism's claim to be anti-utopian and its scorn for 'utopian socialism', marxism in fact motivated millions of activists and working people throughout the world with a semi-religious vision of a socialist society – but they differed from marxism in stressing the aspect of the ending or annihilation of caste.

Inventing and Reinventing India: The Subaltern Vision

Finally, the discussion of India's sociopolitical situation today very often focuses around the issues of communalism, on the one hand, and that of the assertion of the dalits and OBCs on the other. Few, however, have taken the theories and utopias (in Mannheim's sense) of the anticaste challenge seriously enough to influence their analysis. This is true not only of the sophisticated intellectual critics of secularism such as T.N. Madan, Partha Chatterjee and Ashis Nandy, but also of many of the more marxist defenders of secular and democratic ideals. Among these is a well-argued study by Stuart Corbridge and John Harris, *Reinventing India: Liberalization, Hindu Nationalism and Popular Democracy* (2000), who conclude by saying, "We agree with Paul Brass that the defining struggle in Indian politics is between the centralizing instincts of the BJP and the Hindu nationalists... and the countervailing forces ...of caste mobilization in general" (238) but then disagree with Brass's emphasis on the particular needs and claims of subaltern groups defined within a regional and local context. Corbridge and Harris instead want to focus on the generalizing role of the state, and the conclusion of their study is that

> The deepening of democracy in India offers India's 'social majorities' their best hope for taking some control over the economic and political situation which governs their lives and which might yet be made to work for their empowerment. As ironic as it might seem to some critics, their attempts to reinvent India still have regard for the invention of India that was proposed in the Constituent Assembly. (239)

While this is well said, in taking the 'tall men' of the period of India's independence to be Nehru (above all), Patel, Rajendra Prasad, Lohia and other 'national' leaders, they ignore not simply the part played by Ambedkar in the Constituent Assembly but also marginalize his basic thinking. While resigning from parliament and his position as minister, not – as Corbridge and Harris seem to think – over issues of 'agricultural labourers' and nationalization of land, but over the failure to pass the

Hindu Code Bill (the first legal effort to give economic and marital equality to women), Ambedkar had warned, "To leave inequality between class and class, between sex and sex which is the soul of Hindu society untouched and to go on passing legislation relating to economic issues is to make a farce of our Constitution and to build a palace on a dung heap" (1995, vol. 14, 1: 1325).[3]

'Building a palace on a dung heap' is a striking phrase; and in pointing to the 'soul of Hindu society' Ambedkar was pointing to where the dung heap existed; and that there was moral and religious debris that had to be cleared. Ambedkar was objecting not to the practice of Hinduism, but to its ideals, to its morality. He was attacking the morality of the 'religion' that had been constructed from brahmanism, in a millennia-old process culminating in the colonial period. His political and intellectual thrust was not simply against Savarkar's 'hindutva' but against Gandhi's varnashrama-based 'Hinduism', and even Nehru—to the extent that Nehru was in his own way a kind of 'soft' apologist for traditional brahmanic Hinduism (see Alyosius' *Nationalism without a Nation in India* (1998) for a critique). These elements of ideals, vision and morality were crucial. Corbridge and Harris are right to argue that class-based politics and the dynamics of capitalism are still central to the analysis of Indian society; but they are wrong to take this in the mechanistic sense that gives no role to the moral and spiritual norms fostered in different ways by different religious traditions.

It is precisely this issue that was foregrounded in an earlier and somewhat ignored sociological interpretation of

[3] As the context makes clear, 'class' is used here the way it had been used during the British period, such as in references to 'Depressed Classes', and at the time of the Constitution to 'backward classes'. It is in fact a reference to castes as a sociological category, not a marxist one; its use emphasizes that their economic position largely reflected their social position.

India's problems. In *India: The Roots of Crisis*, Satish Saberwal attacked the 'easy agnosticism' of those who refuse to take religion seriously (1988, 247–58) and claimed that problems of communalism, caste-based politics, corruption and the erosion of moral authority – indeed we may argue the failure to establish a moral centre to many Indian social institutions – can be attributed to certain aspects of tradition. He compared the historical role in European modernity played by the Catholic Church in providing an institutional continuity (including traditions of reason in universities, common cultural traditions and a common ethics) to the lack of these in India. Neither brahmanism, nor bhakti, nor Islam, claimed Saberwal, could provide these.

Partha Chatterjee objected to this in a review, arguing that *dharma* could be seen as a 'unifying master code' (1988, 105). Saberwal responded that even on its most favourable ground, which postulated a ruler's commitment to righteous conduct, dharma had the main problem that its 'universalizing function' was incomparably weaker compared to that of Christianity in Europe because it did not legitimize a general, nonsegmented and nonsegmenting code. Dharma, according to Saberwal, was above all particularistic. "If it be the logic of cleavage between groups…which its 'shared ideas' stress, we may then speak of the constitution of society only in a weak sense" (256).

A similar point had been made in stronger language by Phule, when he wrote in his last book, *Sarvajanik Satyadharma Pustak* [The Universal Religion of Truth], that because of "the false self-interested religion of the Aryans, the cunning Arya Bhat-Brahmans consider the ignorant Shudras to be inferior; the ignorant Shudras consider the ignorant Mahars to be inferior; and the ignorant Mahars consider the ignorant Mangs to be inferior…since marriage and social relations are forbidden among them all, naturally their various customs, eating habits, and rituals don't match each other. How can such a conglomerate of 18 grains be united to become a 'nation' of integrated people?" (1991, 494). Here was not only a question of cleavage, but of scorn; with the lower groups considered ignorant and inferior. Phule and his colleagues, and after him Periyar and Ambedkar, experienced the scorn and cleavage created by brahmanism, and saw this as the main obstacle to the development of a democratic national unity.

The privileged caste leadership of the national movement, the 'tall men' discussed by Corbridge and Harris, never really contested the claims of the Hindu nationalists in their ranks; most of them were in one way or another themselves Hindu nationalists. Their mild saffron laid the basis for the persistence and later political growth of the more virulent 'Hindutva' trends. This was true even of Gandhi. Savarkar had defined hindutva by identifying the 'holy land' (*punyabhumi*) with the 'fatherland' (*pitrubhumi*), thus giving Hinduism a territorial/nationalist foundation. But when Gandhi opposed conversion by arguing that 'Hinduism' was by birth the religion of the untouchables and they should reform it rather than reject it, he was implicitly using a similar definition: in fact, he opposed conversion, even to Sikhism, more strongly than even the Hindu Mahasabha. At the same time, Gandhi's Ram Rajya expressed a stagnant, village-centred idealized version of Ram's kingdom, which ignored much of the story of the avatar Ram; but the dalits and most bahujans never forgot Shambuka, the sudra slaughtered for the 'sin' of practicing *tapascharya* (penance). This gandhian vision of Ram in crucial ways laid the foundation for the development of the harder, hindutva Ram Rajya which culminated in the massacres of Muslims in Gujarat in 2002. In turn, the marxists and the nehruvian socialists were unable to counter hard-core hindutva because they did not contest it at the level of ideals and religious morality. Their socialism was also a utopia but it ignored some of the crucial realities of Indian life.

Thus, in a larger sense, there is no need to 'reinvent' India; what has to be done is to turn to the India 'invented' by or envisioned by its dalit-bahujan intellectuals and leaders. The alternative to Ram Rajya and *Hindu Rashtra* is the *Bali Rajya* of Phule, the Begumpura of Ravidas, the *Dravidastan* of Periyar, the 'Buddhist commonwealth' of the Sakya Buddhists of Tamilnadu. These were formulated as ideals and as frameworks for specific socioeconomic policies and programmes at the same time as the privileged castes–led national movement was explicitly or implicitly looking to Ram Rajya. They had a specific developmental thrust. This included an urban orientation (as opposed to a 'nation of villages'), a need for prosperity and the industrialism that would fuel it, a sense of collectivity and the assertion of an anticaste equality. In later years they drew upon many of the ideas of socialism, but they also fought many of its aspects. Leaders like Ambedkar and Periyar were friendlier to the idea of Pakistan than the elites because they shared much of the Muslim critique of the Hindu orientation of the Congress.

In other words, this study will argue that the positions of Gandhi and Nehru – representing an implicit 'soft hindutva' and a mild socialism that ignored the realities of caste respectively – have defined India for too long. It is time to look at the dalit-bahujan alternatives in imagining India, and in formulating the utopias that can motivate and guide our struggle out of the current morass.

ii

New Message
Whispers in the Kaliyuga

khele mandiyela valvanti ghaaii

They've organized a game on the river sands
The Vaishnavas are dancing, ho!
Pride and wrath they trample underneath their feet,
at one another's feet they're falling, ho!
They dance in thunderous joyousness
singing sacred songs and names, ho!
to the dark ages challenging,
one is stronger than the other, ho! (refrain)
Sandal paste on foreheads, rosaries and garlands,
they parade themselves with pride, ho!
Cymbals and tabors, a shower of flowers,
an unparalleled festival of joy, ho!
Engrossed in music and entranced
are my simple sisters and brothers, ho!
Pandits, meditators, yogis, mahanubhavas,
all have won unequalled powers, ho!
Forgotten is the pride of varna and of caste,
each humbling himself before the next, ho!

Minds have become as pure as melted butter,
the stones themselves will melt at last, ho!
Cries of victory reach up to the sky!
The Vaishnava heroes feel their power, ho!
Tuka says, you've made an easy road
to cross the oceans of our life, ho!

(Tukaram 1973, #189)[1]

The early modern centuries (fifteenth to seventeenth) brought out in Europe new themes of democracy and an emerging modernity—emergence of ideas of citizenship in a nation that went beyond just the king's household, individualism, challenges to priestly dominance and religious literature in the vernacular, rationalism, science and empiricism.

In India these were centuries of Muslim rule, and as we shall see, this opened up certain new opportunities for mass expression. In various ways, especially for the radical sants of the bhakti movement, themes of democracy, equality, opposition to priestly power and ritualism, and emphasis on experience were expressed. Caste, however, remained strong, and among other things, hampered the kind of access to education and expression that allowed intellectuals of Europe to have some links with the masses, with technologically oriented artisans. The intellectual elite of India, primarily brahmans, remained caught in the throes of caste pride, and developments in Sanskrit stagnated (see, for instance, Pollock 2001), though Persian continued as an important means of communication.

Nevertheless they were centuries of important change, when some of the new ideas of modernism came to be seen through the radical bhakti movement. Beginning around the end of

[1] All the translations of Tuka used here and elsewhere in this study are by Gail Omvedt and Bharat Patankar. The numbering, using #, refers to the Maharashtra government edition (1973). I have given a romanized Marathi first line so that those using other editions can refer to them.

the fourteenth century, radical sants brought a new message to people across the subcontinent. It was one that renounced the old advaitic goal of moksha, or freedom from rebirth, for a religion of ecstasy in devotion, often expressed as being sought in life after life. It denounced the rituals and restrictions of brahmanism, often taking pandits as a curse, proclaimed the equality and dignity of women and men of all castes, and sang of love of a god seen not as a distant deity but as a familiar loving father (often mother–father). They brought the theme of ecstasy for all the people, collectively finding devotion and love—in dancing, in singing, in collective dining.

The sants emerged on their own. They were part of a tradition that can be called a movement, and they acknowledged their forerunners, but they had no real gurus in the brahmanic sense, though the hagiographic traditions kept giving them gurus—Ravidas and Kabir and others are made rather improbably the disciples of Ramananda (a follower of Ramanuja who came north and settled in Varanasi and is the main figure who is said to link the bhakti of north India with the southern *Bhagawata* tradition). Namdev has to be convinced (finally by the god Pandurang) to have a guru, and Tukaram finds his in a dream. Little of this has any real base in the corpus of their poetry, and in fact goes against their trend that was one of strong individual thinking and a rigorous search for truth. "Kabir puts on a gown of love and dances in the world; they shine with beauty who speak the truth with body and with mind," sings Kabir (sakhi 58). The emphasis is on truth and seeking, for it could be a theme for all of them.

Their poetry was not only in the vernacular, it was in the colloquial language of the masses, full of Prakrit forms rather than the sanskritized speech of the upper classes. It was also marked with imagery drawn from their work, from the life of production—weaving, spinning, dying, farming, trading. These were, in other words, the poets of the people.

The Dark Ages

The era prior to the modern (including the early modern) can be loosely called 'feudal'. But it would be useful to describe it in indigenous terms. Traditional brahmanic thinking had to cope with popular religions, had to absorb some elements from them as a counter to the challenge of Buddhism and other samanic faiths. One of the ways it did so was to interpret the 'way of devotion' as the form allowed to the 'weak' – to sudras and women who could not follow the hard path of brahmanic ritualism or renunciation – in the kaliyuga.

The notion of kaliyuga or 'the dark age' was for nearly two millennia in India the guiding metaphor of brahmanism for understanding the historical world. It was the fourth of the cyclical ages or yugas envisaged in a cosmology of vast expanses of time, shared with Buddhism but lacking the ethical twist and human agency given to Buddhism's notions of eras and time. In the eloquent words of the *Vishnu Purana*:

> All kings occupying the Earth in the Kaliyug will be wanting in tranquillity, strong in anger, taking pleasure at all times in lying and dishonesty, inflicting death on women, children and cows, prone to take the paltry possessions of others, with character that is mostly *tamas*, rising to power and soon falling.... People will follow the customs of others and be adulterated with them; peculiar, undisciplined barbarians will be vigorously supported by the rulers.... Money alone will confer nobility. Power will be the sole definition of virtue. Pleasure will be the only reason for marriage. Lust will be the only reason for womanhood. Falsehood will win out in disputes. Being dry of water will be the only definition of land. The sacred thread alone will distinguish Brahmins.... Boldness and arrogance will become equivalent to scholarship. Only those without wealth will show honesty. Just a bath will amount to purification, and charity will be the only virtue.... And any water hard to reach will be deemed a pilgrimage site. The pretence of greatness will be the proof of it, and powerful men with many severe faults will rule over

> all the classes on earth. Oppressed by their excessively greedy rulers, people will hide in valleys between mountains where they will gather honey, vegetables, roots, fruits, flowers and so forth. Suffering from cold, wind, heat and rain, they will put on clothes made of tree-bark and leaves. And no one will live as long as twenty-three years. Thus in the Kaliyug, humankind will be utterly destroyed. (Dimmitt and van Buitenen 1978, 41)

This theme of degeneration set the tone for the hegemonic understanding of all periods up to late 'colonial modernism' when the orthodox finally gave up the metaphor, at least officially. Until then, notions of the kaliyuga prevailed. Descriptions of the kaliyug begin Mahipati's story of the sants in *Bhaktavijaya* and appear throughout the literature of the sants themselves. A similar 'orthodox' example, a long *abhang* in the collected edition of Tuka's writings, gives a picture of what this means from an orthodox point of view. It is not an abhang by Tuka himself, rather it is signed 'Sevak Tukyachya' (servant of Tuka) and is likely the work of one of his brahman followers. This abhang depicts castes being mixed, the dreaded *varna-samkhara*. It shows the ritual practices defining the life of the privileged castes being ignored, '*homas*, obligations' being lost. Family relations, traditionally so fixed and hierarchical, are thrown into turmoil: "The son takes service from the father, treats him as slave, the mother-in-law is bonded to her son's wife … the wife treats the husband as a subject." Land revenue and service are given to infidels. Religion is brought into ruin, and part of this is the appearance of alien Islam; though "brahmakarma is above all things, people throw it away and run to Muslim shrines." With this background, the depiction of famine, the withering of crops, the death of cattle appear as a natural accompaniment to heresy in culture and social practice (Tukaram #3035).

As we shall see later, the sants' own version of this is different, and Tukaram in particular depicted the kaliyuga in much more socially radical terms, while at the same time stressing the power of the sants to overcome it. But kaliyuga is a strong metaphor, and while it was applied by the orthodox to all known eras of historical – in contrast to mythical or puranic – time, it remains a good trope for the much-debated concept of feudalism in India.

The 'medieval' period in India, beginning from roughly the middle of the first millennium, can be appropriately conceptualized as 'caste-feudalism'. There is no doubt that a major social transition took place in India around this time, expressed at religious, cultural, economic and political levels. R.S. Sharma, the major historian arguing for 'feudalism', has defended his position steadfastly throughout all the debates. Of his opponents, the most recent has been Andre Wink, who describes the period in terms of the advent of Islam in India and argued that in fact the economy gained in depth after the eighth to tenth century or so, with extension of cultivation. As he describes it:

> [I]t was the power of the kings which was decisive in the restoration of the new Brahmanic order. Brahmanism, culminating in the cults of Shiva and Vishnu under the patronage of regionally entrenched kings, with huge stone temples clustering in newly arising regional capitals which accommodated peripatetic courts, and sedentarization and settlement of nomadic or mobile groups, accompanied by agricultural intensification—this was the 'vertical' pattern which, with its more solid forms, descended on the open-ended world of the itinerant trader and the Buddhist monk. (1991, 230)

Wink and similar scholars see an economic expansion, not feudal stagnation. Some have argued for the power of 'Hindu' civilization, with Ronald Inden stressing the 'hegemonic' rulers such as the Rashtrakutas, and Sheldon Pollock writing of the 'Sanskrit Millennium', noting that it became a court and high literary language linking peoples and regimes throughout much of South and Southeast Asia.

Wink's characterization above is ambivalent: if the brahmanic order was restored, how was this 'new'? In fact, the ancient period, characterized by the hegemony of Buddhism, had seen a flourishing in political capabilities and commerce that was more than just 'itinerant' trade. With the 'new brahmanic order', the earlier empires of Asoka, Kanishka, the Guptas, and Harsha were replaced by regionally-based regimes with ill-defined boundaries that rose and fell, and struggled for hegemony as their rulers embarked on endless rounds of conquest or *digvijaya*s. If the earlier empires were 'shallow', the later ones could hardly be delineated. In the Deccan, the earlier Satavahanas yielded to a fluctuating variety of powers with ill-defined boundaries—the Chalukyas, Rashtrakutas, later the Yadava's of Deogiri, jockeying for power regionally and moving across the subcontinent. In spite of the occasional glories of these empires, archaeological data indicate a 'significant gap in occupation' in the Deccan between the fifth and thirteenth centuries: these famous dynasties left little actual record, and Dandekar raises the question whether they were actual states or rather 'warring pastoral chiefs' (2003, 85). By the time occupied sites were restored, the era of Muslim domination in India was in sway.

However, the power of brahmans in society increased at two prongs—at the local level, where they gained new control over land and the people on it as the proliferating land grants after the seventh and eighth centuries attest; and at the top where they were temple priests, administrators and legitimators of the often barbarian kings. Huge temple complexes, arising everywhere during this period, testified to the new orthodoxy and its appropriation of popular but non-Buddhist deities like Siva. It is to this era, after the defeat of Buddhism and between the eighth and twelfth centuries, that most social scientists trace the beginnings and spread of a village-based *jajmani* system.

On the whole, the period of 'the new brahmanic order' was

in many ways a retreat from an outward-reaching civilization, one that left the subcontinent vulnerable to conquerors from outside. Then came the advent of the Muslims.

Muslim Yuga

The Muslims cracked open the system in a new way. Not even the *Vishnu Purana* had predicted that 'peculiar undisciplined barbarians' would not only be favoured by rulers but themselves become the rulers. India had always known 'invaders'—the subcontinent, with its rich, lush Gangetic plains, had lured people from outside, from the mountainous inhospitable terrain of Afghanistan and beyond, throughout its history; these gradually settled as pastoralists or cultivators and produced conquerors and kings. But earlier peoples from the Hunas onward had adopted much of indigenous religious and cultural traditions, including Buddhism and Saivism, though not always brahmanic varnashrama dharma. In contrast, from the time the Arabs first arrived in Sindh and the Malabar coast, they brought with them their own religion, Islam—the desert-born faith of submission to a single rigorously conceived monotheistic god. This was a new phenomenon.

Jotirao Phule was later to hail the advent of Islam, praising it for the same reason that brahmans denied it. He described Mohammed as a "king of daring, world hero" who stood "alone before the truth" and with "the sword of fortitude in his mind... raised the flag of the creator."

> He established the book that God is one, and made humans all
> over the world as brothers....
> The majority became his disciples, so many came to Balisthan,
> they learned after coming of the Aryas' evil, they freed the
> Shudras from slavery....
> The contentiousness of Aryadharm was broken by Islam,
> people ate together without distinctions,
> Along with Mangs the Aryas were led to the mosque, one clan,

as blood brothers all.
Defeating the Kshatriyas and becoming Rajas
the Mughals freed many,
took advantage of caste differences and became great.
They took the Untouchables slowly to themselves,
shamed the Aryans all the time,
and so the Aryas are whining and yelling, like Brahma...
The Bhats praise the Aryadharma as superior,
call the Mughals tyrannous,
But say, Dada, who freed the Shudras from the Bhats' slavery
and led them to God?

The debate about despoiling temples (Eaton 2000, 94–132) is relevant here: Muslims did at times both plunder and smash them, but not so extensively as they are pictured, and as Eaton points out, attacking the main temples of 'foreign' rulers was a political act engaged in by all kings because the temples themselves were political, representing a major symbol of power and embodying a good deal of its substance. Even today they are huge accumulators of wealth.

Nevertheless, Muslim rule had major cultural, political and economic effects. First, it brought a higher level of political consolidation, culminating in the Mughal empire. At the same time, a monopoly of power for any one religion or cult was made practically impossible throughout the subcontinent. Whereas in the earlier 'feudalism' nearly all kings and feudatories enforced varnashrama dharma, there was now a real ideological plurality of power. Organized groups could always emigrate, and somewhere or another shelter might be found for religious dissidents. Even orthodox Muslim rulers were not strong enough to properly regulate the 'kafirs' or enforce the Shariat on Muslims themselves in a society largely made up of non-Muslims. There was in many ways a great social and philosophical gulf between Islam and the traditions of brahmanism (or for that matter Buddhism). Muslims often recoiled from both brahmanical social exclusiveness and the efflorescence of divine and semi-divine beings that populated the imaginative universe of people in both villages and towns. One was an affront to their social solidarity, the other to their hostility to idolatry. Nevertheless India held a fascination for them, and there emerged forms of exchange and even that coming together of diverse traditions called 'syncreticism'.

Culturally, Islam had never been so closed and fanatic as it is depicted today by anti-Muslims in the US and India. As Karen Armstrong has pointed out, Muhammad's message was seen as crowning the achievements of earlier West Asian faiths like Judaism and Christianity. Abraham, Moses and Jesus were all considered to be 'Muslims' whose teachings were distorted by their proclaimed followers (Armstrong 1993, 159–67). Muslim rulers might see these followers as heretics but usually tolerated them as 'people of the book' and allowed them rather more freedom than non-Christians were given in Europe. Exchange of scientific and philosophical ideas with people of other religions, from astronomy and mathematics to medicine, were a constant feature. It was harder to interpret the people who followed various religious cults of India as 'people of the book'. Even here, some syncretically oriented rulers (Akbar, Ibrahim Shah II of Bijapur in the Deccan) provided openings at the highest level for religious spokesmen of various kinds, while popular exchange was constant, often centring around Muslim holy men or *pirs*, revered by non-Muslim peasants as well as conscious followers of Islam.

The material background for this was the commercial vigour, openness and bureaucratic strength of the Muslim empires. This culminated in the Mughal empire, one of the largest centralized states of the premodern world. Covering most of the Indian subcontinent, though fitfully to the south of the Vindhyas, the Mughals ruled a population estimated between 100 to 150 million. It was far larger – in size and resources – than the other premodern Islamic empires, Persia and Turkey. Europe, raucous but divided, was only an aspiring power, at the time far behind (Richards 1997, 197–98). The empire had bureaucratized and formalized methods of extracting the agricultural surplus and using it to maintain a flourishing bureaucracy and nobility. This power apparatus included brahmans and other literate castes, primarily kayasthas and khatris, who were essential to the administration of empire, who wrote and functioned in Persian. Warrior sections of society, rajputs in the north, and Marathi and Telugu speakers in the south, were also absorbed into the nobility of the empire. Most of Shivaji's relatives and forerunners were in the service of Muslim rulers. Though 'Turks' remained in much of popular culture as a fundamentally different and threatening ethnic–religious group, yet a symbiotic relationship including marriage was established with rajputs in north India.

By the time of the Mughal empire, a monetized society existed, with land revenue paid in cash providing the base for an extensive use of coins at all levels of society. Mughal coinage – in gold, silver and copper – was extensive, with mints located in numerous places; the silver *rupiya* has given its name to today's rupee. Domestically and internationally, commerce flourished. Indian textiles, along with spices and narcotics, became world famous. The seventeenth century, just before the establishment of the factory system in India, saw a wide variety of cotton cloth – both ordinary and luxury types – becoming dominant and popular in Europe. Within India itself, regionally specialized economies were linked. The fact that Tukaram, from a substantial but still sudra, landowning family in a small village of the Deccan, was a merchant indicates the wide prevalence of trade. That he traded in grain, chillies and salt (he was a *mahipati*) indicates that commerce went far beyond luxury items.

Brahman dominance has never gone unchallenged throughout

the historical eras of India, and various anticaste movements have taken varying forms. Before the actual rise of the radical bhakti we discuss, and before any real influence of Islam through Sufism or any other form, two such movements are important, namely the *Virasaiva* movement led by Basava which was influential in the Telugu- and Kannada-speaking regions, and the *Nath-panthi* yoga cult led by Gorakhnath, which had a wide spread in much of north and south India. Both are generally dated from the twelfth century. First, however, let us look at the situation of the first major religion of India, the Buddhist dhamma.

The Silence of the Buddha

Avatar of Buddha, O my invisible one,
with mute countenance, fixed attention.
Dark blue, four-armed for the people,
you speak in whispers to the sants.
The kaliyuga has come, this has fallen to my lot;
However I move my eyes I cannot see you thus.
What have you done to me, Narayana,
Why no compassion? says Tuka
(#4160)

Within this complex system, the old indigenous traditions continued. The counter-traditions to orthodox brahmanism and the new Islam were many. One was Buddhism. Buddhist traditions did not of course suddenly die away, and many scholars have traced their influence on bhakti. Very often this is seen, as Linda Hess does, in terms of the links of Sahajiya Buddhism, a late form of tantric or Vajrayana Buddhism (see her afterword to Kabir 1986, 139–41). While this may be true in northern and eastern India, it does not appear to be so in regard to the *varkaris*, where in some ways the 'early modern' bhakti originated.

Here, in the Deccan, there is less apparent influence of Vajrayana. Buddha instead appears, as the Marathi scholar R.C. Dhere has pointed out, as silent, as 'naked' and as representative of, above all, compassion (Dhere, 1984).[2] Dhere's conclusion to his chapter on Vitthal and the Buddha argues that though the Buddhist community disappeared as consciously 'Buddhist', it did so only with a merger into other sects and left its mark especially in the form of compassion. Dhere's interpretation, however, is to suggest that in so doing the 'negative' side of Buddhism – it's anti-vedic thrust and its rejection of the brahmanic social order – was left behind:

> And then it naturally comes to mind that Jñândev and Nâmdev must somewhere have had an unbroken connection with the Buddha's limitless compassion.... Eknâth, who picked up and placed on his hip an Untouchable Mahâr child who was floundering in agony on the beach, and who gave a pot of Gangâ water to a thirsty donkey to drink, is a footsoldier in this tradition of compassionate action. Tukârâm believes that the only true holy man is one who calls his own those who are rusty and dirty and that it is only with such a man that God abides. When Tukârâm holds himself to be closely related to both castes of humans [male and female?], he does so with the support of this tradition! And therefore I say without hesitation that as the Buddha, who had abided in Maharashtra for a thousand or fifteen hundred years, left in the twelfth or thirteenth century, he overturned the water pot of the compassion in his heart, and that then the saints, so that its stream would remain flowing even more generously, added to it many currents of their loving faith and devotion. At least in Maharashtra, Buddhism pushed aside all its Tantric distortions and other inferior forms, and became reincarnated in the form of the Bhâgavata religion. Even in this new incarnation it kept up its accusations against the Vedas; but it wiped away its non-Vedic stamp.... This new Bhâgavata incarnation of Buddhism has ushered in a new intellectual era in the cultural life of Maharashtra. (Feldhaus' translation, unpublished)

[2] Dhere's *Shri Vitthal: Ek Mahasamanvay* (Vitthal: A Great Confluence) being currently translated from the Marathi by Anne Feldhaus.

It is hard to understand 'evil powers that harm the social order' unless there is a subtle reference to Muslims. What Dhere is trying to do here is fairly obvious: he wants to maintain the varkaris within the framework of brahmanic tradition, even with caste and gender orthodoxy (for instance, the 'unrestrainable' attraction of women to motherhood and the 'Vedic stamp') and he wants to integrate into this the power of Buddhist compassion.

Thus Dhere's presentation of the Marathi sants' interpretation of the Buddha shows that the Buddha is seen as silent, as a 'lord of yoga' and as naked. (This suggests more Jainism.) The 'nakedness' may be a reference to the supposed asceticism of the Buddha; nevertheless it is puzzling. And why silence? Perhaps the sants themselves stood before Buddha images, which could be seen in caves throughout the region, which no longer had monks or spokesmen to interpret for them.

Similarly, Dhere makes a valuable point in noting that everywhere Buddha is seen as the ninth avatar, the one inaugurating the kaliyuga. This was a more or less orthodox (puranic) story, but he describes the way the sants wrote about this as 'contradictory'. The brahmanic interpretation of the 'Buddha avatar' is that it was designed to deceive men; it is because of this deception that afterwards a destructive and murderous cleansing force is needed. This does not fit the compassion stressed by Dhere. However, there were variations among the varkaris themselves, reflecting their varied interpretations of a traditional and imposed discourse. Among the sants it is especially Eknath, with his brahman education, who gives us the more traditional interpretation of the Buddha as an avatar, the ninth among those of Vishnu, where he is seen as the avatar who opens up kaliyuga but does so by playing the role of a deceiver:

> 4.272. *Know that he himself will later, in the form of the Buddha, keep strictly silent. At that time, no one will be able to decide between karma and non-karma.*

273. *He always, silently, will move to great arguments. Under the pretext of argument, he will increase intoxication and great infatuation.*

274. *Infatuation will give rise to difficulty; it will cause some people to be ritualistically involved in ceremonies; some will fall away from karma; they will not understand the pure welfare of their own soul.*
4.277. *When the situation is thus one of infatuation, the inclination to conflict will become strong. Then those kings will become low; they will rob their subjects like thieves.*

(Cited by Dhere, 1984)

But this overwhelmingly negative interpretation does not seem to have greatly influenced the other sants. They accept the Buddha as 'silent', even 'naked', but what they stress is not his role as a deceiver, but (again) his compassion and his inauguration of the age in which they live—which they do not necessarily see in the black colours of the kaliyuga. In a recent article the classic European scholar of the varkaris, G.A. Deleury (2004; see also 1994) has stressed this in looking at Namdev. He argues that Namdev did not simply take the avatar theory as such, but reinterpreted and sometimes mocked it, calling the various avatars *bagul* or 'scarecrows', and insisting that god/Krishna was not like this—just as Kabir was later to insist that his Ram was never the fish, the tortoise, the boar, the dwarf or the other supposed avatars of Vishnu. Deleury insists that Namdev was a more radical thinker than Dnyandev, citing his poem:

1053. *The incarnation in Gokul was husband to 16,000 women. As the Buddha he was a lord of yoga.*

1096. *In order to break vows, the Buddha incarnation became naked on earth.*

1098. *Becoming hard-working this way, you remained bauddha.*

2105. *In the middle he became the silent god, deep in meditation on the Self. He was to be enlightened (bauddhya), therefore he was named Buddha.*

(Namdev, cited by Dhere)

Thus, where Dhere uses his material to stress the 'incorporativeness' of the varkaris who are seen as blending various vedic and non-vedic interpretations, Deleury's recent article sees rebellion and differences *among* the Sants. While 'scarecrow' is only one possible translation of *bagul*, the more usual meaning of the term is also negative—the 'heron' who is sly, cunning, deceptive, is always seen in contrast to the pure swan in social and religious literature in India. Various poems on the avatars appear throughout the work of Namdev and other sants, and very often they seem to be using, critiquing even as they use, and transforming a discourse that was presented to them. This relationship to the existing brahmanic, puranic discourse goes on at several levels; the critique and denial of the received wisdom was a major characteristic of the radical bhakti tradition.

Speaking of Siva

Virasaivism, or 'Heroic Saivism', dates from the twelfth century in the Karnataka country just south of Maharashtra. Thus it was a kind of intermediary bhakti between early Tamil bhakti and the Maharashtra–northern network that began with Namdev and the varkaris. Yet there is no evidence of a connection. The varkaris never refer to the Virasaivas. Perhaps the political divisions, or the fact that the western–northern network was based on Vishnu, provided the reasons. In any case there were both important similarities and also some differences.

The founder of Virasaivism is Basava (1106–67/8), who was a brahman and a minister in the court of Bijjala, the king of Kalyan. However he is reported to have torn off his sacred thread, being repulsed by caste differences, and when he formed his community, he ignored criteria of caste, sex and class to accept all. Among the important members of this community, Allama Prabhu and the unconventional, daring woman Mahadeviakka (Akka Mahadevi) were noted.

Virasaivism was firmly monotheistic, and fought fierce battles against both the devotees of Vishnu and Jains, who were predominant in the region. Akka Mahadevi was most renowned in this sense; her husband (or the man who aspired to be her husband) was a Jain, and furious when she rejected him for Siva; she is said to have wandered around without any clothing except her own long hair. Basava expressed this contempt for multiple gods in many *vachanas* (the *vachana* was a kind of free-verse poetic form), as can be seen in A.K. Ramanujan's translations:

The pot is a god. The winnowing
fan is a god. The stone in the
street is a god. The comb is a
god. The bowstring is also a god. The bushel is a god and the
spouted cup is a god.
Gods, gods, there are so many
there's no place left
for a foot.
There is only
one god. He is our Lord
of the Meeting Rivers.
(1973, 84)

Another characteristic was the freedom from temples: the Virasaiva devotees substituted instead a *linga* (phallus, symbolising Siva) worn on the body. This was one of their main characteristics, and it also separated the linga from its sexual connotations. The *jangam* was characterized as the 'moving' locus of Siva, as contrasted with the stable one, his temple. As a famous vachana (the first cited by Ramanujan) put it:

The rich
will make temples for Siva.
What shall I,
a poor man,
do?

My legs are pillars,
the body the shrine,
the head a cupola
of gold.
Listen, O lord of the meeting rivers,
things standing shall fall,
but the moving ever shall stay.

(1973, 19)

Caste was decisively rejected. Not only did Basava accept people from all castes into his new community, but he himself proclaimed his rejection of his brahman birth and his kinship with the oppressed castes. "Our Cannayya, the untouchable, is my father, and our Kakkayya, the tanner, is my uncle" (in Schouten 1995, 52). Many vachanas from the twelfth century movement – often by oppressed castes and untouchables themselves – proclaimed equality, and Basava's uncompromising attitude was prominent:

What does it mean which background you have?
He who wears the linga of Siva is well-born!
Should we inquire about background among the devotees,
after the castes have been mixed?
This is the saying:
Who is born in the caste of Siva's lore, free from rebirth is he;
Uma his mother, Rudra his sire, and verily the Siva fold his tribe,
so I will take the leftovers at their place
and I shall give my daughter to them,
for I believe in your devotees,
O Lord of the Meeting Rivers.

(Schouten 1995, 55)

The freedom from and rejection of caste distinctions, the role of the community of devotees, the householder status of the main devotees and gurus (Basava himself had two wives), the emphasis on devotion and freedom from ritual—all linked the Virasaiva movement with later bhakti. However, the role of the guru was strong; the guru was practically an object of worship and taking his *prasad* or consecrated food, drinking the 'water of his feet' were important marks of devotion that were not found in later bhakti movements—where the guru or *sadguru* was more often used not for an earthly object of devotion but for god himself.

The radicalism of the early movement culminated in a marriage organized between a former untouchable boy and a former brahman girl. This brought the fury of the orthodox to the fore, and when the fathers of the bride and groom were sentenced to death by the king and dragged by an elephant through the streets of the town, the radicals of the Virasaiva community took over. At this point the movement appears to turn into a full-fledged revolt by the oppressed castes. The king Bijjala was assassinated, and riots and persecutions followed, which ended in an orthodox victory; the movement was driven out of the kingdom (Ramanujan 1973, 63–4). The story suggests why similar intercaste marriages remained unknown (or at least unrecorded) in other bhakti movements: the power of the orthodox was too strong, even in the case of the Virasaivites when there was a ruler sympathetic to them and the leader held a strong ministerial position; the king was in spite of all obliged to enforce the deepest admonition of varnashrama dharma, the prevention of *varna-samkhara* or mixture of castes.

The first generation of Virasaivism faded away; when it underwent a major revival a couple of centuries later it was not nearly so radical; caste was no longer challenged and caste-like distinctions began to prevail among the Virasaivas themselves, with the jangams becoming hereditary much as brahmans were (Schouten 1995, 15). This may well have been a reason for its failure to have much noticeable influence on the varkari and later bhakti movements—by the time they rose, it was no longer a shining symbol of equality, and language barriers prevented the radicalism still expressed in vachana poetry from being known to them.

Nath Yoga traditions: The 'Secret in your Body'

It is the Nath-panthi yogic tradition that is said to have been most widespread throughout India in the period of the origin of radical bhakti, and is credited with strong influence on it by many scholars. The main figure in this is a rather mysterious Gorakhnath, usually located in the twelfth century. The sect was first studied thoroughly by the British writer G.W. Briggs (*Gorakhnath and the Kanphata Yogis*, 1938), who also calls them *Kanphatas*, from the custom of having their ears cut for large earrings. Gorakhnath is taken as the main figure in the Nath-panthi tradition. The term *nath* means 'lord' and most, following Saivite customs, added 'nath' to their name.

As Gordon White describes them, the Nath-panthi yogis were part of a much broader network of tantric Saivism, which drew on older traditions of the Pasupatas, Kalamukhas and the fearsome Kapalikas—linked with magical, alchemical and medical tantra. Their cosmology saw a homology between macrocosm and microcosm, between the human body and the universe; the universe was the outgrowth or emanation of Siva's play, in particular of the sexually conceived and ecstatic interaction of Siva and Shakti. The goal of various practices, whether these were actual practices of 'left-handed tantra' (that is, imbibing meat, alcohol, sexual fluids and engaging in intercourse with outcaste women), or forms of yogi practice that stressed control of the body and its nervous system, or use of chemicals such as mercury (conceived of as homologous to semen) or sulphur (homologous to menstrual blood) was liberation of a particular type (White 1996, 1–8).

This could be given a more orthodox interpretation, that of achieving a 'spiritual' simple identification with the universe. As Briggs argues, quoting Vasant Rele:

> A Yogi when he develops his automatic nervous system, becomes so engrossed in it that the somatic function of his *susumna nadi*

> and the knowledge of the relation with the external world are held in abeyance and he sees his own self which pervades the whole universe and becomes one with it.... When this *kula kundalini* is awakened or made active, it forces a passage through the distinct *cakras* and excites them to action, and as it rises step by step, the mind becomes opened and all visions and powerful powers come to the Yogi, when it reaches the brain. The Yogi then is perfectly detached from the body and the mind, and the soul finds itself free in all respects. (Rele in Briggs 1938, 320–21)

However, White, based on a detailed study of the texts, argues for a rather different type of 'freedom'—different from both traditional brahmanic moksha and from later bhakti devotional identification. The yogic practitioners sought to become like Siva—to achieve "eternal youth, immortality of the body, and the attainment of an identity of nature with Siva, that is, liberation in the body [*jivanmukti*] which is difficult even for the gods to attain" (quoted in White 2000, 173–4). These are the first words of Siva given in a major alchemical tantric text, the *Rasarnava,* dated around the eleventh century, a text that White feels was probably compiled in an area near the upper Godavari in Maharashtra, prior to the founding of the Yadava dynasty in 1175 (114). (This was north of where the varkari movement was to emerge, on the Krishna river, which had been considered since the earlier brahmanical period a 'heretical' river and area—that is a Buddhist centre).

A story from the Virasaiva tradition about Allama Prabhu and Gorakhnath, the supreme name in this yogic tradition, illustrates the difference: it was a contest of powers, since Allama was also a practitioner. Allama whirled a sword at Gorakhnath, which shattered on his adamantine body. However, when Gorakhnath did the same to Allama, the sword simply passed through him as if through air. The Virasaiva story represents a critique of the 'materialism' of the Nath-yogis, in comparison to their own implied ability to reduce the self to nothing (cited in Ramanujan and White).

Linda Hess has stressed the similarity between Kabir's language and many of his ideas with Sahajiya Buddhism (itself said to have merged into yogic tantric traditions) in the translations of Kabir she did with Shukdev Singh. In her more recent work with a Madhya Pradesh Kabir troupe, she emphasizes this more (though Hawley contests this interpretation; see Hawley 2005, 104) and the focus on the body can be seen in many of the songs in *America mai Kabir yatri*, a wonderful VCD on a tour of this group in September–November 2003 organized by Hess:

> *Where did you come from, where are you going?*
> *Get the news from your body*
> *If you find a true guru,*
> *you'll get the secret, the window within.*
>
> (Kabir 2003)

In some ways the idea that sant poetry reflects a Nath-panthi yoga tradition has helped to fit them into a largely brahmanic framework, the 'Indic' great tradition. While admitting that the Nath-yogis themselves represented a protest against brahmanism, they are still incorporated, with Buddhism, into an 'Indic/ Hindu' identity that is defined as a counter to traditions linked to Islam (or Christianity). The logic of this is seen in the writings of Hazariprasad Dwivedi, who sees Kabir as representing the "Hindu–Indic tradition's response to the Muslim challenge" (Dwivedi cited in Lorenzen 1996). As Milind Wakankar points out in a discussion of the changing uses of Kabir among the nationalist and literary elite, the effect of Dwivedi's work is not only to marginalize the Islamic influence on Kabir; it also evades the issue of caste injustice. Dwivedi sees Kabir as the quintessential romantic rebel and religious seeker, with his individualism contrasting to the collectivity embodied in Islam. As Wakankar puts it:

> Dwivedi seeks to read the best of Bhakti ethically for its response to Islam as historical adversary ... but what continues to interrupt the movement of Hindu ecumencisim is the essential wound ... at the heart of Dwivedi's high Hindu society, which is caste and the spectre of conversion.... The perennial achievement of Hindu society (for Dwivedi) was that it had subsumed the problem of the social within the principle of tolerance towards individual spiritual and religious seeking. (2005, 138–9)

In Wakankar's critique, Dwivedi can exalt the individualism of Hindu tradition only by ignoring the oppressions of caste hierarchy. This also points to the issue that Satish Saberwal had discussed in the debate over the 'weak social norm' in Indian society. If Hindu 'orthopraxy' that supposedly substitutes for 'orthodoxy' allows more freedom at one level, the acceptance of varnashrama dharma implied in it means a drastic reduction not only of social solidarity but also important forms of deprivation of freedom for the oppressed castes, who were forbidden religious access by Vedic traditions and had to win it at some cost.

A similar framework emphasizing the role of Nath-panthis is applied by Vijay Mishra to the entire bhakti movement. In *Devotional Poetics and the Indian Sublime* he takes up the *Bhagawad Gita*, then looks south to Virasaivism; then brings in the *Gita Govinda* and the thirteenth century brahmanic interpreters of bhakti such as Shandilya and Narada; then discusses the Sufis and Namdev and culminates with Kabir. In fact, the songs translated are selected, it would seem, for this very purpose of having yogic themes. Mishra's chapter order itself suggests that the ideological influences of puranic traditions were most crucial. Concurrently, he denies that there was any real rebellion against caste, arguing that Chokhamela and his family never really rejected caste or their untouchable status, and that they were never looked on as predecessors by the dalit movement of today (1999 38–41).[3]

Mishra analyzes the bhakti movement of the early modern period as the product of the subaltern castes, mainly artisan and similar OBC groups, who were becoming nearly independent in an increasingly commercialized society but at the same time were affected by the traumas of an era marked by "the enormous unease within Hindu society in the wake of Muslim invasions begun in earnest at the turn of the second millennium" (122; also 126–7, 132). In formulating their response, these subaltern caste groups were said to draw primarily on the Nath-yogi traditions and this was made acceptable to the mainstream tradition through sanskritic texts which cast the love of the bhaktas into a Krishna-devotional framework which maintained orthodoxy by reading the sexuality out of the poems—treating the cowgirls' extramarital love in metaphorical terms and ensuring that the god himself, Krishna, was not in reality subject to desire but (in contrast to his female lovers) was capable of controlling his sexuality.[4] Like Dwivedi, then, Mishra sees the sants as defenders of an indigenous 'Hinduism'.

Dhere, one of Maharashtra's most sophisticated scholars of the varkari movement, also discusses the nath-yogi tradition as the crucial predecessor of the movement. His *Shri Vitthal: Ek Mahasamanvay*, cited earlier, provides the theme which continues to be argued—that the varkari movement was, above

[3] From the very beginning Ravidas was looked upon as a forerunner by dalits in north India. While Ambedkar clearly rejected Chokhamela because of the clear cooptation the varkari movement of his day illustrated, today the large intellectual class among dalit Buddhists, given birth to by the policy of reservation, is beginning to debate the nature of the varkari movement, arguing for its Buddhist roots and in the process turning to recover not only Chokhamela but also Tukaram. (See the discussion in Zelliot and Mokashi-Punekar 2004.)

[4] Hawley (2005) has given a powerful critique of the male chauvinism involved in this ('the Gender of Longing') which Mishra defends himself against—before the fact, as it were, but arguing that hardly anyone was free from patriarchal ideas at the time.

all, 'syncretic' or *samanvay*, and represented not rebellion or revolt but a bringing together of diverse 'Hindu' traditions. Buddhism, this way, can be absorbed. Dhere's interpretation of the Nath-panthis also sees this as a widespread 'revolt' not against brahmanism but against the 'left-hand' sects – sects that actually practised drinking, sexual intercourse as part of tantra – in other words one that remained within the framework of behaviour acceptable to brahmanic notions of the 'pure'.

Mishra, Dhere and Dwivedi ignore the 'materialistic' goals of the Nath-panth yogis, and also they never really confront the textual problems involved in using the songs of the sants. For instance, Mishra's arguments rest primarily on taking the writings of the sants (as available in whatever preserved manuscripts we have) as reflecting the real person. Thus he writes as if the Namdev of the texts, or the Kabir of the texts, were the real thirteenth or fifteenth century individuals. However, the poetry of the bhaktas itself is filtered throughout the presumptions of those who transcribed them, those who kept the manuscripts, and the minstrels who sang (and sing) their songs, added their own, and both maintained and shaped the tradition. To take every composition claiming *kahat Kabir* or *Nama mhane* as the actual 'sayings' of Kabir or Nama can be, as we shall see, unwarranted.

There is no doubt that the yogic tradition is part of the heritage that the sants responded to, that it provided the imagery of many of the songs of the 'wandering minstrels' associated with bhakti—but it was not the sole or main part of the message of the sants. Dnyandev, who is considered by orthodox interpretation the founder and philosopher of the varkaris, was clearly himself highly influenced by Saivite yogi traditions; Chitre, his best translator, has stressed the role of 'Kashmiri Saivism' in his philosophy (see Chitre's introduction to his translation of Tukaram's poetry, 1991). However, the question of the actual relationship between Dnyandev and Namdev remains unresolved. The sants, especially those in the north, very often used the language of Nath-yogi traditions, but they also heavily criticized yogis. Finally, the aims of bhakti were totally different. While interpreters like Dhere emphasize compromise, comprehensiveness and incorporativeness, and see the varkaris as a harmonious 'flowing together' or *mahasamanvay* of various positions, most of the sants were, in fact, pointed and often radically harsh in their positions.

The Rags of the Sufis

One went to the door of the Beloved and knocked.
A voice asked, 'Who is there?'
He answered, 'It is I.'
The voice said, 'There is no room for Me and Thee.'
The door was shut.
After a year of solitude and deprivation he returned and knocked.
A voice from within asked, 'Who is there?'
The man said, 'It is Thee.'
The door was opened for him.
(Jalaluddin Rumi cited in Shah 1964, 356)

I know not what place it was where I passed the night just gone:
all around me were bodies half-slaughtered writhing in a dance;
There was the beloved nymph, her body a cypress tree,
her face tulip red;
Ruthless wreaking havoc in every heart.
God himself was the master of this ceremony
in that otherworldly place.
O Khusrau!—Muhammad was the lamp that lit up this party,
where I passed the night just gone.
(Hazrat Amir Khusrau cited in Kalidas 2002, 74)

It is the Sufis who are usually credited with being the main actors in a great process of syncretism of Islam and brahmanic Hinduism in India. For example, Charlotte Vaudeville argues that Kabir

> is the first great Indian poet to appear in North India after two centuries of Hindu–Muslim symbiosis.... When the Khalji Turks from Afghanistan displaced the Slave Kings at the end of the thirteenth century, the process of Indianization of the invaders was already well under way. For the first time, historians and chroniclers refer to the local Muslims as 'Hindustanis.'... In the field of music and literature, the cross-breeding of the two cultures brought remarkable developments. The most brilliant representative of the period is Amir Khusrau (c. 1254–1324), the greatest Indo-Islamic poet in the Persian language...[whose] poetry is full of pride in his native land.... Muslim missionaries, generally known as 'Sufis', were active in Oudh, Bihar and Bengal during the twelfth and thirteenth centuries...facilitated by the anti-Brahmanical disposition of the common folk who had been influenced by a somewhat degraded form of Buddhism. (1993, 65–72)

The name *Sufi* comes from a word for 'wool' and refers to the rags stitched together and worn as clothing. This is a rule similar to the requirements in early Buddhism that monks wear rags; it signified a disinterest in the world and a style of life directed to god rather than worldly affairs. Sufis are also famous in non-Muslim circles for dancing; they have given us the stereotype of the 'whirling dervish' and feature in novels as such. They are also known for a poetry of love, developing the mystical, dreaming, innovative side of Islam.

In the extensive debates about the role of Islam and in particular Sufis with respect to 'Hinduism', most Indian historians argue that the mysticism, flexibility and even inchoateness of the 'Indic' tradition helped to bring about that great shift in Islam known as Sufism. Sufi advocates argue, to the contrary, that it was Sufism which represented the first and most pure forms of mysticism, that brahmanic versions in contrast were derivative (Shah 1964, 402–03). Still other historians, for example Richard Eaton (1978) have denied that the Sufis can be considered 'missionaries' at all, noting that their teachings were primarily for those who already considered themselves Muslims.

Linkages between Sufis and sants are hard to trace because they are usually denied by both sides. 'Hindu' interpretations claim sants such as Kabir and Dadu to be only accidentally 'Muslim'; some hagiographies do not recognize their Muslim identity at all (see Deak 2005, for an exception in an article on the guru of Janardan, who was in turn the guru of the varkari Eknath). Muslim histories, in turn, usually ignore them. The stories of Hindus and Muslims fighting over the dead body of Kabir – with one side wanting to cremate, the other to bury him and both instead getting a shower of flowers – are apparently only stories; in fact, Kabir himself did not attempt a synthesis but ruthlessly criticized both pandits and qazis, both veda and Koran, in his brilliant poetry. 'I am neither Hindu nor Turk' is a theme common to Farid, Kabir and Nanak—though one is considered today a Muslim, the second a 'Hindu', while the movement begun by the third has indeed achieved a separate religious identity through organizational innovation.

The first impact of the Sufis was in north India, where the Chishti Sufis entered quite early. Among these were Kwajah Moinuddin Hasan Chishti (died 1236), the founder of the order in the subcontinent known as 'Gharib Nawaz', (Patron of the Poor); Fariduddin Mas'ud Ban-e-Shakkar, also known as Baba Farid (1175–1265), the most important and popular of those Sufis who pioneered Punjabi literature; and Nizammudin Auliya (1238–1325), who died in Delhi. All of these stressed the love of god and humanity, often giving up all their worldly goods and living in careless poverty. In spite of often being courted and patronized by rulers, they took an antagonistic attitude to the courts and the rich, illustrated by a reported reply by Nizamuddin to a request by the Sultan to see him: "This faqir's house has two doors. If the Sultan comes in from one I shall leave through the other" (cited in Sikand 2002, 14). The Sufis engaged with society at a mass level, not only distributing their wealth to the poor but carrying on some forms of organized charity such as community kitchens – the *langars* – that later came to be widely seen among the Sikhs. Along with this is the other reputed and well-known Sufi characteristic of ecstatic dancing and singing, in which love is not simply silent and passive meditation, but active use of the body. This again was a new phenomenon in India, but it is unclear that it preceded bhakti.

While Sufism entered from the north, it is said that bhakti came to northern India from the south. This however, is by no means self-evident. While the *Bhagawata Purana* was written in the Tamil areas (see van Buitenen 1966 for an interesting discussion) there was still a gap of five centuries between the *Bhagawata Purana* and later developments. What, then, happened during those long centuries? There is more likely to have been a direct influence of the Basava-led Virasaiva movement on the varkaris, but there is little historical evidence. And what about Sufi influences on the earliest of the early modern bhakti movements, the varkaris?

'Deccan' comes from *dakhan*, the Prakrit word for south, and it was known as such to the Greeks, a region distinct from both the north and south of India. The early Buddhist-oriented empire, the Satavahana, was succeeded by a brahman-dominated flux of kingdoms. The Deccan was never absorbed fully into the Mughal empire and Muslim influence was more tenuous than in the north. During the sultanate, the conquest of the south ended with a breakaway Muslim ruler establishing a sultanate (1347–1527) and taking his title of Ala-ud-Din Bahman Shah from the Prakrit pronunciation of 'brahman'. The Bahmani kingdom in turn broke up into five regional sultanates, which the Mughal empire sought without too much success to dominate; only the northern Maharashtra regions were brought within the empire. While trade and commercial ties between north and south remained important, there was no significant Muslim landed class or local nobility; and brahmans predominated in the administration at almost all levels. Among the feudal nobles or sardars, Maratha and Telugu warriors dominated. This was especially true of the Adilshahi kingdom based in Bijapur. Thus, though Sufism and the cult of pirs spread, the heresies of the kaliyuga were undoubtedly less prevalent in the south and brahmanism remained stronger.

Namdev and his fellow sants in Maharashtra came before the message of Islam could have reached them. Whether the dates of Nama and others were really at the beginning of the thirteenth century or in the fourteenth, it was not until the fifteenth century that the Chishti Sufis (the most unorthodox and mystical) reached the Deccan in any thorough way. There were earlier 'warrior Sufis' who sought to propagate Islam, but there is little evidence of any deep penetration. It was only with the phase of Bijapur's strength beginning in the last half of the sixteenth century, and especially in the time of Ibrahim Shah II, that a real outreach took place. Ibrahim – whose reign was parallel to that of Akbar – sought to make a broad appeal with an interest in Sanskrit literature and a policy of tolerance for Hindus:

There are different languages;
But there is one emotional appeal
Be he a Brahman or a Turk.
He is only fortunate on whom
The Goddess of learning (Saraswati) smiles.
O Ibrahim, the world only seeks knowledge....

(Cited by Eaton 1978, 99)

This syncretism at an elite level provided space for a more radical syncretism at the mass level. But the process is not yet very clear, in spite of the material given in Eaton's detailed study of the Sufis of Bijapur.

The Sufi position, as Eaton describes it, included a critique of the yogis. The Chishti Sufis not only rejected their physically-oriented practices as hypocritical and ostentatious, but also as based on a radically different spiritual tradition. To them, hatha yoga practices of nakedness, striving for breath control, physical mortification of the body and suchlike were 'ludicrous'. The Chishti Sufis wanted their followers to shed his "concern for his mortal body and to train his soul for meeting God. The yogis, on the other hand, regarded their bodies as the universe in microcosm, and accordingly attached cosmic significance to their physical self-discipline" (154–55). This critique, in many ways, was shared by the later bhaktas.

While Eaton does not believe the Sufis actively sought to convert, he describes an indirect effect of absorption of people drawn to the dargahs of the Sufis and gradually becoming incorporated. These were primarily women, it seems, for as Eaton points out, while men were at the mosques, the dargahs served as a gathering place for women, who sought the pir's intervention for fertility and other family problems, just as they had sought the intervention of other holy men or local goddesses. Sufis were the pioneers of Dakhani (the southern version of Urdu, which developed in a different process from Punjabi roots and only later merged with what was to become the Urdu of the north). This was first in a mystical literature oriented to Sufis themselves and with a large use of Persian and Sanskrit vocabulary; but later a folk literature developed that was almost entirely songs, and, again, mainly directed at women. These included the *chakki-nama*, sung while grinding grain; the *charkha-nama*, sung while spinning thread; *lori-nama* or lullaby; the *shadi-nama* or wedding song; and *suhaik* or eulogistic song. Most of these forms had already existed among the common people belonging to subaltern castes; what the Sufis did was to inject Islamic themes and use Dakhani instead of Marathi or Kannada, something Eaton considers "a major development in the cultural history of the Deccan" (157–58). Dakhani itself became a local language, as is shown by the fact that Eknath, and later Tukaram, composed in it as well as Marathi. However, Namdev and his contemporaries apparently did not use the language (so far as we can tell from the texts, a rather questionable issue).

Christian Missionaries through the Ages

Buddhist influence on bhakti is by now admitted by many scholars. As yet, that of Christianity has come in for little study, outside of Christian activists and intellectuals. These, however, make some interesting points. Advocates of 'St Thomas Dravidian Christianity', for example, argue that elements of monotheism and compassion in a salvation religion coming through Christianity from the first century onwards – presumably after St Thomas visited the subcontinent coming through Kerala – influenced developments in Vaishavism, Saivism and the rise of Mahayana Buddhism. While this is an extreme interpretation (the opposite of the 'Jesus died in India' school), there are evidences of Christians in the Madurai region of South India at the time of the Portugese. (For some of these arguments, see Deivanayagam and Devakala n.d., Devakala 2005 and Kurikilamkatt 2005.)

The crucial developments for our period come with the conquest of Goa by the Portuguese. Jesuit missionaries from different parts of Europe began spreading out through India from 1545. These were literate; they left letters and records and engaged themselves in translations and often in fairly high-level debates with brahman pandits. It was natural for Italian noblemen such as Matteo Ricci and Roberto de Nobili to associate with the Confucian, samurai or brahman aristocracy of different societies, though in India especially they often strained themselves to interpret customs as 'social' and not 'religious'. Dominicans, Franciscans and other orders were less likely to be literate, perhaps more inclined to identify (if they identified with indigenous traditions) with antibrahmanic currents; but we have almost no record of their activities. In some ways they have gotten a bad press for their reportedly harsh condemnation of all 'indigenous' traditions in contrast with the Jesuit policies of accommodationism (for instance, in the popular Japanese novel *Shogun*) but the debate about accommodationism may well have gone on without being so intellectualized among the other orders.

Thus, while it may appear unrealistic to argue that Kabir's 'Sai' was actually 'Isa' (Jesus) and to make him into a kind of crypto-Christian, it remains quite possible that among the later poets using the name 'Kabir' one was indeed influenced by Christian ideas. After the sixteenth century, specifically after 1545 when Jesuits began to spread through north and south India, a wide impact of ideas can be seen. In Maharashtra, a *Krista Purana* was reported as composed in 1626, as one of the earliest Konkani/Marathi writings, written by Fr Thomas Stephen (1549–1619), an English Jesuit, one of the first of these Jesuit translators.

In the end, however, any discussion of 'influence' has to remember that ideas go all ways, that they interact with different frameworks in a way that frequently changed their significance. At the personal level, missionaries eager to assimilate their message to indigenous frameworks and themes can end up themselves being 'corrupted' by these. The greatest of the sants appear to us as creators, using influence and speaking in the framework of traditions – various traditions – but often giving new meanings to these. They used existing discourses, but often subverted these—and their message was a new one, emerging not under the impact of feudal conditions (as seventh–eight century Tamil bhakti had done) but of early modern conditions, at a time when kaliyuga had not quite given way to 'colonial yuga' and new themes of rationality, equality, and messianism were pervading the world.

iii

Nama
Dancing Open the Temple

They saw the whole world flock around me
and the great Brahmans seethed with rage.
They called me a Sudra, they beat me and chased me away.
What should I do, my Father?
But suddenly the world was filled with wonder,
a miracle happened unsurpassed.
The temple doors swung open for Namdev, the bhakta.
And slammed shut in front of the Pandits.
(Namdev 1989, 219-220)

The Puzzle of Namdev and the Power of the Name

Though Dnyaneswhar (also Dnyandev, Dnandev, Dnana) is credited in a famous varkari poem with 'laying the foundations' for the bhakti movement in Maharashtra, and Namdev is relegated to the position of a 'mason', it is Nama who is known throughout northwestern India as the originator of the devotional movement. "The first bhakta who lived in the Kali age was Namdev," says Anantadas in the earliest hagiography written in 1588 (translated by Callewaert and Lath 1989, 2). Dnyandev is unknown outside of Maharashtra, and one of Tukaram's powerful *abhangs* – a metric form unique to the varkaris – gives a kind of 'historical' account of the varkari movement with Nama, relegating Dnyaneshwar and his brothers to the following verses. In what could be a more accurate depiction of what actually happened than the hagiographic version, Nama "made Vitthal the leader," while Dnyaneshwar and his brothers and sisters identified Vitthal with Krishna (Tukaram 1973, #190).

Namdev's dates are uncertain. The traditional dating, accepted in Maharashtra, is 1270–1350. But many scholars, including the French doyenne of bhakti studies, Charlotte Vaudeville, see him as living in the middle of the fourteenth century or later ("Maharashtra Santism", in Schomer and Macleod 1987, 218n; see also "Introduction to Namdev", Callewaert and Lath 1989, 15–20). The latter would allow for some Sufi influence, but there is no evidence for this and little appears of Persian words in the Marathi texts. In any case, the usual brahmanic effort to make Ramananda– a southern follower of Ramanuja who had moved to Varanasi – the guru of all the subaltern bhakti sants, and the supposed transmitter of bhakti itself from south to north, also cannot work in the case of Namdev.

Generally, problems of dating and analysis of bhakti trends are tremendous. The methodological problems have to do, as many scholars have pointed out, with the fact that we have almost no clear evidence about the dates and exact compositions of any of them. Of existing manuscripts of any famous sant, it is only the Dehu collection of Tukaram's *gathas* that even makes a claim to be an original (see the summary in the introduction by Dilip Chitre to Tukaram, 1991). In fact, as John Stratton Hawley has pointed out, putting together 'critical editions' of the sants is an entirely different problem from that in Europe because the whole tradition of 'authorship' is different (2005, 10–11). The manuscripts we have are written down from the songs of wandering bards or minstrels; these followed the works of the great bhaktas but they were under no compulsion not to change words or verses or create new compositions which they saw as following that sant's path. The earliest manuscripts date from the end of the sixteenth century, often centuries after traditionally accepted dates of the sants. And the versions they present us also reflect both regional–linguistic differences and different intentions of those who collected the poems. The *Adi Granth* collection of the Sikhs, for instance, takes a stern *nirguna* stance, rejecting all compositions that imply a worship of god envisaged 'with form' (Mann 2001).

This issue has been much studied regarding Kabir. As Winand Callewaert and Swapna Sharma have shown in his *Millennium Kabir Vani* (Kabir 2000) – an exhaustive attempt to arrange compositions from manuscripts they collected throughout Rajasthan and Punjab – not only is there a problem of different versions, there is also little correlation between these 'western' collections and the 'eastern' tradition of Kabir which has been collected in the *Bijak* manuscripts. And there is almost none at all with the living oral tradition of Kabir with songs passed down through the centuries and continually innovated. Only one of what they call 'Kabir's greatest hits' even appears in the *Millennium Kabir* collection and Callewaert writes that it is unlikely that Kabir himself composed these songs (Callewaert 2000: 23).

There has been no similar effort to collate varying manuscripts of the varkaris, and most of the scholars of this movement (Dhere, Chitre, More) write as if the attribution of the songs is unproblematic. But it is not. With Namdev and the early sants in particular, there are many puzzles. We seem to know almost nothing for certain, in contrast to the much more accessible and historically attested Tukaram and Kabir. Vaudeville stresses a Saivite origin of Namdev's movement, noting that the name of Nama's supposed guru, Visoba Kechare, is actually iconic: it means 'one who rests on air', and probably refers to the yogic traditions (the Nath movement) which she and others feel have been a major predecessor to Maharashtrian Vaishnavism (in Schomer and Macleod 1987, 220). But the fact is that *all* the Maharashtrian founders have iconic names: *Namdev* (who lays stress on repeating the name of god), *Dnyanadev* (known for his knowledge or *dhnyan*), Nama's maidservant *Janabai* (a woman of the people), Dnyana's sister *Mukta* and so on. It is beyond the realm of logic that these could have been their birth names; they were undoubtedly given by movement followers for whom these men and women were symbols of varying forms of religious achievement. This does not mean that Nama, Jani and others were not real people; rather they meant so much to the masses who followed him that they attained iconic status very quickly—and the result is that very little of what is written about them or attributed to them can be taken at face value.

What was the significance of Namdev? What were the major themes of this new bhakti movement? In the Hindi selections (see Callewaert and Lath 1989, who make a case for what would be the oldest and presumable most authentic poems) many themes are evident—including the love of god, a great sense of the power of access to god even for someone of a subaltern caste, and occasionally a yogic concern for and use of symbolism of the body (Callewaert and Lath, 205). But perhaps the most pervasive theme is that of the power of the name. Repeating the name or names of god is sufficient; nothing else – neither caste status, nor rituals, nor yogic achievements – is seen as necessary or even helpful. This is put very strongly in a Marathi poem repeated at least twice in the collection of Namdev, and given almost unchanged in the Tukaram collection.

Don't read the Vedas, don't worry about shastric wisdom,
Memorize the book of the name.
Neither consciousness of Brahman nor renunciation,

Take the glory of bhakti in the company of sants.
Others may do the rituals in this age,
But tell me – what is the power that has saved me?
Nama says, the sants told me,
There is no other peace like this.
(Namdev 1999, #1368)

A couple of abhangs later this is made even stronger:

No need of doing vows, austerities, or pilgrimages –
Be content with hymns to Hari at home.
You don't have to exclude anything of life or food,
Place your every mood at Hari's feet,
You don't have to sacrifice, meditate or give up sex;
Your devotion will suffice, laid at Hari's feet.
Nama says, hold the name firmly on your tongue,
It will give you a meeting with Pandurang.
(#1371)

Na lage is the Marathi term for 'You don't have to....' Devotees, the sants argue again and again, don't have to subscribe to any of the rituals, paths and means prescribed by brahmanic theory or by other religious sects. It is a theme that is constantly repeated in many poems of the varkaris, a chant of freedom and a challenge to all ritualism. The power of the name, linked to the love of god, is sufficient. This is reminiscent of, yet different from, the repeating of the name of 'Amitabh Buddha' which a follower is supposed to do, and which is capable of bringing a rebirth in Sukkavati, the land of joy, if done at the time of death. Here, the stress is on the grace and gift of the saviour or Boddhisatta. These themes are indeed there in bhakti, but they are more often linked to the idea that the devotee controls the deity through his devotion.

What is also very much present is the engrossment in singing and dancing. This represents ecstasy, in contrast to the earlier Buddhist (and brahmanical) stress on eradicating passion. The dancing may be said to be a Sufi note; in this respect, if Islam did not lead to the formation of radical bhakti, it certainly strengthened it. The temple, in a frequently repeated and important 'miracle' story, revolves and opens up for Namdev, but the temple itself is not very important; indeed, there are many stories of problematic relations with temples, where subaltern devotees are excluded or discriminated against. The northern sants – Kabir, Ravidas, even Nanak – had no specific temple they were associated with. The varkaris had Pandharpur, but the poets write more often of dancing on the river sands and meeting Vitthal everywhere, much more than of the viewing in the temple itself. The 'sighting' or *darshan* itself is usually an imaginative one. What matters is the *seeing*; the poets are great seers – visionaries – and part of the power of their imagining is they bring the deity to walk, talk and dance with them. Janabai gives us a powerful picture of this celebratory vision:

A single beat resounded on the river sands,
my Dhanraj gave out popcorn to the devotees.
Namdev sang the stories, dancing in front was Pandurang –
Jani pleaded, O Dnyandev, sing for us a song.
As the song was sung, there came a rainbow glow,
in the passion of this love, Vitthal began to dance.
Dancing, dancing, the god's gown began to fall,
take care, O God – from Kabir this call.
The grandeur of such stories is greater than all else,
The ignorant devotees have found a simple path.
Nama's Jani rolls at the feet of the saints –
give love's nectar without end, O Mother Vitthai!

(Janabai in Namdev 1999, #132)

The word *kirtan* in this, which I have inadequately translated as 'stories', is usually a performance, built around a song or abhang[1] but filled with exhortations, jokes, and stories, not

[1] In contrast to the northern sants, there is no practice of associating the varkari compositions with *ragas*.

necessarily of the gods or even sants but very often parables or illustrations taken from daily life. In this song, however, the kirtan is a collective entrancement: the sants danced together. (We will deal with Mother Vitthai later).

The main varkari tradition, as Engblom has noted in the historical survey given in his introduction to the translation of a book on Pandharpur's pilgrimage (1987), has always remained outside the temple—it is on the river sands that they come together. This is understandable; after all, the dalit devotees were excluded from the temple itself and even lower OBCs, as Nama's story of the 'revolving temple' shows, were often also not welcome. In spite of the stories of temples revolving and opening up, or of the god leaping out to meet his devotee, in fact the Pandharpur temple, like those throughout India, has remained under control of the same hereditary priests who continue to exploit their position up to the present day.

Singing and Dancing with God

The meaning of singing and dancing becomes strikingly clear in the first long part of the *pravachana* – the stories about Namdev that stand at the beginning of the Marathi collection of his poems – and which themselves were a popular part of the repertoire of all *kirtankars* (singers and storytellers). A 'dialogue between Gonai and Namdev' is, in turn, a lengthy part of this. Gonai is Nama's mother, and the setting is the story of his birth, his work as a tailor 'sewing night and day', his first meeting with Pandurang and his resolve to write poetry. Then Gonai runs looking for Namdev, finds him unconscious in the ecstasy of devotion to Vitthal, grabs him, and when Namdev comes to consciousness his mother begins what are several long verses of complaints and accusations against Nama and the deity. There is much repetition, and much bitterness is expressed. Gonai's tone is illustrated in one of these verses:

Mother said, Namya, what divine being pulled you
to play at the temple,
You've been made to live in humiliation,
calumniated with laughter throughout the land.
Leave this madness, don't do this,
how you have ruined a great house!
You've been born to conquer,
why have you become a burden to the world?
How can you describe yourself as a child of fortune,
you've become a loss to the family!
I find it a great marvel
that you have no shame before the public,
Throwing aside all worldly pride and egotism,
you dance and sing in gaudy clothes.
...Sons and wives face household calamities,
your attention is given to Pandarinath.
Nothing remains of caste –
see this god, he's a homebreaker!...
Gonai says, Nama, it's not good
what Vithoba has done to you!
(Namdev 1999, #113)

This goes on for long verses, repeating the accusations of 'dancing and singing in gaudy clothes' and ruining caste and clan. Gonai turns to pleading with Vitthal: 'Why have you made my Nama mad?' and accuses the god of being a useless and dishonourable deity, with a frequent repetition of the theme, 'you're not a god, you're a homebreaker' (*dev nahi, gharghene*). The repetition itself is compelling: *budawale kriya, budawale karma, budawale dharma*.... The theme is clear: Nama has thrown away everything, ignored caste, rejected rituals, disregarded family, ruined his wife and children; everything is gone. She accuses Nama of becoming an enemy to all, to her, his family, and in turn he accuses her. Namdev finally replies:

You don't know my heated mind....
I'm exhausted from casteism, from the sorrows of birth and death,

you've never asked me about this anguish,
and so I've found refuge in Vithoba, he's done this much good for me.
Sons, wives, all worship their own welfare,
no one shares the sorrow....
Wandering through endless wombs is our low fate,
and this is the toil you tell me to do!
But my Vithoba's service is sweet and joyful,
there is nothing to be done and nowhere to look,
He has not asked my caste and clan,
I don't know on what merits I have been accepted....
When I'm weary of the clamour I look out –
O come, my mother Pandurang!
At that instance a word falls on my ear
and the god comes leaping,
knowing all my life without a single word,
giving assurance of security, caressing me
and spreading the shade of the silken gown.
A true mother-father, beloved friend,
all in all of my worldly life.
Nama said, it's the peace of my heart,
singing songs makes life sweet for me.
(Namdev 1999, #125)

This explanation resolves nothing. 'Namya, this is great boasting!' says Gonai and returns to her accusations, ending in pleading to Pandurang: "Give me back my Nama." But almost to the end, Vitthal remains for her a homebreaker—*gharghene*. Why was this dialogue included at such great length in the collection? (Mahipati gives only a vastly shortened version.) Though the section is called *atmanivedhan* (autobiographical preface), it does not appear to be 'by' Nama; it is likely not of his time. It was an addition that has no prestigious literary or religious significance, and was clearly not included as a means of coopting Nama into a puranic tradition. Rather, it must have appealed enormously to the varkaris who came into the movement, perhaps especially to the doubts and preoccupations of the men.

All of this provokes a new image of what bhakti was. Consider the situation: here is a young man, perhaps in his teens, bright and creative; married at an early age, and burdened with wife and children; forced into the toil and drudgery of work assigned to a caste considered low, work that has to be carried out under conditions of poverty and even humiliation. Why wouldn't he be weary of these responsibilities? What is more natural than a really creative person in such a situation running away—to a dance, to a nightly *bhajan* show. Disco today or bhajan then, there may not after all be so much difference. After all, singing and dancing were so important in religious movements.

The songs of the radical bhaktas have been compared by Mukta (1997; Patankar and Omvedt, 2002) to freedom songs, which express under conditions of powerlessness the deep longings of oppressed sections in language that their oppressors cannot easily understand. However, there is more than just the message. Freedom songs do not inspire simply by their intellectual message; they grip the emotions and the body itself as the entranced worshippers dance and sing. Music is not an incidental but a crucial part of worship; and also a crucial part of revolt. *Mutiny: Asians Storm British Music*, a recent documentary film produced by Vivek Bald, tells what seems like a double story of young Bangladeshis in England, who form bands partly to find refuge in the drumbeats and music of a new integrated culture—and to fight the police and the oppressions of racism. 'Why do you dance so violently,' the one-time 'skinheads' were asked. 'To keeping shape to fight the police,' they replied. The varkaris were not fighting the police in this way – though some of Tuka's abhangs express their self-image as fighters – but the element of rebellion in their poetry cannot be denied.

Homebreaking, Householding

If Vitthal is a homebreaker, then what is Namdev? Someone who lets his home be broken? Yet he remains a householder, and it is a characteristic of the radical bhaktas – one that differentiates them from those bhaktas who were part of *maths* and who had therefore institutional support – that they remained throughout their lives in some sense 'householders'. This was a revolutionary change in Indian religious tradition. Up to that time, the real religious authority, whether in brahmanic or samanic traditions, had belonged to the 'renouncers'. Brahmanic householders had authority in society, but for others the only way to achieve any kind of religious prestige was to renounce. In Buddhism too, most of the Theravada *suttas* are addressed to monks; when the Buddha gave teachings to lay people, it was considered as a special event. Mahayana Buddhism had developed a major role for householders but even this was problematic; the householder Boddhisattas or high-level practitioners, for example, were supposed to be 'in the world but not of it'; and this meant specifically that they were not supposed to keep relations with their wives. Thus, the fact that Namdev and most of the other sants remained householders – carrying on their businesses and supporting themselves by their own labour (rather than depending on maths and institutions, or on begging) – was a significant innovation.

It was not easy, as stories like those of Gonai make clear. Almost all the hagiographies depict the sants as ineffective householders. They are seen as unable to really carry on their business or support their family, due partly to their bhakti and partly to personal characteristics. As Hawley and Juergensmeyer remark in relation to Kabir, "In suggesting why Kabir's business habitually lost money, Priyadas seems eager to soften Kabir and make him conform to the kindly, abstracted type that lies at the core of Priyadas' own vision of sainthood." Priyadas – who authored the *Bhaktirasbodhinitika*[2] in 1712, emphasizes Kabir's

[2] A major hagiographical work on north Indian sants that added 634 verses to the extant 214-verse compendium *Bhaktamal* compiled in the 1600s by Nabhadas.

timidness and generosity, and relates how once he gave away all his clothes and "became so frightened of the reception he would get if he returned home that he simply did not go. He hid in the market for three days, while his family languished in hunger" (Hawley and Juergensmeyer 1988, 37–38). A similar story is told in Mahipati, the eighteenth century Marathi hagiographer of the sants, regarding Kabir's mother (Mahipati 1999, I: 81–85) and he gives a similar depiction of Tukaram and Namdev. These sants who were otherwise powerful voices – and we know from Tuka's poetry that he could be fiercely and sometimes nastily critical of the pandits, the wealthy, and religious frauds, often in language that would be considered borderline obscene – are shown as soft, even timid.

The obverse of this is the depiction of women of the family, not simply as suffering from neglect, but as shrews and god-haters, carrying their hatred of god beyond reasonable bounds because of the helplessness of the men of their household. This is a constant theme in Mahipati. Gonai and Rajai (Nama's wife) are both shown as hating Vitthal, and as giving some credit to the god only when they get something out of it—such as a gift of money (288–94). Mahipati's version contrasts with the Namdev collection, where Rajai is given some abhangs expressing devotion and a desire to learn about Vitthal (Zelliot 1995, 91–2). (Generally, in the Namdev collection and others, the relatives of the sants are all depicted as bhaktas to some degree or another.) Similarly, in making Tukaram's wife a bitter hater of Vitthal, Mahipati exaggerates a dialogue given in the *Gatha* (translated by Chitre 1991). An even more telling story is that of Gora Kumbhar. He is described as so engrossed in meditation and devotional ecstasy that he tramples on and kills his own child while pounding the mud for a pot. He neglects his wife; she thinks that it is because she is unattractive to him and has him marry her sister. He blithely goes through with this and then, when the marriage remains unconsummated, the sister curses both of them. Mahipati concludes the story by showing that Vitthal restores the child to life and instructs Gora to return to his duties as a husband.

There is reason to think that this was not simply a matter of innocent narration. For instance, James Laine (1998) takes the hagiography at face value and describes the depiction of family life as a result of the very problematic nature of being a householder-devotee. But it is problematic only within the framework that emphasized renunciation. Brahmans had every motivation to show the sants as ineffective householders and the women as shrews simply because they wanted to discredit the idea that anyone but brahmans could be at once holy and a householder. Hagiographers such as Mahipati were clearly caught between their loyalties to brahmanism and to the new ideas of bhakti, which proclaimed both a strong opposition to varna and ritualism, and the reality of a householder's life. The result is the ambivalent and often perplexing mixture we seem to get. Mahipati's description of kaliyuga, for instance, includes all the traditional brahmanic notions of the upsetting of family life and the turn to Muslim sants, and in general the depredations of Muslims; but it also refrains from mentioning *varna-samkhara*, miscegenation of castes that is otherwise a deadly sin for brahmanism. He praises the equalitarianism of bhakti and of a god open to people from all social backgrounds—but continues to emphasize the holiness of brahmans, calling them *bhudev*s, gods on earth, and depicting them as endlessly praised by the sants. It is crucial that though the deity Pandurang dines with the subaltern caste tailor Namdev, in Mahipati's account he accepts to undergo the brahmans' ritually prescribed 'penance' for having eaten the leftovers of a low caste man; the 'necessity of obeying Vedic rules' of varnashrama dharma has to be followed even by gods! (229, 245–47). Similarly, in the case of the householder life and women, it is Mahipati who stresses the depiction of women as shrews. Though he finally – as in the story of Gora Kumbhar – gives a kind of sanction to a family life for the sants, the total effect of his stories is quite the opposite: being a true householder looks impossible for a man of devotion. We have to, then, use the hagiographies with care if we want to analyze the position of women in the society of the sants, or any other aspect of the bhakti movement.

Imposed and Imagined Gurus

What the question of the householder's life illustrates is true of many issues. Another example is the case of the sants and their gurus. It is part of brahmanic traditions, including the traditions of some otherwise dissenting sects (such as the Naths, for example) that a *guru-parampara* or line of gurus, giving hereditary sanction to the holiness and wisdom of any particular religious person, has to be established. In her study of *Sant Mat*, Vaudeville (in Schomer and McLeod 1987, 34) calls the position of sants 'somewhat ambiguous' on this issue, noting that the story of Ramananda is unsatisfactory (there is no evidence in the poetry of either Ravidas or Kabir that he was their guru, and their tendency was to see god as the satguru).

Similarly, Tukaram's supposed guru, one 'Baba', appears to him in a dream, gives him the mantra of 'Hare Krishna' and connects him up with Chaitanya (abhangs # 368–371, Tukaram 1973, 60–61). All of this appears to be concocted. The dissident scholar A.H. Salunkhe (1997) has argued that this is one of many interpolations, though he has failed to establish a textual basis for analyzing what is 'interpolated' and what is not; this kind of scholarship has simply not yet been done regarding the varkaris. In regard to Namdev, as Vaudeville has pointed out, nothing is known about the real existence of Visoba Kechare. Even the story about Namdev has him questioning the need for a guru;

he has to be convinced by Gora Kumbhar and Vitthal (Namdev 1999, 89–90).

This ambivalent relationship to the guru is characteristic of the radical bhakti movement after the fifteenth century. Earlier religious dissident movements, such as Virasaivism and the Nath-panthis, stressed gurus and were particular about them. But the teachings of the sants went against the guru tradition in one significant respect. This was the idea of thinking for oneself, whether this is meant religiously, socially or philosophically. *Satya-asatya man kele gwahi, maniyele nahi bahumati* ("I made my own mind the witness to truth and untruth, I never heeded the opinions of the majority," says Tuka in his famous autobiographical abhang (#1333). Similarly, a famous line from Kabir goes: *Ved-kitab kahan kin juta, juta jo na vichare.* ("Which is false, Veda or Koran—false is he who does not think!") (*Bijak*, #97). The theme is pervasive, and harks back to the Buddhist dictum 'be your own lamps, be your own refuge'—a stress on self-discipline, experience and self-reliance which runs all the way through the radical sants up to Phule's Satyashodhak Samaj and to Ambedkar's own warnings against the guru tradition and exhortations to his followers to think for themselves.

The imposition of gurus on the sant's traditions was thus a method of cooptation: the implied puranic pedigree worked to establish their legitimacy in the eyes of orthodoxy, and vice versa—it established the puranic stories and the whole line of veda-brahman–accepting tradition as legitimate among the mass followers of the sants. It is perhaps not surprising, then, that the guru or 'hero-worship' tradition that Ambedkar decried was, for him, embodied in bhakti itself. When he warned in his speech on the Constitution that liberties could be lost by 'laying them at the feet of great men,' he went on to say:

> This caution is far more necessary in the case of India than in the case of any other country, for in India Bhakti or what might be

> called the path of devotion or hero-worship plays a part in politics unequal in magnitude… [to] any other country in the world. Bhakti in religion may be a road to the salvation of the soul. But in politics, Bhakti or hero worship is a sure road to degradation and to eventual dictatorship. (2000, vol. 13, 1215–16)

The fact is that bhakti did end up being absorbed and to a large extent brahmanized, a process that shall be sketched out here. The imposition of and imagination of gurus was a significant part of this process.

This process can be seen, in fact, in the very story about Namdev and his guru. While he himself is depicted as reluctant, the process of convincing him gives opportunity for, verse after verse, exalting the greatness of the guru; it is Pandurang himself who is made to declare:

> *"If you say God can be seen, it is not good speech Nama,*
> *without destroying the idea of 'me' and 'mine'*
> *how can you meet the Ram inside?*
> *There is no liberation without a guru."*
> *Hearing this, Nama quaked and fell swooning on the ground,*
> *his eyes filled with tears.*
>
> (#271)

Visoba Kechare may be, in the view of scholars, a member of the Nath-panthi yogic tradition, but the message he is made to give to Nama is purely advaitic. The idea that runs through much of the varkari's saguna bhakti – that life after life of 'dualistic' devotion and relationship to god is their goal – is put in its place, and the advaitic notion of 'everything is god' is stressed. Thus, there is reason to think that the guru aspect of the sants was a later addition—part of the coopting process of brahmanism.

Janabai and Chokhamela

With Namdev, beginning the great bhakti tradition of Maharashtra and symbolizing the times, was a cohort of women and men from all castes, including Gora the potter, Savata the gardener, Kanhopatra the prostitute and many others. His own household was a huge joint family amounting to fifteen to seventeen people, including sons and daughters-in-law and dependents, a *mela,* a 'factory' as Chokhamela described it (1998, 140). And as with all households, others in it also wrote songs.

Among this extended family of sants, Namdev's maidservant Janabai and the 'untouchables' stand out. Of the latter, the most famous is Chokhamela, but here it is striking that a collective is presented: Chokha and his brother Banka, their two wives (also sisters), Soyra and Nirmala, and a son, Karmamela. In contrast to the way wives and husbands are normally depicted in the literature on sants, especially the hagiographies, is a relatively equalitarian family group in which the women come across as quite assertive. The stories about Chokha and Soyra, for instance, include a striking depiction of the birth of Karmamela, in which she gets pregnant by god's intervention, and while Chokha runs away from the 'bloody mess' to his brother's house to lose himself in devotion, Vitthal comes to tend to Soyra, taking the guise of her sister Nirmala (Zelliot, in Zelliot and Mokashi-Punekar 2004, 149–54).

The characterization of this group of 'untouchables' is striking, and in its own way iconic. Chokha himself represents a kind of 'ideal untouchable'—bemoaning his lot, stressing the continual presence of impurity, of always 'standing on the threshold' but serene and making no real protest. Banka, his brother, takes him as a guru and praises him. The women stress the bitterness of *samsara*, their burden of daily life and housework. All interpret their lot in terms of karma and rebirth, but it is only one, Karmamela, the son, who is allowed to be rebellious and bitter:

You have made us low caste: Why
don't you understand the fact,
O god of gods? Our whole life:

spent in scrounging for leavings.
Have you no shame?
You ate rice and curd in our house: do you dare to deny?
Says Cokha's Karmamela, why have you given me this life?
(Trans. by Rohini Mokashi-Punekar, in Zelliot and Mokashi-Punekar 2005, 147)

Even Chokha's death, caught in a landslide while working as a bonded labourer on a road, seems iconic. As Zelliot has pointed out, there is no authenticated collection of this poetry at all, nothing to show that any writing had been preserved. There is indeed a great body of songs attributed to the dalit sants; but it can be argued that these reflect the outcries and creations of dalits only as they have been filtered through the guardians of tradition across the centuries.

Janabai's poetry may be similar: she is an orphan, and her songs reflect that status, but there is at least one in the Namdev collection (cited above) which is clearly a later interpolation as it refers to Kabir.

Still, iconic or not, whether actually from the period in which Jani, Chokha and others are said to have lived or gathered up from centuries of suffering expression by the most oppressed sections of the caste system, the songs of this group have real power. Chokhamela and Janabai represent the beginning of a unique tradition of varkari experience of the divine, in which the god comes to share their life and even labour. From this period on, through Tuka's powerful climactic expressions of the theme, the god becomes a weaver, a gardener, a maidservant, a cobbler, a potmaker, a common labourer forced into bondage. It is Vitthal who cares for Jani, combs her hair, washes her, feeds her; and when Chokha is accused by the brahmans of polluting the temple and whipped, it is on Vitthal's back that the marks appear.

How rebellious were the sants in their time? Joseph Challer's discussion of the bhajans and stories of Raidas (Ravidas) in contemporary dalit settings shows that it was much more radical than the stories that have come through the collected and largely brahman-written traditions (in Zelliot and Mokashi-Punekar 2005, 221–27); this must have been true throughout the centuries, and the original sources of such stories may have been equally rebellious. But we cannot know. The sources of their writing that we have give no hint; they are the songs that were maintained throughout the ages in which brahmanic domination, though challenged, remained hegemonic. Thus what remains of Chokha and the most subaltern sants is an outcry of pain:

> *Run, Vithu, don't be slow,*
> *The* badwes *are beating me,*
> *As if I've done some sin....*
> *They are cursing the Mahar,*
> *saying he's polluted the god...*
>
> (1998, 134)

The Origin of Vitthal

Finally an important historical question remains: who or what was Vitthal? The varkaris seem to have been inspired by a specific temple and the 'form of the formless God'. Here they contrasted with the northern sants as well as with the lingayats, who had specifically rejected a location of god. Instead, the varkaris, from Namdev to Tuka, celebrated the unity of *saguna* and *nirguna*, and looked to the form of god as Vitthal of Pandharpur.

Though Pandharpur and the *varkari sampradaya* are said to represent the very epitome of Maharashtrian culture, the city was for a long time in the Karnataka region; the original form of its name was almost certainly Kannada—Pandarige. It is only from the thirteenth century, under Hoysala rule, that we hear of the connection of Pandharpur with the god Vithoba or Vitthala. The Yadavas, centred at Devagiri (now Daulatabad) were the first Marathi-speaking dynasty of the region, and their power reached its zenith under King Krishna (1247–1260); a period in which Marathi was becoming a literary language. There are many more inscriptions from the thirteenth century which make it clear that by then the cult of Vitthala had spread among Marathi-speaking people. The coming of Dnyaneshwar to Pandharpur and Alandi at the end of the century is taken as the real beginning of the tradition (Deleury 1994, 22–36).

But what was Vitthal (also Bittala) before this? Vaudeville (in Schomer and McLeod 1987, 215–28) argues for a Saivite origin; dalits today believe that the site was originally Buddhist (see, for instance, Javale 1999). Deleury (1994, originally published 1960) and more recently Dhere (1984), the greatest of the recent Marathi interpreters, have argued that Vitthal was originally a god of nomadic pastoral tribes.

Though this apparently represents some resolution to the debate, it seems to have missed a point. Laminated pictures of Vitthal are now sold all around Pandharpur, as modernization has hit the region. Two major forms exist: clothed, as the priests normally show the deity for any *darshan*, and an unadorned depiction of the statue. Bharat Patankar, my husband, has received several pictures of Vitthal as a result of his work with dam evictees and drought-struck farmers in the region. Looking at one large splendid lamination of the unadorned Vitthal, a striking new question came to our minds: was this a man or a woman? The deity was black, arms akimbo, clothes in bare outline much as early Buddhist statues appear, with what may have been small genitals—everything as described in the iconographies. Yet the overall appearance was that of a woman, a goddess, quite female and mother-like: wide hips, narrow waist, busty, long hair, straight though harsh face. We wondered. None of the long discussions of iconography and Vitthal's origins had mentioned this. They had discussed it being black; contemporary dalit-Buddhists had stressed this blackness as evidence of indigenous origins and argued that its hands on hips and lack of weapons was a proof of nonviolence, and called it a Boddhisatta. Deleury, the first great scholar, discussed this and other features, concluded that there was no proof of Vitthala being Buddhist.

Is there in Hindu iconography any other instance of an image with arms akimbo? There are indeed very few, and it clearly demonstrates that it is a unique characteristic ofVithoba. Although as we have noted, Buddha himself has never been represented with arms akimbo, there are some other Buddhist sculptures showing the arms in that position.

But the Buddhist sculptures Deleury identifies are those of Sri, the pre-Buddhist goddess who survived through Buddhist times and eventually became identified as the goddess of luck or wealth, Laxmi (1994, 163). Sri is shown, in a Rhys Davids' depiction, not with arms akimbo but with the same dress (*pitambar*) as that on Vitthal (Rhys Davids 1997, 40).

Deleury goes on to ignore this evidence. Mother goddesses were apparently outside the realm of the thinking of Jesuits, just as they were of brahmanical Hindus.[3] The other striking example of ignoring the possible female origins of Vitthal is Dhere (1984). Just as he has a chapter on Vitthal and the Buddha, Dhere also has a chapter on Vitthal Mauli (Mother Vitthal). He had earlier authored a remarkable study of an indigenous goddess, Lajja Gauri. But he is concerned to show in his *Vitthal: Ek Mahasamanvay* that Vitthal's origins are as a pastoral deity, and apparently he considers that pastoral deities are inevitably male—though, after citing in the beginning a song by Namdev describing the image in a consistent feminine gender as 'my Krishnai' (mother Krishna) he also notes that statues of 'Vithalai'

[3] However, Deleury's more recent work, after he moved back to France, suggests that he would be much more open now; see Deleury 2001 on Namdev.

are found throughout Maharashtra and that rather than 'Vitthal' being a corruption of the sanskritic 'Vishnu', Vishnu was a sanskritization of 'Vitthal' or 'Vithu' (Dhere 1984, 10–13).

I initiated discussions on this issue, showing the photo of the lamination to many friends, asking, 'If you look at this without any preconceptions, who or what is it? Is it a god or goddess?' It is difficult to avoid preconceptions. Invariably, Maharashtrians identified it as 'Vithoba'[4]—but all non-Maharashtrians, who had no prior 'knowledge' of the tradition of Pandharpur, identified it as a 'goddess' or on sometimes as 'androgynous'.

Were we then being eccentric in our ideas about Vitthal as mother? Perhaps not. One other significant group has seen the deity thus, and that is the varkaris themselves, from Namdev, Janabai and Chokhamela in the thirteenth and fourteenth centuries through Tuka in the seventeenth century. Invariably they have some references to mother, and often address or refer to the deity in the female gender (using *ga* as opposed to *re* in addressing Vitthal). Ironically, using English breaks this: the form 'Vithoba' and the use of masculine gender in translation has become normative. In Marathi, however, there are three major forms of the name, matching the three genders of Marathi: *Vithoba* (male), *Vithumawali* or *Vitthai* (female) and *Vitthal* (unidentified).

Other bhakti poetry in the northwest circuit we are focusing on is male-oriented, even the nirguna poetry. Krishna, the god, is male; the lovers are female. And, as Hawley shows in his sensitive essay on Krishna and the *viraha* poetry of longing for the god, "Krishna and the Gender of Longing" (2005, 165–178), it is

---

[4] An artist friend insisted that mother goddesses/females are invariably depicted in Indian sculpture as much more big breasted than the photo. However, as the Gazetteer account makes clear, the statue, only three and half feet high, would have been worn down through constant hugging by the devotees (see Government of Maharashtra 1984, 423–24).

also male chauvinist—the lovers are tormented and hurt, but even where the male is shown as longing for the encounter, he is shown as able to control and sublimate his desires through yoga, whereas the female devotees are not given credit for this.

Hawley adds that love need not necessarily be male in this sense; that Mughal court poetry, with Persian influences, visualized the divine either as a beautiful woman or an elusive adolescent boy, with the human being as male (166–67). It can be argued that the male chauvinism can also exist with the divine visualized as female. Another study by Carla Petrievich (2002), describing the ideology of 'manly' poetry of Urdu argues that the earliest mixed poetry was Dakhani and Laknavi; what later became male *rekhta* poetry was *rekhti* in Laknavi; this also often used 'low' and even 'obscene' language and was connected with courtesans; later stigmatized for this. But Dakhani ghazals of the seventeenth century could not be called frivolous; they were quite sophisticated, though they did see the divine in female terms, perhaps due to indigenous ('Hindu') influences. The Dakhanis were later discredited for being sensual, profligate and extravagant (Petrievich 2002, 245–46), and the greatest among them, Wali Dakhani, who was the link with northern Urdu after he moved to Delhi, was treated as if he had no forerunners when in fact he was the last of a great series of Dakhani poets.

The possibility of Vitthal having a female origin is intriguing. We know that there were originally independent female goddesses. We know also that there was a process of supercession of these by males, sometimes through a simple takeover of a site and replacement of one image by an earlier one, sometimes through the goddesses being 'married off' to a well known vedic or vedicized deity. Siva is often seen as most prominent in this; the yoni gets united with, and then taken over by, the linga—but it happens also with Vishnu and the domestication of Laxmi. In one process of cooptation, the goddess becomes

Mahisasuramardini, literally the 'killer of the demon *Mahisha*'. She emerges as stronger than the gods, and does what they could not—but at the service of the gods. On the background of all these histories of absorption, a similar process could have gone on with Vitthal.

Maharashtra is, in many ways, at a crossroads in India. Just below the Vindhya mountains, it has been historically a part of south India, though its language is identified as 'Indo-Aryan' and not 'Dravidian'. The ancient *dakshinapatha* – the road to the south – ran through here, down from Bihar through what is now Ujjain, Maheshwari and Paithan (see the *Sutta Nipata*) on south, undoubtedly through the Pandharpur-Solapur region. Nearly all sources, including Dhere and Deleury, give Vitthal a southern origin, and even songs speak of the deity as 'Kannada Vitthalu'. Islam and Sufi influence may have come through here; Buddhism, even Christianity from the times of St Thomas could be argued. The Basava-led Virasaiva movement in the twelfth century took place just south of Pandharpur; indeed one of the cult sites, Mangalvedha, where Chokhamela died, was the town where Basava served the Kalyan state for many years. Here, a very de-mythologized and monotheized version of Siva becomes the centre of devotion. It was this crossroads of moving goods, people and ideas that produced, by the twelfth and thirteenth centuries in early modern India, the new flourishing of radical bhakti which expressed the mass yearnings for a life of simplicity, love, equality and reason. It may have drawn on the earlier, suppressed lingayat movement initiated by Basava, but it had its own themes and message, brought by Namdev to the wide-ranging regions of northern and western India.

iv

Kabir and Ravidas
Envisioning Begumpura

This is the big fight, Raja Ram
he who solves it is free of bonds –
Is Brahma great or where he came from?
are the Vedas great or who gave birth to them?
is this mind great or what it believes in?
is Ram greater or the knower of Ram?
Kabir wanders the world detached,
is the holy place great, or the devotee?

(Shabd 112, trans. based on Hess and Singh 1986)

The traditional stories make Kabir and Ravidas contemporaries. These two most renowned sants of northern India were both associated with Banaras. They were both subaltern: one a chamar, with the traditional occupation of leatherwork and the traditional duty of disposing dead cattle; the other a weaver, most likely one of the poorer, struggling coarse-cotton weavers of the region. The caste is described as julaha for Muslims, *kori* for Hindus, and dalits today argue that koris are in fact a Scheduled Caste—'dalit' not only in identification but in actuality. The two are not only considered contemporaries, but often compared and posed against each other, in what is a famous though historically unlikely confrontation of *nirguna* and *saguna* bhakti, represented respectively by Kabir and Ravi. In the accounts offered by Anantadas (in Callewaert and Sharma 2000) and Sain (see Lorenzen 1996, 34–59 for a translation of Sain), Kabir emerges first as victorious and is accepted as his guru by Ravidas.[1] And then a *saguna* vision is given of Vishnu appearing to both the saints and both, somewhat ambiguously, appear victorious in the debate (see Anantadas in Callewaert and Sharma 2000, 124-40 and Lorenzen 1996, 169-181). Kabir and Ravidas have also been claimed as disciples of Ramananda, linking them to the safe, south Indian brahmanic *saguni* Vaishnava tradition.

This, however, is an imposed interpretation of their contributions. While the Ramananda story places them in the 'Hindu' tradition through a satisfactory brahman link, the *nirguna–saguna* debate frames their theology in brahmanical, philosophical terms. In fact, the writings of both poets are ambivalent, and we cannot assume that their views of the divine fit traditional Indic philosophies. Kabir, in many of his contributions, especially the popular *dohas* of the oral tradition, sees god in what appears to be a monotheistic form, and stresses a major *guna* of love and compassion. The Sikh renderings, in turn, interpret Ravidas as solidly *nirguna*, which of course itself sees the divine in that way.

At the same time, even more than the earlier message of Nama, their songs give us a social message, and this social message is indissolubly linked with their identities. This message, born out of protest against the inequalities of caste and the uselessness of

[1] Anantadas was a Ramanandi, writing in 1588 in a way that moved towards brahmanic incorporation; Sain was a member of the Rajasthan-based Niranjani sect, which was also fairly orthodox in its views of caste.

priestly ritualism, climaxed in a new vision of a utopia free from class and caste oppression, a heritage for later ages.

Kabir

The traditional dates assigned to Kabir are 1398–1518, which suggests he shared a whisper of the immortality (a very long lifespan) aimed at by the Nath-Siddhas. Scholars have debated his actual dates: did he flourish in the first or second half of the fifteenth century? The full truth is lost in the shadow of non-documentation of popular life in India, though there is now some agreement around the dates 1398–1448 (see Dharwadker 2003, 2–3).

Just as hard to access are his actual compositions. There are at least four major categories of collections, all of which seem to suggest different Kabirs. The Adi Granth collection brings us primarily the *nirguni* Kabir; many of the Rajasthan collections are more *saguni* and devotional, because these reflect in part the influence of Krishna-based devotionalism (though those associated with Dadu Dayal, another originally Muslim *nirgunai* sant, also reject the forms of God) so strong in much of the region; the eastern or *Bijak* collection gives us Kabir the great iconoclast and philosopher. There is also the oral tradition, which has in fact very little overlap with the written collections (see among others, the Introductions in Callewaert 2000 and Dharwadkar 2003, and the essays in Hawley 2005). Finally, there is the most popular version of Kabir in the West—Robert Bly's freewheeling translations drawn from one set of popular translations from the oral Kabir, and the romantic mystic presented in Tagore's Kabir, of which scholars take a dim view (Hawley 2005, 267–78).

Were there, then, many Kabirs? Scholars and devotees alike tend to shrink from this conclusion. The most recent assessment, by Dharwadkar, stresses a 'collective Kabir' but with a commonality of philosophical and social positions, and argues that this involved a polishing of the poetry (2003, 2–97). Yet there is a good deal of evidence for almost irreducible variety, certainly in terms of language and also in the ideas that Kabir was associated with. The justification for arguing for pluralism is that India, even before Kabir's time, was a meeting place of markedly different religious traditions. The most obvious of Islam, which had been marking its presence on the subcontinent for several centuries, but there was also forms of Christianity dating back traditionally to the missionary work of St Thomas in north and south India, as well as Zoroastrianism (seen in the Parsis, who generally kept to themselves but still had a presence in the subcontinent) and the Jews, whose arrival predated that of even St Thomas. It is precisely Kabir's placement – or the placement of the numerous Kabirs who added to and polished the poetry – at the meeting place of Islam and the Indic religious traditions which give him his power.

The most well-known Hindi Kabir scholar, Hazariprasad Dwivedi (1942) has stressed the Nath-panthi connections of Kabir and emphasizes his individualism as a way of seeing him representing the 'Indic' tradition's response to a Muslim challenge. However, while Kabir knew the language of the Nath-panthis and often used it, he also seems to be simply playing with it, and very often placed the 'yogi' along with the 'pandit' and the 'qazi' as representatives of religious traditions that were ultimately fraudulent. As Hawley notes, the 'earliest' collection of Kabir songs specifically refutes the Nath tradition: 'Kabir does not drink' (Hawley 2005, 302–03). This may simply reflect the Krishna-bhakti orientation of this area of collection; however, it is consistent with Kabir's general rejection of the Nath-panthis. He was aware of them, he may have dialogued with them, but as an antagonist. It makes more sense to see a Kabir for whom the Nath-panthis' proclaimed practices and beliefs completely missed the point of what was, to him, not simply an internalized but also an ethical divine force that required humans to behave morally in a way that was incompatible with caste divisions, wealth and power.

The idea that Kabir knew 'Hinduism' from the inside but not Islam is not as justified as scholars seem to think. As a recent subaltern caste convert to Islam, Kabir could read neither the Sanskrit vedas and upanishads nor the Arabic Koran. Yet a general knowledge of what both said was available to a bright subaltern boy. Kabir writes of such stories as Adam and Havva (the Arabic name for Eve). He seems to have been as familiar with the rituals and externalities of Islam as he was with the popularized puranic stories of the avatars, the well-known sexual symbolism of the Nath-Siddhas, and the Sufi tradition. Thus, though Dwivedi and others read Kabir as standing at the apex of a long tradition of Hindu/Indic thought, drawing on the individualistic religious seeking of vedantic philosophies, as well as tantric Buddhism and Siddha traditions, it is also possible to read him as standing at the apex of a tradition of Islamic mysticism which had become by his time the main popular force in a far-reaching global civilization.

A Eurocentric mentality that has tended to see the fifteenth–sixteenth centuries as those of the ending of Islamic creativity and the beginning of European military and sociocultural ascendancy is now being contested. Islamic civilization, argues David Eaton (2000, 36–38, 42–44) was strong, and new empires – Mughals, Ottoman Turks, Safavids in Iran – were being created. There were conservative trends that sought to check the potential heresies of the Sufis, announcing the 'gates of *itjihad*' closed: in other words, human reason could no longer be applied to the interpretation of the Koran, and the authority of traditional interpretations had to be accepted. Yet Islamic civilization remained a major global force with considerable creativity. On the other hand, the European 'breakthroughs' of the Renaissance and Reformation were uneven achievements, marked by anxiety, warfare and trauma. Karen Armstrong's *History of God* – really a history of the developing, dialoguing ideas of the divine in the major traditions of Judaism, Christianity and Islam – contrasts the tolerance illustrated by Akbar's syncretic and innovative policies and the flowering of bhakti with the increasing anti-Semitism in Europe, and the chauvinism and superstition shown by reformers such as Martin Luther (1993, 257–75). Kabir would have lived in the years just before the establishment of the Mughal empire by Babar (1530), at the beginning of the 'early modern age', after the full flourishing of Sufism. If we go outside the boundaries of the subcontinent to take into account these global trends, he can be seen as a modernistic reformer linked to Islam, taking some Sufi themes to their extreme.

But Kabir's identity was to be linked in the end with 'Hinduism'. Both the orthodox trends of Islam and Brahmanism rejected and attempted to ignore him, while he remained popular among the masses of each. Only since independence has he been decisively identified as a 'Hindu' reformer, one of the 'bhakti' side of a 'Sufi-bhakti' division. At the same time, though famous in India, he has remained much less known or appropriated in the new 'Muslim' countries of the subcontinent as an increasingly fundamentalist culture veered away from admitting heterodoxy to its fold.

With this in mind, let us look at a few of the 'several Kabirs' relevant to this study.

Kabir the Individualist

Kabir as a rebel and denouncer of hypocrisy is a familiar voice. Hess draws our attention to Nabhadas' short note on Kabir in *Bhaktamal*—written around 1600 and one of the earliest and least orthodox of the hagiographies. Though Nabhadas was a member of the Vallabha *math*, he belonged by origin to a subordinated caste in contrast to the later brahman hagiographers (see Pinch, 1999). Nabhadas writes:

> Kabir refused to acknowledge caste division or to recognize the authority of the six Hindu schools of philosophy, nor did he set any store by the four divisions of life prescribed for Brahmans. He held that religion (dharma) without devotion (bhakti) was no religion at all (adharma), and that asceticism, fasting and alms-giving had no value if not accompanied by adoration (bhajanas). (Hess in Schomer and McLeod 1987, 139n)

Nabhadas' concern was to bring Kabir and other sants belonging to subordinated castes into a framework that could be acceptable to the orthodox. Nevertheless, it seems he was not in a position to say much regarding Kabir, and he does not mention the 'Ramanand' story at all or any legend of the poet's life. His description of Kabir mostly relies on negatives, on his rejection of hegemonic traditions. It is this 'negation' that Hess sees as most characteristic of the Kabir of *Bijak*:

> Kabir is famous for his solitariness, vigor, fearlessness and iconoclasm; for his swift and original mind that pierces dark places with sudden probes of light and finds a natural idiom in paradox and obscure metaphors.... [He] shouts and attacks, challenges and teases...is strong and self-reliant, dares everyone to be strong and self-reliant, and never takes a stance that emphasizes the individual's weakness and impotence.... He refers to his loneliness, to the rarity of individuals who can understand him, to the joy of meeting now and then a kindred spirit. (Hess in Schomer and McLeod 1987, 139)

This striking individualism of Kabir is seen, above all, in his refusal of the collective authority of both the major traditions of his day, Islam and brahmanic Hinduism. More than this, it is not simply a matter of stressing the inability of religious traditions to create a path to god, it is also an occasional assertion that god – Rama himself, in the language most often used in the songs we have – is a human creation. "Which is greater – Rama or the mind that knows him?" is a line that gives something more than an interiorized path to divinity. Similarly, *Bijak* gives us evidence of a Kabir refuting some of the major 'frameworks' of his time—the theory of avatars, the sanctity of the Vedas, even the idea of rebirth. "Human birth is very rare, it comes but once to men—once the fruit falls from the tree, it won't go back again"; and "Kabir sings dohas every day, at the decided time; those who die will not come back, they'll not return again" (*Bijak*, sakhis 115 and 320, my translation).

Kabir the Prophet

Prophets use an ability to speak the language of divine authority to address very earthly sins and inequalities—and the anger with which they speak was relatively unknown in the Indian subcontinent before the coming of Islam. With Kabir this anger takes on force, directed primarily against caste and priestly ritualism. It is these ideas that he most often refused: though he is severe on the book-reading Muslim qazis, what he most often denounced was the hierarchy of caste and the pride of brahmans.

Worship, libations, six sacred rites,
this dharma's full of ritual blights.
Four ages teaching Gayatri, I ask you, who won liberty?
You wash your body if you touch another,
tell me who could be lower than you?
Proud of your merit, puffed up with your rights,
no good comes out of such great pride
How could he whose very name
is pride-destroyer endure the same?
Drop the limits of caste and clan,
seek for freedom's space,
destroy the shoot, destroy the seed,
seek the unembodied place.

(Ramaini 35, tran. based on Hess and Singh in Kabir 1986)

Kabir wrote about 'untouchability' in a way that took up and transcended earlier dalit laments. Chokha had seen the whole world as polluted:

The vedas and the shastras
polluted; the puranas inauspicious,
inpure; the body, the soul contaminated; the manifest
Being is the same.
Brahma polluted, Vishnu too;
Shankar is impure, inauspicious.
Birth impure, dying is impure.
Says Chokha,
pollution stretches
without beginning
and end.

(Trans. Rohini Mokashi-Punekar, in Zelliot and Mokashi-Punekar 2005, 139)

Kabir, instead, in the perfected poem given in *Bijak* makes it clear that this is only pollution from the brahman's standpoint and turns the theme around to strike at the 'pandit':

Pandit, look in your heart to know.
Tell me how untouchability was born –
untouchability is what you made so....
We eat by touching, we wash by touching,
from a touch the world was born.
Says Kabir, only he's untouched
who has no link with Maya

(Shabd 41, trans. Hess and Singh in Kabir 1986)

This tradition of fierce opposition to caste inequalities as unjustified is carried on in the popular songs:

baman se gadaha bhalla, aan jaat se kutta,
mulla se murag bhalla, raat jaagaave suta

A donkey's better than a brahman, a dog beats other castes,
a cock is better than a mullah to tell us night is past.

(Das' edition, Kabir 1991, shabd 85, my translation)

janmate maanus hot sab, yah jaanat sansaar,
bancak suud karaavahii, kahai kabiir pukaar

All are born as human beings, this is known by all,
Sudras are made by lying rogues: this is Kabir's call.

(Kabir 1991, shabd 69; my translation)

Kabir's anticaste attitudes come from being a subaltern, a man of the people. His language is filled with themes of weaving and production, and he also prophesies justice for the elite: "Water never stays on heights, it flows to lower ground; the lowly drink it to the fill; on high their thirst abounds" (Kabir 1991, 34–35).

Kabir the Moralist

The Kabir of popular dohas is an individual and a rebel, but he is also a moralist. He warns of death, of little time left to lead a righteous life, and he defines a righteous life quite simply in terms of behaviour, a love of god and other humans, a rejection of wealth and status. As with the entire bhakti tradition starting from Namdev, he rejects rituals vociferously, harshly questioning and condemning the practices of both 'Turks and Hindus'.

Kabir kahe pukar ke, do bata likh le
kar ssahib ki bandagii, bhukho ko kucch de

Kabir calls out, write two things down,
Worship god and feed the hungry

pothi padh padh jag mua, pandit bhayaa na koy
Dhaaii akshar prem kaa, padhe so pandit hoy

The world died of reading tomes, no one turned out wise;
from the single word of 'love', wisdom will arise.

Simple messages, however, have a philosophy (theology, in western terminology) behind them. Kabir contrasts the divine with the world of maya,[2] and speaks of this divine as being found within the individual, not in any place. For instance, "Look in your heart, in your heart alone; there live Ram and Karim" (Hess and Singh's translation in Kabir 1986, shabd 97)

There are various versions of the internalized divine. With traditional brahmanism, which favoured an advaitic philosophy, this meant an identification of the internal atman with the universal brahman; self and universe are ultimately the same. With the yogic tradition, this meant the identification of the self with Siva in a way that sought *jivan-mukti*, immortality of the body and magic powers. Yet Kabir rejected advaitic identification fairly clearly in at least some of his *Bijak* writings (see, for instance, Ramaini 8):

> *'That art thou' is what they preach;*
> *this is what the upanishads teach....*
> *They are so stubborn on this theme,*
> *they propagate to all around.*

He is sarcastic about the way in which the heroes of brahmanism 'madly' hold on to this, and concludes: "If you can't see what's before your eyes, you're as good as blind."

Kabir the Visionary

Finally, we have Kabir the visionary, though there are again varied versions of this. In *Bijak*, consistent with its high mysticism, the visions were not of a geographically definable utopia, but rather of a place that is a non-place, a time that is beyond time:

---

[2] Dharwadkar sees this separation as his essential message, but argues that this is a 'secular' way of seeing god—because all human institutions including religious institutions (beliefs, practices, rituals, faith) are part of the world of maya, none can offer a real entry to the divine (Dharwadkar 2003, 93–4). It is hard to see how the conclusion follows that the "process of attaining mukti...is also a secular process" except in the limited sense that no human attribute ("caste, class, birth, gender, upbringing, rank or status" in his terms) can obstruct anyone from reaching this goal.

Pandit, your thinking's a sham,
there's no creation, nor creator,
Tangible, intangible, pure nor impure,
sun nor moon, no earth or water,
No form of light, no place or time,
no word and no flesh are there.
Neither action nor faith is there,
no worshipping or chants,
Sacred texts have no value there,
is it double or alone?
Nothing like Gorak or Ram is there,
nor any thought of the Ved,
There is no Brahma, Hari, Shiv or Shakti,
no actions of pilgrimage,
Where there's no mother, father or guru,
can we say it's two or one?
Says Kabir, if you can understand, you're guru,
I'm at your command.

(Shabd 43, trans. adapted from Hess and Singh in Kabir 1986)

'No actions of pilgrimage, no worshipping, no chants'—this is again the rejection of ritualism that is common to all bhakti. Kabir repeatedly asks, as if the question were not already resolved, whether there is duality or unity, *saguna* or *nirguna* in orthodox philosophical–theological terms. He seems to be insisting that neither answer is correct. This is a theme we shall meet with again in Tukaram; indeed, as scholars like Hawley have argued, there are in all the radical sants themes of both dualism and unity.

Bijak's abstract, pointed and philosophical Kabir seems to have little feeling of the love and emotion of bhakti that pervade many of his popular *dohas*. It may well have borrowed from earlier, more austere forms of Buddhism. It is likely, however, that *Bijak* also reflects the philosophical concerns of those – Kabirpanthi pandits, we might say – who amassed this collection. Devotional spirit flowers in other versions of Kabir, and Tagore's translations are full of these. *Bijak* has one brief *sakhi* on dancing — "Kabir puts on a gown of love and dances in the world; they shine with beauty who speak the truth with body and with mind," (sakhi 58, Hess and Singh's Kabir 1986) – but Tagore's Kabir (1915, 1997) revels in it:

Dance, my heart! Dance today with joy.
The strains of love fill the days and the nights with music,
and the world is listening to its melodies:
Mad with joy, life and death dance to this rhythm of this music.
The hills and the sea and the earth dance.
The world of man dances in laughter and in tears.
Why put on the robe of the monk and live
aloof from the world in lonely pride?
Behold! My heart dances in the delight of a hundred arts,
and the Creator is well pleased.
(#44)

This is quite unlike the Kabir of *Bijak*, but Tagore's Kabir harks back to the themes of Namdev and the varkaris who took their lead from him: dancing together, in collectivity. The vision is of a gathering, of celebration in this world. And this is done not in a temple – explicitly or implicitly, from Basava onwards all the radical bhaktas rejected or were uninterested in temples – but within the world, on the river banks, where the 'robe of the monk' is rejected. The vision of a full life within the world is expressed; what remained was an explicit envisioning of this place, and here we come to Ravidas, the creator of Begumpura.

Ravidas

In contrast to Kabir's sharpness and denunciatory individuality, Ravidas appears in almost all the extant songs as serene. If Kabir is the great negator, Ravidas is affirmative. He is as hard to date as the other sants (c. 1450–1520); many hagiographies have him and Kabir as coevals, if only to meet and debate on the *saguna–nirguna* issue, where Kabir is taken to represent nirguna bhakti and emerges (ambiguously) victorious in the debate (see Lorenzen 1996, 169–81).

Both men were born in Banaras. If Kabir belonged to the weaver caste from a family of recent converts to Islam, Ravidas was a chamar, an 'untouchable'. In his songs he refers to himself as such, as still doing the work of carrying dead cattle around Banaras. Though he expresses his caste status frequently, it never seems to disturb him in the way that Tuka (not as subaltern) was later to be disturbed, nor provoke him to express the fierce outcry of Kabir. He writes,

O people of the city, everyone knows
I am a cobbler by trade and tanner by caste.
One of the low-caste, and yet within my heart
I meditate on God.

(Ravidas 2007)

This so far can be taken as a simple expression of the bhakti tradition that could, reputedly, give openness to god to all but without challenging the social order. And much of Ravidas' songs seem to express this in elegant and simple fashion:

A family that has a true follower of the Lord
is neither high caste nor low caste, lordly or poor.
The world will know it by its fragrance.
Priests or merchants, laborers or warriors,
halfbreeds, outcastes, and those who tend cremation fires –
their hearts are all the same.
He who becomes pure through love of the Lord
exalts himself and his family as well.
Thanks be to his village, thanks to his home,
thanks to that pure family, each and every one.
For he's drunk with the essence of the liquid of life,
and he pours away all the poisons.
No one equals someone so pure and devoted –
not priests, not heroes, not parasolled kings.

As the lotus leaf floats above the water, Ravidas says,
so he flowers above the world of his birth.
(Hawley and Juergensmeyer 1988, 25)

Yet, in the stories about him, there is an air of defiance to brahmans that comes through even in the sanitized versions. These stories in fact centre around conflicts with the brahmans. A semi-legendary queen, Jhali, desires to become his disciple; the brahmans in her court protest, denouncing Ravidas and questioning the ability of a dalit to be a sant. "Mean himself, he has a mean job, he is from a mean family and from a mean house," they mutter about him, in the *Raidas Parcai* of Anantadas (1588). They are depicted, with some sarcasm, as greedy, constantly hungry, profiteering from their religious monopoly and hysterical about having been questioned by a 'low-caste' man. Ravidas in turn tells them, "Ram is not your private property. Anyone giving all can have Him" (see Anantadas in Callewaert and Sharma 2000, 314; a major excerpt is given in Zelliot and Mokashi-Punekar 2005, 232–44). The miracles he performs are enough to convince the queen, and in the end, the brahmans themselves.

In this story, however, the brahmans are shown as having no power of their own: they seek to kill themselves in protest and thereby provoke the state power to support them: "Some sat in the burning sun, while others threw themselves on the ground. Some of them bit their tongues, some of them rent their clothing. Some of them swallowed lumps of poison, some of them ran off to court. Some of them sliced open their bellies with daggers, some of them threatened they would kill themselves in the king's house" (Anantadas, 323). This situation also tells us something: brahmanism was, relatively speaking, out of power in northern India. Muslim rule meant at best a lax enforcement of orthodoxy; the trade and vigour of the commercial society that was coming to be provided opportunities even for those of low caste. In Ravidas' poetry, there are not only references to specific occupations such as working leather, dyeing it, and carrying carrion through the streets of Banaras, but also of merchant activity. "I am a peddler for Ram, I traffic in his easy ecstasy" (Hawley and Juergensmeyer, 29)—this and many other songs address the itinerant merchant. Some, then, from the artisan castes could move into a new life, seek a new mobility, and have new aspirations.

Ravidas' poetry is also strikingly different from those of Chokhamela which we have available to us. This may reflect not simply individual differences, but also the way in which institutionalization has taken place. Chokha has become absorbed in the varkari institutionalization, in which the temple remained in control of brahman priests throughout. Kabir, in turn, saw the later formation of Kabirpanthis, influenced in many ways by brahmanism. Ravidas, in contrast, was relatively ignored; his temples were independently those of dalits, except for his photos placed in Sikh gurudwaras

The Sorrowless City

Ravidas' songs can be used to argue how radical bhakti was, and to see to what extent their subaltern status was accepted by the sants of whom we have some records. However, there is one among the remembered songs of Ravidas that is strikingly different, in giving the images not only of low status, not only of longing for and achievement of the divine presence, but of a very earthly utopia. This is the "Begumpura" poem.

> *The regal realm with the sorrowless name:*
> *they call it Begumpura, a place with no pain,*
> *No taxes or cares, nor own property there,*
> *no wrongdoing, worry, terror or torture.*
> *Oh my brother, I've come to take it as my own,*
> *my distant home, where everything is right.*
> *That imperial kingdom is rich and secure,*

where none are third or second—all are one;
Its food and drink are famous, and those who live there
dwell in satisfaction and in wealth.
They do this or that, they walk where they wish,
they stroll through fabled palaces unchallenged.
Oh, says Ravidas, a tanner now set free,
those who walk beside me are my friends.

(Hawley and Juergensmeyer, 32)

This is in many ways quite 'modern': no property, no taxes, no political torture, no king and no temple in Ravidas' utopian city; neither is there the religious 'ecstasy' of singing and dancing. There is prosperity and equality. Ravidas hails companionship, and notes that 'they walk where they wish', indicating that the rich and privileged castes cannot impose restrictions of place upon the subordinated castes and the poor. The meaning here of being 'set free' is quite this-worldly.

"Begumpura" is so different in tone from most of the devotional bhakti songs that it may well have been preserved only because it was so remarkable, because it drew for its audience of the poor and deprived an image of the society they aimed for. It was an expression, in the early modern age, of a utopia, perhaps the first one in Indian literature. In some ways it seems to stand alone, yet it was a harbinger—of the kind of social vision that would underlie all the later struggles and theorizing of anticaste intellectuals. Begumpura was, for Ravidas, an imagined city, without a geographical location, without a history: it was to be a later task to build it in space and time.

V

Tuka The City beyond Time and Death

One of the most well-known songs of the varkaris is attributed to Bahenabai, Tuka's brahman woman disciple, though it was probably composed later, at the time of the brahmanic recuperation and cooptation of the movement. It offers what we might call the orthodox 'history' of this particular section of the bhakti movement.

sant krupaa zhaali

The sants gave their blessing
and the building arose.
Dnyandev laid the foundation,
he structured the temple.
Namdev was its mason,
he gave it this expanse.
Janardan, Ekanath,
raised the flag of Bhagwat.
Slowly sing the bhajan,
Tuka became the pinnacle[1]

[1] This song appears in the Tukaram collection and also (in slightly different form) in

Though the idea that Dnyandev 'laid the foundation' and Nama was only a mason can be contested, Tuka (1608–1649) was undoubtedly the 'pinnacle' of the movement of radical sants of the early modern period—not because he was the greatest but because he was the last of the greats. Furthermore, his poems and songs have a 'modern' quality that is not seen in the early sants—their subjectivity, their expression of a variety of mixed feelings and experiences, their very individuality gives them a quality not seen earlier.

These attributes can be related to his age and times: the first half of the seventeenth century, the climax of the early modern age and standing on the verge of a major transition. The seventeenth century was the height of the Mughal empire, but it was also the period when that empire was beginning to crack. By the end of the century Aurangzeb would be running into trouble in south India, and the empire would begin to become fragmented, solidly challenged by rising 'proto-nationalist' powers such as the Marathas and the Sikhs. During Tuka's time its strength was firm north of the Narmada, while in the south the heir kingdoms to the Bahmanis held sway, notably the Bijapur Adilshahi rule. The overall political unity was solid enough to support extensive trading and communication.

Western Maharashtra, though most of it was not an agriculturally rich area, shared in the prosperity brought by trade: the famous *dakshinapatha* (road to the south) of ancient times had run through Khandesh, close to the Ajantha caves, Paithan, and from there through western Maharashtra south to Karnataka, Andhra and Tamilnadu. Just south of Pandharpur lies the region (now in Karnataka) where the Virasaiva movement

---

the Bahenabai collection. The numbers given in this chapter after the other abhangs cited are from the Maharashtra government edition (Tukaram 1973), but I have given a romanized Marathi first line so that those using other editions can refer to them. All the translations of Tuka used here are by Gail Omvedt and Bharat Patankar.

had exploded and was then defeated and dispersed in the twelfth century; one of the towns where Basava had served for years, Mangalvedha, is now in Maharashtra and is associated with the dalit varkari Chokhamela. A recent song sung by women uses Mangalvedha as a locale as it expresses their identification with the women sants Kanhopatra (supposed to be the daughter of a prostitute) and Janabai, a maidservant.

Clearly, ideas as well as commodities flowed through the whole region, and Tuka himself represents both the culmination of previous religious currents, and a cross-cutting point in the hierarchies of caste and class. He was born into a fairly well-off family. He identifies himself both as a kunbi and a merchant; kunbis, now mostly known as marathas, are the major cultivating community of Maharashtra. While most were simple peasants, some easily made their entry into trade. Yet Tuka suffered a life of poverty: the famine that killed his wife must have revealed the fragility of some of the erstwhile prosperity in the region. Nevertheless, it was a new era. Tuka's training as a merchant apparently gave him access to writing in spite of general brahmanic discouragement of learning for the sudra castes. Against this background, Tuka stood on the threshold of modernity.

Witness to Truth

Though he signs himself only as 'Tuka', the poet is known in more orthodox terminology as Tukaram[2] and the controversy about his life begins from this simple point. The orthodox version takes off from the presentation of Mahipati (1715–

[2] 'Tukaram Maharaj' is the formal expression. The 'Ram' ties him in with a brahmanic framework in one way, while the 'Maharaj' also carries a caste marker as nonbrahman though it was used for all the varkari sants (as Dhere (1984) points out, the Pandharpur deity itself was not as 'pure' as a brahman deity since it was touched and hugged by devotees). He himself invariably used 'Tuka' in his 'signature line'. 'Tukoba', meaning 'father Tuka', is a favourite and affectionate form of address.

1790), whom we have already encountered in the chapter on Nama, and is represented in an early, award-winning Marathi film of 1930, *Sant Tukaram*, a classic by Prabhat Talkies which is still shown annually on television at the time of the Pandharpur yatra. This depicts a gentle, innocent man, a simple devotee of Vithoba whose unworldliness conflicts with the cares presented him by wife and world, who in the end achieved 'union with the Absolute' and is carried off miraculously to Vaikuntha. As noted earlier, Mahipati stresses his naive innocence: Tuka is simply unable to make a living as a merchant, and his whole worldly life ends in ruins. Mahipati's Tukaram tells Shivaji to follow varnashrama dharma, and throws his own manuscripts into the river in remorse when he is told by the brahman Rameshwar Bhat that as a sudra he has no right to write and teach (Mahipati, 1999). He is a kunbi who may 'tell what the vedas say' but knows his place as a humble devotee.

D.D. Kosambi, the most famous and independent-minded marxist scholar of Indian history and society, nevertheless characterizes bhakti as 'feudal' and thus has no trouble in accepting this depiction of Tuka, saying that he 'survived grim famine, the unremitting jealousy of contemporary folk-poets, and the contemptuous hatred of brahmins, ultimately to drown himself in the river' (Kosambi 1975, 34). Another modern version of this orthodox perception is offered by Dilip Chitre, Tuka's most well-known translator. Chitre depicts him as the greatest Marathi poet; but his translation and the arrangement of poems overall stresses his orthodoxy, and some of the most well-known, radical ones are simply omitted (Introduction to Tukaram, 1991). Finally, a recent study by Richard Eaton, though noting that the arrangement of the *dindis* (processions to Pandharpur) and much of the social aspect of the varkari cult had been formed after Tuka's day, nevertheless takes the hagiographies uncritically and argues that "from its very beginnings that movement was concerned not with revolution – certainly not the overthrow of the caste system – but with reform" (2005, 153).

A dissident tradition has survived in rural and antibrahman circles. Pioneered in some ways by Phule and his compatriots, it was expressed most recently in *Vidrohi Tukaram* (Tukaram the Rebel), a book published in 1997 by A.H. Salunkhe, a small-town Sanskrit professor. This depicted Tukaram starting his career by casting his moneylending records in the river, and going on to defy brahmans until he was murdered by the most ferocious of his enemies. The book sparked a debate throughout Maharashtra, both in oral and printed cultures, with the most eminent writers and translators of Tukaram (including Chitre) jumping into the fray with articles in *Maharashtra Times* and finally the *Times of India*. Nevertheless though he stressed Tuka's social radicalism, Salunkhe remained within the framework of orthodoxy in assessing Tuka's spiritual position. He concurred with the brahmanic view in describing him as *veda-pramanya*—accepting the authority of the vedas, but able to interpret them better than the brahmans. We might say that Salunkhe was following a kind of kshatriya antibrahmanism; he views the upanishads (the supposed source of advaita) as representing a basic kshatriya point of view against brahmanic ritualism (see 1997, 35–46). In contrast, an emerging dalit-Buddhist view sees Vitthal as a version of Buddha, and the sants as Boddhisattas (Javale 1999).

Tuka, however – perhaps as befitting a poet of the seventeenth century, a century emerging into modernity – gives his own extended commentaries on his life and these are quite different. The most thorough one is quite prosaic:

yaati shudra vansh kela vevasaay

By caste and lineage a sudra, I took to business.
At first he was just the family god.
I shouldn't talk, but I'm honoring the pledge
to answer your question, O sants (refrain)

My worldly life turned into extreme pain
after my mother and father passed away.
Drought wiped me out, took away wealth and honor
and one of my wives died crying for food.
I was ashamed, my soul tormented by pain,
and I saw my business fall into loss.
The temple of the god had fallen into ruin,
it came into my mind to repair it.
At first I would do songs on the holy days.
My mind was not inclined to study.
I memorized some sayings of the sants,
in reverence and faith repeating them.
After that I would sing refrains after them,
making my mind and emotions pure.
I served the sants, took the water of their feet.
never letting shame enter my mind.
I helped others as much as I could,
making my body strong for toil.
I never followed the advice of friends,
I was nauseated by the whole material world.
I applied my mind to discern truth from untruth,
never heeding the opinion of the majority.
I respected the guru's advice of my dream,
held firmly to trust in the name (in Nama).
After this I was inspired to poetry –
my mind held to the feet of Vithoba.
A blow of denunciation fell on me,
paining my mind for some time.
My manuscripts were drowned, I sat in protest,
and Narayan gave me satisfaction.
If I told all the details
it would become late; enough.
Now my thought is what it seems.
God knows what will happen next.
Narayan never forsakes his devotees,
I have learned his compassion.
Tuka says, my only assets are
that Pandurang has made me speak.

(#1333)

This reviews some essential landmarks of Tuka's life: a famine and a subsequent loss of life and livelihood, identifying without explicitly saying so, his business loss with the famine—not due to ineptness, or (as Salunkhe has it) throwing away his own records of debt. (As for naivete in business, a very explicit abhang has him saying, "I'm a merchant by profession and suspicious, no frauds will stand before me"; #1859). It describes taking up the worship of Vitthal almost casually but humbly; then comes 'a blow of denunciation' which results in his manuscripts being drowned. Other autobiographical poems refer to his persecution in the courts and a resultant decision to leave settled, village life for one of wandering in the forests: here there is indeed renunciation, but not as a religious injunction, rather as something forced on him: "How shall I eat? Who can I meet? Who will support me living here? The headman's angry, the people upset...they do decisions in their courts.... Tuka says, I don't want their company, I'll go and search for Vitthal now" (#678). This fits the pattern of the other radical bhaktas: they are not basically renouncers but they are quite often forced into a life of wandering. They are at odds with the establishment, and are often persecuted.

The most famous lines in #1333 are *satyaasatya man kele gwahi*—"I made my own mind the witness to truth and untruth." But perhaps just as crucial is his signature line: "My only assets are that Pandurang has made me speak." The word used is *bhandwal,* now usually used to translate 'capital'. It is a reference to what appears as important through so many poems—the ability to speak, and to write.

Part of the problem of interpretation of Tuka is the matter of dealing with the 'tone' of a poem. For example, in many places the theme is heard that as a sudra he is not supposed to read or write: that this was the judgment of society was something that he learned through bitter experience in his life. But did this mean he accepted the caste hierarchy and his assigned position in it? In fact, the tone of his writing suggests a rejection. A famous example is the well-known abhang that begins *bara kunbi kelo* ("good you made me a peasant"). The words *bara* or *bara zhala* are very often ironic in Marathi, and it seems clear that, in contrast to some interpretations, Tuka is using them in that way here (see, for example, Eaton 2005, 132–35).

Though there are poems expressing humility and the greatness of his sin, this (like songs on Krishna and Rama) is a 'stock theme' of much of bhakti (see, for example, Hawley's discussion of Surdas in Schomer and McLeod 1987, 205–09), and often this humility seems rather rhetorical. However dramatically he may call himself a sinner, Tuka's self-image is not low: the voice that we hear very often is one of power; one that expresses his own sense of achievement and spiritual-moral power, and his awareness of his ability to inspire people. "As long, as long as the stone looks bright the diamond will never shine; as long, as long as the lamp gives light, the sun's rays will not open; as long, as long as they prattle of sants they'll never meet with Tuka" (#2784). The phrase "I made my own mind the witness to truth and untruth," in fact, is one of determined self-reliance, and echoes the great theme of the antibrahmanical tradition, from the Buddhist *atta deepa bhav* (Be your own light) to Kabir's *veda-kiteb kahaa kin jhuuthaa, jhuthaa jo no vicaare,*[3] to Phule's 'truthseeking'. If he decided this early in his life, it would have led him naturally to a revolt against caste humiliation; and his spiritual seeking and the great response he began to get from the subordinated groups who flocked around him, must have confirmed his position. With such support, he clearly began to work his way through the brahmanical interpretations of the deity and of human life which were hegemonic in his time.

[3] From the *Bijak*, (Kabir 1997a, shabd 97), "Which is false, Koran or veda? False is he who does not think".

We thus have many abhangs in which he claims a status almost of a prophet, of bringing a great message to all the people:

kaas ghaaloni balkath

Girding my loins with strength
I've wrestled with time and death,
I have made a pathway
across the ocean of life.
Come, come, young and old,
women and men of all castes,
Nothing to worry about,
just think...
Tuka says, I've come,
I'm the bearer of the name
(#519)

Thus two things stand out regarding Tuka as a person. First, compared to the earlier sants, there is more of 'autobiography' in his songs; he examines and expresses his own subjectivity, something that might be taken as a sign of modernism and a new concern with the individual. Second, in a society in which the ritualism of brahmanism was being rejected, where the heritage of Buddhism, the Nath-yogis, and later Sufi and Islam were strong, where Christianity was beginning to permeate from Goa, Tuka was forging his own religious and cultural message.

The Lineage of Dissent and Heroism

Communities are both real and imagined. Tuka, who often wandered along in the forests or sat in meditation, had an imagined community which he saw as gathered around Vitthala, or 'Pandhari's lord'. It was undoubtedly realized to some extent in the support he received from followers of Vitthala in his day, but he drew much of his strength from the vision of a community stretching backwards into time (and potentially forward) and he passed this strength on to his followers. With a few notable exceptions, his followers were primarily from the subaltern castes. Of all the legendary heroes and saints available to him, he chooses the subalterns. He celebrates them as such – and does so with the tone of rejection that characterizes so many of his song-poems: "Which of your books have saved the fallen?' In fact, in many of his abhangs, brahmans and the brahmanized sections from the sudras represent the 'Other'.

> ***pavitra te kul paavan to desh***
> *Blessed the lineage, holy the land*
> *where the servants of Hari are born.*
> *Karmadharma's become Narayan,*
> *it's he who has purified the worlds* (refrain).
> *Who is purified by pride of varna,*
> *tell me if you know!*
> *Untouchables are saved by hymns to Hari,*
> *legendary stories are told by bards.*
> *Tuladhar Vaishya, the potmaker Gora,*
> *the leatherworker Rohidas.*
> *the momin Kabir, Latif the muslim,*
> *the barber Sena are Vishnu's slaves.*
> *Kanhopatra, Khodu, cotton-carder Dadu,*
> *sing hymns to Hari without discord.*
> *Banka, Chokhamela, by caste Mahar,*
> *have united with the Lord.*
> *What is the worth of Nama's Jani*
> *when Pandhari's lord eats in her company?*
> *Can you tell the lineage of Mairala?*
> *What greatness did he have, do tell!*
> *Vishnu's servants have no caste,*
> *the veda's science so decrees.*
> *Says Tuka, which of your books*
> *have saved the fallen – I know of none*
> (#4299)

This song of his heritage, of the 'Vishnudas', is a line-up of subalterns. His writings repeatedly stress the working-caste status and the collectivity of the 'company of the saints' that gather on the river sands. More than almost any other bhakti poet we have access to, his songs suggest a class sense—one in which 'the last are first':

aahmii bhaagyaace bhaagyaace

We are blessed, so blessed,
we have gourds for vessels.
Others have cattle and buffalos,
our houses have rats and mongoose.
Others have elephants and horses,
we have leather sandals.
Tuka says, we are so decrepit
even death shies from us.

(#2955)

He stresses that he has no 'establishment'; he does not seek to win over people with frauds; he has no army of followers, no hermitage, no institutional land to support him; all those who do and exploit people through religious chicanery are 'crazed citizens of hell' (#272).

In the famous incident about the meeting with Shivaji, Tuka's own poems tell a different story from that of Mahipati. Whereas the brahman hagiographer shows him advising the king not to renounce his political responsibilities to become a devotee but to follow his varnashrama dharma of rulership, Tuka's songs emphasize his rejection of a meeting with Shivaji and his horrors of courtly honours and life:

Torch bearer, parasol, a horse,
these would not be good for me!
Now why, Pandhari Raya,
are you involving me in this?
Honour, hypocrisy, scorn,
these are all pig's shit!

(#1884)

In the house of the kings there is honour for the fortunate,
but no honour for ordinary people there.
Seeing gorgeous clothes for the great,
I feel like dying instantly.
(#1888)

Thus he celebrates the common soldier (the *paik*) rather than the nobles (songs #1062–72). His choice is not simply for the forest and a renouncer's life but a refusal of patronage and an acceptance of uncertainty:

Now life flows like this,
now it's a bed of bliss.
Just as the time commands,
so we flow with its demands.
Now we dine in luxury,
now we eat dry bhakri.
Now we ride in style,
now we plod a weary mile.
Now we wear fine clothes,
now it's cast-off rags.
Now we roll in wealth,
now we live by stealth.
Now the company of the good,
now we live with rogues.
Tuka says, you should know
joy and sorrow together flow
(#2819)

Dancing to the City of Sants

There has been little critical work on the varkaris done of the kind that is now common with regard to the north Indian sants. Nearly all translators and commentators take all the songs that are given in the collections as actually the words of that particular sant. Only Salunkhe (1997) has argued that many of the abhangs attributed to Tukaram are interpolations, but he gives no other criteria for determining them to be so except for the inconsistency with his other themes.

The arrangement in the collected *Gatha* published by Government of Maharashtra, which has by now gone through many editions, is largely by theme. These range from events in Tukaram's life to Krishna stories to village games, common village characters, and idiosyncratic poem themes such as the common soldier (*paik*) or quarrels with Tuka's wife. It often appears that of the many songs on the same theme, some were written at different stages; some appear to be almost 'rough drafts' of a complete masterpiece; some appear to be interpolations and some are in fact 'signed' by others. In addition, it is normal for collections of sant poetry in Marathi to contain songs by members of the leading sant's family, occasionally friends and followers. Thus the Tukaram collection contains many by his brother (though none by his wife, who is depicted in this case as an almost complete shrew), and a few by unnamed followers, as well as some by Rameshwar Bhat, the most famous of his one-time enemies who became a follower. The volume also includes songs in Dakhani (#438–444) as well as a more northern Hindi, called *sakhis* (after the word used in the *Bijak* for the *doha* form) (#1173–1202).

Of the themes, the most striking is that of games, and one of these, *tipri,* gives us some of Tuka's most beautiful songs. The song cited at the beginning of Chapter 2, *khele mandiyela* (#189), symbolizes the new message of bhakti. It offers a characteristic look at the whole movement, the dancing on the river sands, the equalitarianism that rejects 'the pride of varna and of caste'; and most striking, it has devotees falling at one another's feet, thus not recognizing hierarchy among themselves, and ends with the resounding victory cry of the Vaishnava heroes. The song immediately following (#190) gives a kind of history of the movement, beginning with 'the tailor's son Nama' who 'made Vithoba the leader' and is clearly, throughout, Tukaram's hero and inspirer; it then describes Dnyandev and his cohort who made 'Kanho the cowherd the leader'—probably an accurate depiction of events, for Dnyandev was in effect the movement's earliest sanskritizer. What is also striking here is a theme that recurs in many songs of Tukaram, the idea of the devotees creating or controlling the deity.

It is in a later one in this series that we get the most powerful expression of the powerful vision of Tukaram in which Pandharpur is the utopia, which time and death cannot reach, so full of love and the company of sants that none would desire to go to Vaikuntha, the Vaishnava paradise, let alone run after the moksha of brahmanic orthodoxy. If we accept the notion that the numbering has some relationship to an order of writing, this would have been written later in his life:[4]

> ***bhimatiri ek vasale nagar***
> *A city sits on the banks of the Bhima,*
> *its name is Pandharpur!*
> *The regent there has four arms*
> *and 16,000 wives!*
> (Refrain) *Let us go dancing, friend, to his city*
> *he will give us joy and rest,*
> *those who went ahead have gone beyond,*
> *they will laud his new horizons,*
> *Bali the unique, protects the protectors,*
> *Time and death cannot enter,*
> *Pundalik Patil was made to toil like a peasant*
> *and liberated from bodily sorrow,*
> *The good sants have opened up shops,*
> *whatever you want is there --*
> *food and liberty, all for free,*
> *no one even looks their way!*
> *Both the markets are jammed with wealth*

[4] The tipri includes six songs; the only one following this is signed 'Tukyaca Das', i.e., by one of his followers.

uncounted varkaris meet there;
We won't settle in Vaikuntha, say
those who have seen Pandhari.
For many days I've had this longing,
today it happened from great exertion,
Tuka says, yes, it's not by your goodness
we meet at his feet.

(#194)

Here Krishna has become simply the *mokashi*, a regent, and the song refers to a supreme deity this time called 'Baliya', evidently Bali Raja. The verse suggests a theme that Phule was to use later: the 'Kingdom of Bali' as a description of an ideal society, with various *sardars* or 'protectors' under him (Phule would spell these out as Khandoba, Naikba, Chandoba, Vithoba, etc—lords of various *khands* or sections of the kingdom).

Pandhari as the 'Begumpura' of Tukaram, is above all a 'city of saints', a city of love and joy. In the more rustic atmosphere of Maharashtra, it lacks the palaces of Ravidas, but it has shops and above all the river sands on which the devotees dance. As in the case of Begumpura, there is no mention of temples, even of the famous temple of Vitthala. Some among the sants, as the famous case of Chokhamela illustrates, were barred from the temple anyway. Vitthal, 'mother-father', comes out of the temple to be with his devotees. A major characteristic is the solidarity and collectivity of the sants; equality is the theme; people 'fall at each other's feet' in ecstasy, 'everyone will be powerful and prosperous' (#1142). Pandharpur, like Begumpura, is above all a place where there is no hierarchy, where 'no one talks of great or small, all are together' (#211), where 'everyone adorns himself before others as he likes, there is no great or small' (#3268). This envisioned Pandharpur of the river sands is not the actual city with its priest-controlled temple, but rather a city beyond time and death.

I've seen Varanasi, Gaya, Dwarka,
they cannot be Tuka's Pandhari.
No one has pride at Pandhari,
people fall at one another's feet.
Tuka says, who goes once to Pandhari
will never see Yama come to his home.

Socio-Religious Critique, Religious Searching

There had always been a theme among the varkaris and many bhakti movements concerning the power of devotion itself—Namdev, for instance, is frequently described as able to control Vitthal, the deity. With Tukaram, in an age entering into modernity which includes the use of rational questioning, this becomes turned into themes of questioning the divine. The devotees even create the divine, as the following song illustrates (here the crucial word is *bhav*, which we have translated as emotion):

paashaan dev, pashan paayarii

God of stone, steps of stone –
we worship one, walk on the other.
Emotion's the essence, emotion's the essence,
God himself came out of experience.
Do different waters have a nature different?
the Ganga is sweet, do the others have no taste?
Says Tuka, this is the devotees' essence –
Others can ask about dharma and adharma
(#2270)

There is much in Tuka to suggest his modernity—an early seventeenth century modernity, a time when in Europe rationalists like Descartes could assert a beginning from the knowledge that 'I think, therefore I am'; when scientists like Galileo would challenge the Inquisition; when the early, 'heretical' efforts at translating the Bible into the vernacular would yield the King James-sponsored 'authorized' translation of the Bible; when Hobbes and Locke would lay the philosophical foundations of an anti-monarchical democracy. These trends had their correlates in India, though we find more of the themes emerging 'from below' and being cut off by their conflict with an establishment.

What should be stressed is that Tuka was not only critical of the brahmanic social system of caste; he also rather openly denounces the traditional goals of brahmanism of absorption in the divine.[5] *Advaita* itself, the privileged theory of brahmanism, comes in for critique. At a more empirical level, he ruthlessly attacks the pride of brahmans, oppressive kings, fraudulent yogis—indeed, all who trade in the name of god, who 'sell their daughters and their stories' come in for special scorn. The puranas are sometimes simply recited as what we have, but in other cases they also come in for questioning, particularly in regard to the notion of avatars. Where Namdev sometimes reverses it, and Kabir rejects the application to the god, Tuka in one memorable poem, *Hari tu nishtar nirgun* (Hari, you're cruel and without merit), turns it into a questioning of the god himself: how can a god do such things as destroy Karna, send the good king Bali under the earth, take the flesh of Sibi? "This is the life you've given to those who praise you with devotion. I have no idea, says Tuka, what you will do next" (#144). In this poem, the famous cosmological-theological notion of *nirguna* is simply used to mean 'without merit'.

Also a somewhat new feature are occasional songs that almost might be called 'god is dead' poems.

maazhaa lekhi dev mela

God has died for me

---

[5] Here I am disagreeing with most of the interpretations of Tuka by scholars such as Chitre, More and others. To maintain their position of a brahmanized orthodoxy, Chitre and More simply have to ignore a large number of songs.

For others let him be.
We don't talk or take each other's name,
we have separated and gone (refrain).
Abuse along with praise,
so went endless days
Tuka says, I'm standing calm,
that's how I've spent my time.
(#2349)

Among other famous critiques is the one that – like Phule would do later – turn the legends around to use them to accuse the god: "Hari you are cruel and without qualities, you've no compassion, you're very hard, you do what is unimaginable—what no one else has done." It goes on to describe the hardships and torture inflicted on Harishchandra, Nala and Damayanti, Sibi (who is celebrated in Buddhist literature), Karna and King Bali, and concludes, "This is the life you've given to those who praise you with devotion; I have no idea, says Tuka, what you will do next." (#133)

In spite of the later period and a greater certainty about his dates, the fact remains that given the vast number of songs in the official collection (nearly 4,000, not counting those attributed to his brother or to others), and the failure to even attempt a critical edition or to work out a likely order of writing, Tuka's life remains as much a mystery as those of Kabir and Mira two centuries earlier. We might imagine a process, in which he gradually associates himself with Pandharpur and its deity, learns to write poetry and composes song-poems using many traditional themes (there are songs to Krishna and to Rama in the collection) but adding from the very beginning a questioning of caste and of ritualism, and a disdain for religious hypocrisy. Then comes the 'blow of denunciation' in which he is brought to trial and his manuscripts are thrown into the river. Some are miraculously saved—but life in his village home of Dehu is no longer stable. He leaves, 'going to search for Vitthal', takes up for a time a life of wandering in the wild; his fame continues to grow, Shivaji attempts to meet him and is rejected along with all of courtly and worldly life (there is no evidence in the collection to support Mahipati's story, which remains popular, that Shivaji himself then came to meet Tuka; there are simply songs about Shivaji, at least one of which is clearly an interpolation).[6] He tries meditation, reportedly in what was originally a Buddhist cave in the hills near what is now the small town of Chakan, north of Pune; there are some songs that present a nondualistic and powerful meditation experience. Yet these are not so predominant in the overall collection as the emphasis on 'dualism', and the need for devotion and a loving relationship to a divine force separate from oneself. There are many songs throughout that express the vision of a 'Pandhari', the utopian city of dancing and singing.

However, there is clearly a period of questioning; the sense of a protecting and caring deity seems to alternate with that of loss; in one reference to the deity as Buddha he complains that he is 'invisible' and asks 'why no compassion?' (#4160) A whole series which Chitre translates and calls 'the cripple' (Tuka 1991) may express something of the loneliness and longing that comes at the end of life. One of these is particularly beautiful:

desh-vesh navhe mazhe

I have neither home nor habit,
I wander naturally;
I have power over none
and no stability.
My eyes and feet are called my own
I've also set them free —
now I'm blind and lame, but none's
a foreigner to me.

---

[6] Song #1886 refers to Shivaji as 'Chhatrapati', though this was a title claimed and won after Tuka's death.

Now he takes care of me,
his gifts are plentiful and free,
I have no one, no family,
I give myself to the sants (refrain).

Going further on the path
my mind is filled with fear.
Many have gone ahead;
none have turned back here.
What's happened I cannot see,
only a whisper in my ear.
I've sat in the twilight zone,
holding you in mind...

I plead for your compassion, Lord,
as I've lost the way;
I have never filled my stomach,
my feet have always strayed.
I've wandered and I've suffered, Lord,
innumerable lands and ways;[7]
I'm holding to you now, Lord,
this is the place I'll stay...

....I've surrendered all I have,
nothing is left to me,
all relation's broken with
money, friends, family.
I've become passionless, Lord,
this was my destiny.

---

[7] This line illustrates the problematic of translation: the Marathi is *lakshchaurasi gav* which Chitre is at pains to translate literally, and in doing so, imposes an interpretation that Tuka is talking of countless rebirths. His translation is: "I have visited all the 840,000 villages/that karma compels a man to go through" (in Tukaram 1991, 56). Why 'villages'? This is a mélange of the literal and the figurative, and brings an explanation into the text. Instead, I would argue that the whole song is about a weary life of wandering and finding final solace in a god. The other interesting point about the translation is that the word I have translated as 'Lord' is *gaa*—the feminine form of address in Marathi.

Tuka says, it's only you now,
my entire Bali.

(#424)

The Conservative Consolidation of the Eighteenth Century

Tuka's life was short—shorter than that of any of the other radical sants. In 1648, he disappeared from his village early on the morning of the first day of what is Holi in Maharashtra—'dust-throwing day', a time of traditional rioting. The orthodox account is that he was carried off to heaven directly; the modern, brahmanic, secularist explanation is that he simply bid everyone goodbye and wandered off on some unnamed pilgrimage (Chitre, introduction to Tukaram 1991, xiii–xiv). Nonbrahmans believe that he was murdered by his enemies, and Salunkhe's recent study cites many bits of circumstantial evidence in favour of this (1997, 232–89).

Tuka died as Shivaji was beginning his career, and it was Shivaji who heralded in India a new upsurge of regionally based powers, culminating in many separate states in the eighteenth century. This period has been much studied and debated by historians, and the emerging consensus is that it was not, as previously depicted, a period of decadence and depression, marked by the breakup of the Mughal empire and the subsequent 'rescue' by the intervention of a dynamic western power and colonial rule. Rather there were new forms of development, a certain amount of economic growth and deepening of political structures in the new regional kingdoms (see, for instance, Barnett 2000; Bayley 1998; Richards 1997) and the regional powers themselves are now seen as representing language-based 'patriotisms' or 'proto-nationalities'.

The eighteenth century may clearly not have been a period of economic decline; the new regional states may have represented a 'proto-nationalism'. Yet, as Sheldon Pollock (1988) reminds us, it would be wrong to see 'vernacularization' and for that matter regionalization as leading in a straight line to nationalism of the European style. Pollock himself notes the limits of Sanskrit, even when 'new' themes began to be taken up (Pollock 2001), but he does not really deal with the issue that Sanskrit had been a caste monopoly, and that the new vernacularization was increasingly defined in the same way. The dynamic of the new regional 'patriotisms' involved a conservative consolidation. It can be argued that in many ways the eighteenth century represented in Europe itself a new kind of crisis with industrialization and its early traumas; it was really only towards the end of the nineteenth century that working-class living standards can be said to improve. Within India, too, before it moved into a decisive colonial relationship with Britain, the eighteenth century in many ways represented a closure of earlier potentialities of democracy and rationalism.

The bhakti movements, which had earlier had local and regional roots but a pan-regional scope, ended by feeding into regional–nationalist unities that were embodied by landed elites asserting themselves against the higher imperial power. But in doing so they were coopted, distorted and sanitized. The landed elites benefited from bhakti equality, but denied these benefits to the subaltern toilers. Thus, for example, the Sikh kingdom saw a resurgence of jat power, but mazhabi Sikhs (converts from untouchables) continued to be viewed as low. In the Maratha kingdom, even under the Peshwas, people of 'low' kunbi background could experience social mobility, but it was more difficult for those from the other subaltern castes, including artisans and those considered 'polluted' and 'untouchable'. 'Maratha' could emerge as a broad category but never broad enough to include the latter.

It is not surprising, then, that the conservative hagiographies come from his period—Mahipati in Maharashtra, Priyadas in northern India. In north India this was also the period in which the Ramanandi cult gained in strength, winning over many subordinated castes to an identity that linked them to Rama and Krishna but at the cost of maintaining the caste framework (Pinch 1996, 23–47; 1999, 379–82). Even here there was a regression after a major meeting at Galta in 1713. A number of scholars (Gooptu 1996; Lele 1995) have seen the eighteenth century as one of regression for the bhakti movements. The popular power of bhakti had forced a compromise from brahmanism which gave the sants a kind of recognition, but buried their original equalitarian and rationalist message, pushing them back to, at best, an assertion of a spiritual equality which was not allowed to (and usually no longer aspired to) spill over into social equality.

The dynamics must have differed from region to region, but they can be seen in the events in the Marathi-speaking areas. Shivaji rose on the wave of popular assertion and the strength of the Mavali soldiers who, as common paiks sacrificing themselves to defend the community, had been sung about by Tuka. Through most of his life he was opposed by the Maratha nobility. Yet to legitimize his kingdom and to win over the capable corps of brahman administrators, Shivaji had to seek brahmanic sanction, and won this finally with a hugely expensive ceremony presided over by a brahman brought from Varanasi, which had him symbolically establish his kshatriya status. The common myths of Shivaji as '*go-brahman prati-palak*', (protector of cows and brahmans) began to be established from this day—this became hegemonic in spite of the subterranean tradition that he had afterwards had a tantric ceremony performed with a marriage to a mahar woman (Laine 1996, 97–115). By the time he died, feudalism was reasserting himself, and his son Sambhaji carried on an unsuccessful struggle against the emerging brahman dominance. What followed this, as grandsons and daughters-in-law struggled for the succession, was a de facto takeover by his brahman administrators, the Peshwas. The nonbrahman nobles under their hegemony moved throughout India and established their own satrapies – also fairly orthodox – in Gujarat, Madhya Pradesh and central India.

The exaltation of Tuka remains, but he has become 'Tukaram Maharaj', with Mahipati's version of his life holding the field nearly unchallenged. Shivaji remains the most revered king and symbol of Maharashtrian unity, but in spite of attempts, from Phule on through movement leaders today, to depict him as a 'farmers' king' it is the brahmanized versions that get the publicity of popular novels, songs and plays. Nevertheless, while the radical upsurge of the bhakti of the early modern period was sidetracked, and Maharashtra with the rest of India suffered the fate of moving into real modernity under colonial conquest, memories remained, and with it the vision that underlay a search for a different modernity—a Begumpura a, Pandharpur.

vi

Kartabhajas Ecstasy and Reason in the Colonial Yuga

Let me tell you a funny story about a king:
in his city, all along the road, are rows and rows of merchants.
In the city centre there's a bazar,
With the seal of the Royal House.
Twelve months a year there's buying and selling,
importing and exporting
whether the weight of the taxes in the warehouse is little or great.
I came here and saw –
everywhere there were so many things!
I had never seen such things in this world!
So much was spread out everywhere;
I'm thinking, how can I speak of it?
And if you understand this straight-away,
you can cross the river of the world and the cosmic age.
The king never takes gifts, tax or tariffs.
That's why the merchants all revere him.
He waives all the taxes on the waterways.
Everyone pays him the capital of respect.
So listen to what I say:
No one has need for brokerage, commissions or such tactics!

The Moon is the assistant and Kalki the Avatar

(Kartabhaja song)

At the juncture of independent India – when bhakti had been absorbed and coopted into a brahmanic unity enforced in new regional kingdoms – and the new colonial framework, a late version of bhakti confronted both colonialism and brahmanism. This was the Kartabhaja movement, rising in Bengal, the earliest centre of colonial rule.

Ecstasy and Bhakti

Hugh Urban's study of the Kartabhajas, a late nineteenth century bhakti movement in Bengal, emphasizes the concept of 'ecstasy': his theoretical work is titled *Economics of Ecstasy* (2001a) and his translations, *Songs of Ecstasy* (2001b). Urban, indeed, explicitly translates the word *bhava* (from *Bhaver Gita*, the main collection of Kartabhaja songs), a word which is generally translated as 'emotion, devotion,' and as 'religious ecstasy' (2001a, 6). This movement, in fact, gives us the first response of radical bhakti to the new situation brought by colonialism—and it is a welcoming response, one that stresses the potentialities of the new society, a response of 'ecstasy'. Strikingly, also, the movement repudiated the established Bengali Vaishnava movement and claimed to be heirs of the 'true Chaitanya'.

The Kartabhaja movement began around the end of the eighteenth and early nineteenth century—the period of early, self-confident capitalist colonialism as a powerful revival of the Bengali bhakti. Their founder, Aulchand, was often described as the 'divine madman'—the fourth in the line of great leaders and avatars after Chaitanya and his major disciples. He was apparently a Muslim and probably a Sufi of sorts. They called themselves *kartabhajas*—'devotees of the creator'. The activists argued that the old Vaishnava movement, founded by Chaitanya, which they called the 'old marketplace', had become corrupt;

they proclaimed a new 'secret marketplace'. Secrecy was a weapon to resist appropriation, to guard themselves from the power of brahmanism. In the new era of the East India Company, they ignored the traditional, sacred puranic and other imagery, and instead used the images of the city, the market, and the Company, celebrating prosperity and an abundance of goods, enjoyment and eroticism. Terms like 'contract' (*kontrakt*), invoices (*inbhais*) and permits (*parmit*) pervaded their poetry. The word *kompani* was a key metaphor to describe themselves; they were the *gorib kompani*, the 'company of the poor'. They did not glorify poverty, but imagined its end, in a new utopia of love, ecstasy and abundance. 'Poverty' and 'madman' were terms that were reversed in meaning in their lexicon.

Theirs was a "company of the poor" where "the Emperor gives no commands; the King punishes no one. If someone, in need of money, commits a theft in this land, the Company freely gives him infinite wealth" (Urban 2001a, 41). This was indeed a revolt against the keepers of the purse and the holders of power.

They were resolutely anticaste, drawing from all kinds of subordinated castes, and anti-ritual, anti-vedic in the familiar radical bhakti style. They also had links to the *sahijiya* and tantric traditions of Bengal, and their songs also made reference to *parakiya* love—to the forbidden ecstasy of unregulated emotion, to love outside of marriage and outside of social rules, love which was more 'holy' because it was more daring and subversive. All these themes, and especially the disregard, even scorn of caste, shocked and antagonized the elite. One satirical poem ridiculing them put it:

> The Kartabhaja sect has recently emerged – now hear some funny things about them!...
> They see no distinction between boys, old men, youths or women; thus they go along...

> Brothers, if any of you wish to go to the Kartabhaja festival,
> you'll have to go where thirty-six castes go—and caste will
> have to be left behind.
>
> (Cited in Urban 2001b, 9)

It is striking that caste was the theme that predominated in this scornful review of the movement. However, the repugnance that the elite felt towards the Kartabhajas was justified mostly in terms of its tantric connections, which were looked upon as dangerous, and individually and socially degenerate. The threat to the family that *parakiya* love involved, and the links with tantra led them to be scorned by the elite as a 'degenerate form of the tantric religion'. They could thus be taunted with a connotation of lowness and filth. In the words of the favourite guru of the bhakdralok, Ramakrishna, the Kartabhaja path was "a secret back door path," a dirty and dangerous one that was like entering a house through the toilet rather than the back door (cited in Urban 2001b, 30).

The Kartabhajas centred their songs around the metaphor and reality of the market, and for them, as in reality, it was an ambivalent phenomenon. It promised abundance, and this was what underlay the 'ecstasy'; but at the same time they condemned the greed of moneymaking. The favourite negative image in the Kartabhaja songs was that of profiteering brokers (*dalal*). As Urban points out, the use of economic metaphors for religious phenomenon was in evidence here; there is, for example, what some interpret as a reference to Christian missionaries as 'brokers from abroad' (2001a, 165). It is quite possible, then, that the term was used to condemn brahmanism, which represented the dominant priestly and ritual intermediacy between humans and the divine; it may in this way have anticipated the later use of the nonbrahman movement which aimed at performing religious–cultural rituals without intermediaries, describing them as *dalals*. As against ritualism and priesthood, the Kartabhaja movement emphasized, along with much of bhakti, *sahaja* or 'natural' and easy devotion and ecstasy as the way to liberation.

The use of modernistic and technological metaphors was not limited to the Kartabhajas; other religious lower-class sects of the time (the Sahebdhanis, for example) also compared the railroads to the body, the engine to the soul. What was unique about the Kartabhajas was perhaps the theme of the *gorib kompani*, the association of the poor who would attain wealth in the new order.

Ecstasy and abundance on one hand, greed and ruin on the other—this was the ambivalence of the marketplace. Somewhat similarly, colonialism, or the advent of foreign merchants, was viewed with ambivalence—bringing goods to fill the market, but also humbling otherwise proud Bengali religious and political elites. In contrast to the elite itself, notably, the Kartabhajas, belonging to the subordinated castes were not so upset with this humbling, but rather mocked the imitativeness of the native elite. "So many merchant ships and as many imported goods are coming!...The merchants do whatever they want, and joyfully, to their hearts desire, they take it from the farmers!...The Broker runs along behind, hoping to buy or sell something!" (Urban 2001a, 66). This sees the weak Bengali elite as more or less running after the imperialists. In a song which Urban titles "The Shameful State of Bengal under Foreign Rule", the tone is one of mockery not so much dismay at being shamed: "You people of this land are all eternally deluded" (61). In other words, the 'shame' was of the elite, not of the masses of people.

This was a different kind of response to colonialism, one that had little to do with the 'debates' that took place among the elites. The Kartabhajas represented a parallel movement to the reformism of upper-class movements such as the Brahmo Samaj; it was a contesting and alternative interpretation, much more radical, more equalitarian, and above all ecstatic rather than rationalistic. The Brahmos and the like stressed a scientific, rational response, harking back to a pure monotheism said to exist in the vedas, while the Kartabhajas stressed the ecstasy of intense devotion, and praised the 'rag-clad madman Aulchand', finding linkages to the bhakti movement.

As Urban notes, "the Kartabhaja vision of a caste-free company of the poor offered the hope of a radical new vision of *community*—a community based not on wealth or class but on the universal religion of humanity (*manuser dharma*) and the recognition of the inherent divinity of all men and women. This was a communist ideal distinguished both from the traditional class-based religious hierarchy and from a secular materialist social order of the sort championed by the subaltern theorists" (Urban 2001a, 37). In the end, the Kartabhaja movement became bureaucratised and failed to live up to these ideals. However, it is significant that, at the beginning of colonialism, the most radically utopian vision came from an anticaste devotional movement with a subaltern base.

Reason and Ecstasy

If 'ecstasy' is a good translation for *bhava,* the central emotion of bhakti, then *jnana,* more valued by the elite, can be translated as 'reason'. Ecstasy and reason, or *bhakti* and *jnana*—these are two major accomplishments of humanity. In the modern age, ecstasy is to be embodied and realized in the world, in a prosperous, equalitarian society, a utopia that can be achieved in history and through the actions of historically struggling human beings. Reason, in this regard, is the analytical understanding of the socioeconomic conditions that would help to delineate the path to be followed to reach such a society. Ecstasy is thus to be achieved not simply by forgetting the mundane existence of the daily world, but eventually solidifying in a class-free, casteless, non-patriarchal, prosperous society.

In the premodern world, characterized by low development of the forces of production as well as persistence of class and caste inequalities, this form of reason and ecstasy was not available to humanity. The elite could find a kind of ecstasy through leisure and enjoyment, the masses had to forget their sorrows, but this required a letting go of the world. Religion thus provided a road to ecstasy. Marx's phrase, 'opium of the people', implied it smothered their struggles and revolts, but this was not invariably true; it sometimes inspired these.

Reason also was not available to all, but rather limited to the intelligentsia. In India in particular, it was monopolized by a birth elite, the brahmans. Ecstasy for all was assigned to the golden age of the past, to the first great yuga when sacrifice was done everywhere; but for the current period, it was given to the masses through bhakti devotionalism. But even with regard to the bhakti movement devotionalism, its theorization, history, and hagiography were in the hands of brahmans. Knowledge or *jnana* remained brahmanic property. Thus, *jnana* and *nama*, Dnyaneshwar and Namdev, symbolized for the brahmanized varkari version of bhakti the originally double achievement, but they were also caste-marked. The achievement of ecstasy through repeating the name was the task of the tailor Namdev. In contrast, *jnana* was a brahmanic achievement, if even by the outcaste brahman Jnyandev ('Dnayndev' in Marathi). Through control of knowledge the traditional elite sought to domesticate and incorporate the challenge of the radical sants, and by and large succeeded. Namdev sought his own control of his destiny through bhakti but it was momentary.

In the modern period, as noted, both ecstasy and reason are given a historical embodiment. However, brahmanism is to a significant extent inimical to modernity because it also brings with it mass assertion, and trends to equalitarianism and spread of reason as well as ecstasy to all. Brahmans, thus, preferred a romantic past in which hierarchy could be exalted as solidarity and harmony. But because modernity in India took place under colonialism, the brahman elite could manipulate knowledge to its end, could continue its monopoly of knowledge in new forms, and find new ways to exclude the masses of sudras and dalits. As long as education was minimal and monopolized, reason could still be used in the service of hierarchy. The masses could be allowed their traditional forms of ecstasy. This, in a sense, defined the reworking of hierarchy and domination under colonialism. Traditional varnashrama dharma was brought into line with the new requirements of 'science' and modernity; the masses had to be incorporated in a different way.

Colonial modernity also brought with it for dalit-bahujan intellectuals both opportunities and a corresponding need to capture the throne of reason, to work out their own analysis and understanding, to project their own utopia. This was what the greatest of them – Jotirao Phule, Iyothee Thass, Periyar, Ambedkar and many others – concentrated on during the colonial period. Their involvement in agitation was crucial, but just as crucial was their theory formation and their formulation of the themes of an emancipated society. However, it took some time for this response to develop.

This chapter will examine the colonial situation, initial anticaste responses, and the Brahmanic production of knowledge.

Colonialism and Caste

India did not enter the modern, industrial era propelled by internal dynamics. It was forcibly brought in under colonial rule. India and Britain entered the modern world together, but one as an emerging manufacturing power whose ships and guns ruled the earth, the other with traditional manufactures weakened if not destroyed and a process of 'peasantization' leading it to specialize in the production of raw materials such as cotton, jute and tea.

There have been constant debates about the implications of this. The earliest themes, dating back to the nineteenth century, revolved around colonialism's economic impact. While British justification for colonial rule stressed the decadence of Mughal imperial rule and the chaos and lawlessness that supposedly reigned, Indian intellectuals, including many dalit-bahujan leaders, from almost the very beginning seized on economic exploitation, high taxation of agriculture, and the 'drain' of wealth from the country. They turned the implications of an economic relationship around to argue that this wealth had provided the basis for Britain's own industrialization: in Marx's terms, who picked up much of this, India and the Americas were scenes of the violence and plunder that marked the 'primitive accumulation of capital'. These themes, however, did not question the sociocultural progressiveness of colonial rule; with Marx they saw colonialism as the bringer of capitalism, as a historical benefactor in destroying the narrow old feudal society and its values. Thus, when Phule was to combine his economic critique of colonial rule with a warning against the scheming of the nationalist elite in caste terms, he was in many ways simply echoing the marxist critique but transforming it into caste–class terminology.

In recent years, however, the focus has turned to the social effects of colonialism. The new theme emerging in the last decades of the twentieth century, as India undertook a new and troubled modernization to break away from its statist straitjacket, was to question colonial capitalism in new ways, as the destroyer of community and of the powerful traditional identities by which men lived. What was imposed was not simple economic exploitation but also the cultural identities of the West, which would forever haunt Indian self-esteem because it destroyed their manhood. The theme was stressed by Ashis Nandy, who contrasted gandhian 'androgyny' with the super-masculinity of colonialism. In his own way, Partha Chatterjee also emphasized the negative cultural role of colonialism.

In response, historians like Eugene Irschick (1994) have more recently argued for the 'dialogical' nature of colonialism. This 'dialogue' however, has been between the elite, now emerging as an English-educated class, and the colonizers. Instead it would be better to think of at least a three-way dialogue. If the elite and British collaborated, it was in an atmosphere where both sensed, and feared, responses from the masses they ruled. And those masses, and their 'organic intellectuals', also responded to the challenge of colonial rule, to the appeal of missionaries, and to the new ideas they brought.

Among the most influential of the social critiques has been the position that much of what we know as 'traditional' India has been a colonial construct. Above all, this is said to be true of caste, and the most influential recent work representing this position has been Nicholas Dirks' *Castes of Mind*, where he argues that

> caste itself as we now know it is not a residual survival of ancient India but a specifically colonial form of (that is, a substitute for) civil society that both justified and maintained an Orientalist vision.This was a vision of an India in which religion transcended politics, society resisted change, and the state awaited its virgin birth in the late colonial era.Thus caste has become the modernist apparition of India's traditional self. Under colonial rule caste – now defined by the dharmic idea of varna, disembodied from its former political contexts, and available as the principle object of colonial knowledge – could take on a new and different form. In this dissociated form it was appropriated, and reconstructed, by British rule. (2002, 60)

Dirks claims that in traditional India caste was not a predominant and religiously determined social form, but rather was shaped by and dominated by political power. He describes in detail the situation in a southern Indian kingdom, Pudukottai, led by a royal family of the Kallar caste. The construction of his foil, however, is unconvincing: arguing for a religious sanction to caste does not negate the fact that those making it required access to power to enforce it. Caste has always been an affair negotiated among the power-holders—kings (often of questionable background themselves) and brahmans. The political determination of actual social position and the linkage of kings and brahmans does not negate the importance of brahmanism or caste. It is clear that however complex the actual caste situation, brahmans continued to dominate in the administration and even landholding; only that they

> were more adamant than most in insisting on the divinity of the royal office.... Although Brahmans lived apart – both literally in special hamlets and ritually in the myriad ways in which they kept to themselves – they lived very much within a world in which the power and authority of the king seemed paramount. (Dirks 2002, 70)

Here the 'divinity' of kings emphasized by brahmans is the simple argument that Dirks uses, posing it against Louis Dumont's argument for the purity–pollution principle and his posing of the brahman–untouchable polarity as central. Dirks in contrast emphasizes power. Yet he notes that by the early period of British control, quite aside from their administrative and ritual power, 45 percent of *imams* in the Pudukottai kingdom were for the support of temples, monasteries, feeding houses for brahman priests and pilgrims and land grants to brahman communities (68). The combination of a 'low' caste that had won kingly power with brahmans legitimizing it, and in control of both sacred and secular wealth, was neither new nor unusual in Indian history: from almost the very beginning, brahmans had legitimized such rule; as long as the king supported varnashrama dharma and the position of brahmans, his own family was given sanction. (The reluctance of Maharashtrian brahmans to grant kshatriya status to Shivaji was in this sense an exception; in fact, the payment of huge sums to win it finally fit the norm.)

A similar linkage between caste and power, between the legitimization of power-holding and the willingness of the power-holders to allow the enforcement of caste rules, also began to exist with colonialism. This can be seen in Dirks' analysis of various colonial ethnographers. In the case of Colin Mackenzie – one of the earliest collecting valuable but disregarded material – Dirks tends to exempt him from his critique of essentializing caste. However, Dirks admits that all of the material depended on brahman informants, brahman genealogists and brahman authors of *vamshavalis* (family histories) (84–106). The same pattern – brahman power and control over knowledge, used to memorialize those nonbrahman families and 'heroes' who gave support to the brahmanic system, even if of 'low' birth – can be seen. It was also the beginning of the colonial collaboration.

The relationship between colonialism and caste should thus be understood as one of collaboration among the power-holders of both systems The old power of the traditional kingdoms and empires was gone, replaced by a new empire and a new economic system. As the British sought to understand – and enumerate, and dominate through enumeration – a turbulent population, they relied heavily on the collaboration of brahmans in defining and placing castes. The censuses, the gazetteers, the various 'tribe and caste reports' were all done with the indispensable aid of brahman assistants. One of the greatest examples is H.H. Risley, who had written first on tribes and castes of Bengal, and then was placed in charge of the Census. Dirks notes that "as Risley took over the reins of the census…he found himself relying once again on varna, and more generally on brahmanical measures and opinions, concerning caste rank" (213). All the local officials who wrote extensive notes and documents on caste ranking for Risley were brahmans.

> In retrospect, Risley's reliance on a Brahmanical sociology of knowledge is astounding. He depended almost entirely on Brahmans and other higher castes. He deferred wherever possible to the Manu Dharma Sastras and other puranic sources that served in part as later commentaries on Manu. And he organized his entire understanding of caste structure and rank according to Brahmanical indices such as the acceptance of food and water, the use of priests, and origin stories concerning duties and obligations towards Brahmans, as well as about degradation in relation to those duties and obligations, and ritual proximity to and functions relating to Brahmans. (218)

Risley also laid great faith in the 'Aryan theory of race' that explained caste in terms of racial division. Here too there must have been an intellectual collaboration: the Aryan theory fit in very easily with the 'brahmanical sociology of knowledge', and was an ideal justification for caste to replace (or supplement) the theme of divine origin. Nesfield, Risley's main ideological foe, used a functional or occupational theory of caste, and argued for an original Indian racial unity. Risley was, in contrast, almost obsessed with the original racial division between Aryans and non-Aryans, and with anthropometry—physical measurements that were supposed to indicate racial characteristics.

It is perhaps not surprising that in the era of modernity with its concern for history and its pride in science, caste would find this new form of justification. As Iyothee Thass had perceptibly seen, the brahmans were learning 'new vedas and sastras', and prominent among these was the justification of caste in terms of science. Race was beginning to be seen as the prominent feature of biological science, and it was natural that the social and political collaboration between British officials and brahmans should be underlined by a presumed, 'scientific' racial commonality. The thesis benefited both, though in different ways. The British could justify their alliance with brahmans, and at the same time use Indian 'decadence' – presumably having come through an infusion of the more inferior, primitive Dravidian blood – as an excuse for the need to rule. And the brahmans could justify their continuing superiority over the 'inferior', 'lower' castes.

Colonialism increased the power of brahmans and the salience of caste. As Dirks notes, Risley himself argued that "technological change such as the introduction and extension of the railways was having a paradoxical effect. Railways worked to diffuse brahmanical influence, as education worked to expand the reach of Hindu scriptures" (2002: 442). His estimate was probably correct. Education, biased towards an elite and towards filling positions in the colonial bureaucracy, gave a new foothold to brahmans; brahmans continued to propagate the traditional scriptures, now using the prestige and power of their position in a more far-reaching and effective bureaucracy. The old power of kings was replaced by the autocracy of this colonial bureaucracy; new transportation and communication connected the country – in a marketplace of ideas as well as goods – and linked it to world trends ever more strongly. Within this framework, there was an updating of the old themes of contention of caste and anticaste. For example, 'modernization', the 'Aryan theory' and the like may have been exuberantly invented by Europeans, but they were just as exuberantly taken up by Indians—first the elite, and then by those who sought to contest their dominance, the dalit-bahujan subalterns who were also coming to a new consciousness of themselves and their history.

The 'Bengal Renaissance': Brahmo Samaj and the Conservatives

We can understand the process better by examining the developments in the first area of full conquest, Bengal. Calcutta became the scene of the earliest cooperation between British and the Indian elite; it was described as a city of amalgamation in 1839 by the *Bombay Gazette*, where "the thaw of social harmony has produced a permeative process of coalescence, which is spreading in every direction and resolving into one community both Europeans and Natives" (cited in Kopf 1969, 9). In this early phase, newly prosperous Bengali aristocrats like Dwarkanath Tagore took British on as partners in joint-stock companies, and became leaders symbolizing a new liberal hope. The *bhadralok* aristocracy patronized arts and culture – European as much as Indian – and Kopf's description of Tagore's mansion gives a striking picture of a heritage looking back to Greece as much as to the ancient Aryans.

The British also involved themselves in a 'discovery of India', looking to old Aryan commonalities, exploring the countryside and unearthing old monuments. In their 'Orientalist' phase they expressed an admiration for Indian culture, at least in its ancient forms, and this was developed, used and encouraged by the Indian intelligentsia.

After the middle of the nineteenth century this began to change. British racism hardened; it was seen in many things, from the exclusion of dalits in the army to efforts to maintain exclusive clubs away from native pollution. Increasing evangelism expressed in missionary efforts tended to depict religion, especially popular Hinduism, as hopelessly decadent: India became characterized as the centre of idolatry, its multitude of multiformed gods not very comprehensible to increasingly puritanical forms of Christianity. The British began to isolate themselves socially. And the development of capitalism began to leave Indians behind, as British capital became more exclusive and the state refused to give any protection or real support to indigenous manufacturing.

The first generation of English-educated intellectuals, emerging in Calcutta, were caught up in the admiration of western culture and rebels against tradition—but only to a point. Their goal was to reform indigenous traditions but not abandon them. Rammohan Roy, considered the 'father of modern India' was a typical example of the bhadralok class, coming from a landlord base but oriented to the modern world. His writing was a broad-ranging effort to recover what he considered the monotheistic, rationalistic foundation laid by the vedas, and present it both to Indians and the British. He argued that "by a reference to History it may be proved that the world was indebted to *our ancestors* for the first dawn of knowledge" (Roy 1958, 580); however, this first knowledge – philosophical and spiritual – had been overlaid by misunderstandings and excrescences. The vedas were the foundation of all knowledge, but their mystical and metaphorical language often left them 'seemingly confused and contradictory'; thus Rammohan translated into 'Hindostani,' Bengali and finally English, a work that presented itself as 'a Vedant' which summarized these. His aim, he argued, was to prove to Europeans "that the superstitious practices which deform the Hindoo religion have nothing to do with the pure spirit of its dictates" (573). Roy thus emphasized rationality and a pure core to the 'Hindoo religion'.

Rammohan Roy's arguments were focused on the elite, with the effect of Brahmoism being to differentiate Hinduism with its pure core from mass idolatry and questionable, ecstatic practices. The Brahmos were to renounce idolatry and meaningless rituals; but he argued that these were often necessary for those with little understanding. In fact, in presenting a religion of rationality and anti-idolatry monotheism, he was increasing the differentiation of the bhadrolok from the subaltern masses—who were Vaishnavite devotees of one or another sect, who looked back not to the vedas but to Chaitanya, who were not troubled by the problems of widow remarriage and sati but were very much troubled by caste. And caste was an issue that did not enter the agenda of the 'Renaissance' elite reformers.

The Brahmos and 'progressives' fiercely debated the conservatives and defenders of 'tradition'. Yet, the progressives also defended traditions and at least certain traditions; the conservatives reinterpreted them in the process of their defence. And in defence and reinterpretation both used the sacred scriptures as their basis. Strategies differed. Among the conservatives, one of the most prominent was Bhabanicharan Bandyopadhyaya, editor of the *Samachar Chandrika*. Bandyopadhyaya had broken up with Roy on the issue of sati, writing in December 1829 after the practice had been abolished: "At this awful intelligence, we have trembled from head to foot, and are distressed, terrified and astonished, for even under the Moosoolmans our law and shastras were left untouched" (quoted in Pennington 2005, 148). The *Chandrika*, launched in 1822 (after Bandyopadhyaya quit Roy's paper *Sambad Kaumudi*), became a rallying point for the defence of traditional ritual. It was ritual that became the focus—from traditional birth to funeral caste-related practices, to reporting on and praising increasingly expensive, magnificently celebrated festivals. *Kulinism* – the practice of men from the prestigious kulin brahman caste taking many wives – was defended. Brian Pennington, documenting the positions of *Chandrika*, argues that this was also an updating of Hinduism, shaping "a modern, popular Hinduism through emergent discourses promoting a centralization of authority and a common, socially cohesive H.l5tindu identity" (149). Thus the newspaper sought to pass judgment on various issues of ritual practice: "It bridged the gap opening up between the sacred past when the texts were compiled and the declining present… [with] creative constructions of tradition" (151). Pennington, who has a tendency to defend the orthodox position, gives almost no concrete example of how tradition was modified; the very fact of submitting their arguments to a newspaper editor shows a shift in the orientation of those seeking sanction. Yet, the yielding to political and social power was, as Dirks reminds us, not a new feature of caste.

What *Chandrika* had most in common with the progressive 'iconoclasts' was that both sought to argue from sacred texts. Roy and the Brahmo Samaj rejected ritual and idol worship, but sought refuge in the ancient glories of the vedic age. *Chandrika*, and the Dharma Sabha which had sprung up in defence of sati (described officially as *samamarana*, or 'dying with'), did not concern themselves much with theology or 'orthodoxy' but rather with practice, with ritual. The two were alternative methods of maintaining the position and prestige of the elite and its tradition.

The 'Bengal Renaissance' set the pattern for similar developments elsewhere in India. 'Conservatives' defended ritual and the orthodox practices of caste, family and religion. 'Progressives' rejected idol worship and the multitude of gods, formulating bold monotheistic ethical religions—but claiming that these had been the actual pattern of India's past, golden vedic age. They fought for the end of such obvious oppressions of women as sati and child marriage, arguing that women enjoyed impressive rights in the vedic period. But by and large they kept silent on issues of caste, interdining and other practices. They observed the rituals of everyday exclusiveness; having untouchables or other sudra castes as part of their social circle was almost something never considered; and they very rarely actually themselves married widows or carried out bold social reforms. When the Maharashtra progressive M.G. Ranade married a young girl of eleven in 1873 after his first wife's death, rather than a widow as many of his friends had hoped, to satisfy his father, the cause of social reform received a setback (Sunthankar 1993, 141). Finally, Tilak and others succeeded in identifying the social conservatives with political radicals—something that had also been presaged with the defence of tradition. In the final analysis, the conservative school could gain the moral ascendancy over the reformers.

Appropriation of Bhakti as Hinduism for the Masses

With the 'Bengal Renaissance', then, the main formation of Hinduism began. 'Hindu' and 'Hinduism' were terms that had not been heard at the beginning of the colonial period. By the end of the nineteenth century they had nearly been given their contemporary meaning. There has been much debate about the 'construction of Hinduism', but it is clear both that there were early traditions of brahmanic Hinduism, though not by that name, and that it was during the colonial period that decisive interventions took place.

The first has been the themes outlined above, pioneered by figures like Rammohan Roy. The notion of the vedas as the fount, of the Aryans as a racial group whose territory was India, of the golden age of the past, of 'Bharat' as the giver of spirituality and monotheism to the world—all these were embodied in his grand vision, his Brahmo Samaj.

However, Roy was little interested in bhakti; the role of ecstasy was lacking. It was the task of other intellectuals, among them Harishchandra of Banaras (1850–1855) whose role has been emphasized by Vasudha Dalmia, to take this up (1995, 1997). Harishchandra himself was a follower of the *pustimarg* of Vallabha, already representing a brahmanic version of Krishna bhakti. He was writing in a context where European scholars, often missionaries, were theorizing the differences between 'Hinduism' (which they had to see as decadent) and Christianity, and at the same time finding parallels.

Harishchandra shared several assumptions of all of the colonial elite: that 'Aryans' represented the main agent of Hinduism, the founder of its ancient glories, and that Hinduism was the religion of the Aryans. He built on work done by Indological research and thought, which looked for similarities with the Christian West in Indian traditions, work done by Friedrich Schlegel, Max Mueller and Albrect Weber who established a parallel between Krishna and Christ; on Monier-Williams who gave a stage development of brahmanism through 'Vedism, Brahmanism, Saivism and Vaisnavism'; and finally on Grierson, who formulated a theory of bhakti as the overarching principle and the most widespread religious system in India (Dalmia 1997,195–98). But whereas Grierson had seen bhakti entering India through early Christianity (the Syrian Christians in Kerala), Harishchandra turned their arguments around to give primacy to Hinduism, embodied most thoroughly in the basically monotheistic Vaishnavism, which had influenced even the development of Christianity. What he called the *prakrt mat*, the 'natural religion', was from early times a form of Vaishnavism. Vishnu was central to the Rg Veda where he is identified with Aditya (the sun), and the vedas were essentially monotheistic, but the age of the puranas brought a diversification and polytheism; both rituals and polytheism represented snares, but beneath them was a true monotheism. However, diversity remained on the surface, and Harischandra argued for a national unity of the *arya jati*—all those calling themselves 'Hindu', whatever external differences, should unite. As Dalmia notes:

> The categories he employs have more or less clear functions: Aryans, whenever the ancient heritage is invoked, Hindus as descendents of these and reared on Hindu milk – a principally all-inclusive cultural-political category – and finally, within the diversity of faiths, which proliferated on Indian soil and as forming the core of tradition, the most steadfast, with an unbroken tradition, with the capacity to accommodate change, that inner core, that path of love, Vaisnavism. (205–6).

Vaishnavism was thus seen as the main unifying force in the country. But it was of course within the framework of Aryanism and the founding role of the vedic tradition. In this sense, it represented a thorough appropriation of what had been a radical claim to tradition – a rejection of brahmanic ritualism and vedic themes – by fifteenth–seventeenth century radicals.

Harishchandra was theorizing what was being carried out in practice 'at a ground level'. Brahmanic control of temples remained throughout, and it was during the nineteenth and twentieth centuries that the contemporary form of sects was consolidated. In the case of the varkaris, for example, this meant the organization of *dindis* (walking groups) along caste lines, the choice of bhajans to be sung, and slogans (such as 'Gyanba-Tuka', combining Dnyaneshwar and Tukaram as the two overarching symbols of the varkari movement).

The result of the appropriation was that subaltern intellectuals like Phule and Ambedkar felt little attraction for bhakti. Northern dalits were different, in that Ravidas had remained 'stamped' as a dalit sant, with relatively little appropriation. Thus ideologues like Acchutananda could analyze bhakti through Ravidas as Buddhistic and as part of the original non-Aryan faith and philosophy. However, Phule, to take a contrary example, appreciated the 'sudra Sant Tukaram' and rejected the varkaris as such. Whereas ambedkarites mocked them, sants like Chokhamela were rather used by the Hindu Mahasabha to link dalits to Hinduism.

Dalit Puritanism: The Matuas

Many of those Bengali dalits who would by the end of the nineteenth century form the Namasudra movement – the major anticaste movement of Bengal – were connected with the Kartabhajas, especially those in the swamp areas of Faridpur and Bakarganj district. In Faridpur itself, as the Kartabhaja movement became more established and hierarchical, a leader named Harichand Thakur, born in 1811 in a family of peasants and small traders, originated a new movement, calling itself Matua. But where the Kartabhajas had emphasized devotion and unrestrained ecstasy, the Matuas emphasized a kind of puritanical effort to achieve in practice a life of abundance. In other words, they sought to supplement *bhava* with *jnana*, emotion with reason, and to contest elite dominance at an empirical level and by dealing with their own origin as a caste group. Also, in contrast to the Kartabhajas, they were mostly drawn from one particular caste—dalits formerly known as chandalas.

'Matua' was a variation of a term that had been used mockingly for them by the elite—*moto*, meaning drunk. They were, supposedly, drunk on spirituality (Kabir himself had composed songs on the theme). Harichand, who believed in his own divinity as an avatar of god, born to bring salvation to the lowly, accepted this epithet and turned it into an affirmative identity. He and after him, his son Guruchand (b. 1846) emphasized the abolition of differences of caste and gender; women were accepted as social equals and given equal rights in the congregational life of the namasudras. Though these provided its main base, members of other castes were also attracted.

The sect also repudiated *gurubad*, the need for a guru emphasized by most traditional Hinduism. Harichand insisted there was no need for any initiation or *diksha*, that only devotion and love for god were necessary. Though his son Guruchand agreed, gradually both he and Harichand gained the status of leading gurus, and became almost deified in the later period. Nevertheless, brahmanic rituals were rejected, the worship of varying deities was rejected, and the singing of *kirtans* was emphasized to provide the focus for the solidarity of community life. The kirtans often directed themselves at generating self-confidence, affirming the power of the devotees.

> *The devotees of Matua, with bare chests and unbridled hair,*
> *stand and say victory to Harichand.*
> *Beat your drums, get rid of all your fears*

and hoist your flag up into the sky.
What are you thinking of,
do you want to behave like dead people while you are still alive?
Though you are great, you have been denied honour.
So awake, O brave men.
Hold your heads high, do not give up self-respect,
even though you have to sacrifice your life.

(Cited in Bandyopadhyay 1997, 41)

These themes of self-respect were crucial for the dalit and much of the sudra nonbrahman movement, and would remain throughout even under more sophisticated, intellectual leadership.

There was enough sophistication in Matua thinking for it to be a self-conscious opposition to the vedantism of the Bengali intelligentsia. Harichand argued that vedanta was a theory of despair that demotivated working people by advocating renunciation of worldly desires, that it mentally conditioned them to accept their subordinate place in society. He thus advised his disciples to 'worship the goddess of wealth'. Guruchand added that "for the hungry, food was God and their duty was to seek the favour of this supreme god, this *annabrahma*" (Bandyopadhyay, 42). Here was an affirmation of wealth and commercialism, as with the Kartabhajas. The most well-known dictum of the Matuas was *hate kam mukhe nam*—'work in hand, name on tongue'. Householder life, maintaining the family and working in the world were affirmed. The sect preached a *garhasthya dharma* and did not prescribe *brahmacharya* or celibacy of the kind that Ramakrishna was preaching to his middle-class devotees during this period. This again was a heritage of the bhakti movement, although the repudiation of ecstasy for the life of hard work was more central to the Matuas.

Unlike the Kartabhajas, however, the Matua sect also repudiated what they considered sexual licentiousness. The Bengali elite had repudiated, mocked and scorned the Kartabhajas for such assumed sexual licentiousness, and the namasudras following the new sect were careful to adjust their culture to a more puritanical norm of family life. The sect sought to correct what were seen as bad characteristics of the subordinated castes. Matua disciples were advised to marry properly and to refrain from adultery, as this would bring infamy to the community. Devotional songs portrayed uncontrolled sexual desire as the greatest enemy of mankind; ideal love was said to be devoid of sexual passion. All of this aspiration to respectability also was part of an adjustment of cultural life to a new form of productivity. Bandyopadhyay notes that as the namasudras moved from floating boats to homestead land and became settled peasantry, accumulated property and elaborated rights of inheritance, this more structured family life played a major role in their modest levels of success (44).

Thus in an indirect way, the namasudras ended up by replicating something of caste ideology. They were described in the late 1880s by Risley as 'very particular as regards caste prejudices', and began to demand simply a higher place for themselves within the varna framework. In a return to some of the traditional stories of caste origins, they traced their origin from brahman sages and many argued that they should be considered brahmans. In a late Matua legend, Harichand was described as a brahman who had lost his caste by marrying a namasudra woman. In the end, then, the idea of varna being determined by 'merit' – meaning not by work but inherent, almost biological, qualities – came to be held by the marginalized castes as well as the elite.

Both responses, the ecstasy of the Kartabhajas and the work-oriented religion of the namasudras, proved inadequate in the end for contesting brahmanism. The dalit movement in Bengal remained subordinate—strong, providing political representation, but incapable of mounting a real challenge. For this, a stronger intellectual response, taking up the 'reason' of the modern period, was required. This was provided first of all by Jotirao Phule in Maharashtra, and then by Iyothee Thass in Tamilnadu. The next chapters will turn to their work.

vii

Phule Remembering the Kingdom of Bali

Let us remember the incomparable lord of our land, firm in battle.
From Balisthan came the brave Bahairoba, Khandoba, Jotiba,
the great governors,
We remember on Diwali King Bali, a model of merit:
"Let troubles and exploitation go and the kingdom of Bali come."
The Aryabhats came and looted all,
made slaves of the sons of the soil, our father and mother,
'Why did Waman send Bali to the underworld?'
This question Joti the gardener asks the priests!

Joti the Gardener

It was Jotirao Phule who first took up the task of reasoning for the masses of people as an alternative to the elite's monopoly. 'Joti Mali, the gardener' was how he described himself, asserting his caste identity as a worker of the soil with a hint of pride. For Jotirao Phule, named not after the lamp (*jyoti*) but after the popular folk deity (*joti*) in Maharashtra who is indeed a symbol of the peasantry, was born in a city of brahmans but from a sudra family with its humble home in Satara district. He undertook as his lifelong mission the task of freeing the 'sudras and ati-sudras', the oppressed bahujans and dalits, from the slavery of brahmanism (O'Hanlon 1985, gives a comprehensive account of Phule's life and thinking).

Colonialism, while in many ways solidifying the hold of the brahman elites through English education as the new way to administrative power and influence, also gave limited openings for those of the subordinated castes, often through missionary effort. Jotirao's father Govindrao ran a small shop in Pune that attained a modest prosperity. His bright young son was first sent to school in Katgun, the home village, then to a Scottish mission school in Pune. Here, boys of all castes were admitted, with some conflict. Notably in 1842 there was a conflict regarding the entry of a mahar boy.

Caste as experienced by Phule was a system in transformation. Men of castes considered 'low' often mixed with brahmans in associations of the educated elite, such as the Paramhamsa Sabha. Brahmans and others attempted to broaden their traditions, some early radicals challenged them more directly through words, if not openly through actions. Jotirao himself had some friends from among brahmans. Yet the limits of reformism were shown when, invited to the marriage of one of these friends, he was excluded from its wedding procession. It was nothing like the bitter experience of discrimination that 'untouchables' like Ambedkar were later to experience, but it was enough to show up the hypocrisy and contradictions in brahman reformism. The brahmans in Maharashtra were moving cautiously, afraid of being socially outcast—which happened even if they took tea with missionaries.

When Phule left school he began to earn his living as a contractor, but at the same time took up a life of social service, propagandizing for his cause, establishing schools and creating organizations. In 1849 and 1851 he founded schools for girls and untouchables, with his wife Savitribai among the teachers. A couple of schools at the beginning led to several more and to an association. Gradually, however, he began to take a harder line than most of his committee would like, as he began to identify brahmans as the main obstacle in the way of education and development of the sudras and ati-sudras. Rosalind O'Hanlon describes how, in 1855, he had a dalit girl from the mang community read out an essay to a visiting Christian convert. The essay, which has since become famous, described in detail the suffering of untouchables under the Peshwas, arguing that

> formerly we were buried alive in the foundations of buildings... we were not allowed to read and write....God has bestowed on us the rule of the British and our grievances are redressed. Nobody harasses us now. Nobody hangs us. Nobody buries us alive. Out progeny can live now. We can wear clothes, can put cloth around our body. Everybody is at liberty to live according to his means. No bars, no taboos, no restriction. Even the bazaar at the Gultekadi is open to us. (Cited in O'Hanlon, 121)

This essay must have reflected the development of Phule's thinking when it attacked the elitism of even progressive brahmans: "Those who are called reformers, and who are so clever, but who from time to time commit deeds so evil they would make your hair stand on end—it is these who are the real Mangs and Mahars" (121). At the same time it illustrated the way in which many of the excluded welcomed the openings provided by colonial rule.

Phule, then, as he began to write and theorize, and with the experience of his educational reform behind him, began to feel an urge to struggle. In 1875, he took his most decisive step in this direction, forming the Satyashodhak Samaj (Truthseekers Society). This was designed as an organizational weapon of the subordinated castes against brahman domination, but in doing so, Phule had to come into conflict also with some of his own colleagues. As O'Hanlon points out, the Satyashodhak Samaj was radical but not so radical as Phule would have liked; it sought to propagate the idea of a monotheism that did not require a brahman priest, but did not include in its membership criteria the rejection of such priests for all religious ceremonies. While reports hailed various weddings performed without such priests, they represented only a small proportion of the life ceremonies of its members (O'Hanlon, 237–39). Even staunch followers often came under community pressure to give up their radicalism.

One of his greatest conflicts in this came with his colleague and caste fellow, Krishnarao Bhalekar, a young reformer. The beginnings of this are unknown, but we do know that Phule refused to allow him to take control of a printing press owned by the Samaj, and this initial bitterness was followed by a later bitter polemic, centring around the issues of women and educational efforts. O'Hanlon, who gives the major account of Phule's life and thinking, argues that "there is no evidence.... [of] reasons of ideological disagreement" (244). However, Bhalekar's own organization, the Din Bandhu Sarvajanik Sabha, formed in 1884, was focused on education and 'practical reform', forbidding debates about religion among members. It was clearly not so antibrahman, and Bhalekar's own writing – for instance, a kind of novel, *Baliba Patil* (1998 [1877]) – was much milder in tone than any of those of Phule. By the end of the nineteenth century it was becoming clear that the nonbrahman masses – most of all the malis and kunbi-marathas, including dalits – were being attracted by a 'kshatriya ideology' that identified them with the Aryans who had formed the hated enemy for Phule. This began to influence marathas especially. One activist, for instance, Madhavrao Rokade (1839–96), stressed the performance of vedic rituals for the masses (297), something increasingly coming in vogue, which Ambedkar himself even toyed with, in regard to mahars for a brief period. This became a major theme in the conflict that the Maharaja of Kolhapur was later to have with brahmans (see Shahu Maharaj, 1985, 1987, 1994), and though it provoked Shahu Maharaj to a good deal of anticaste reformism, including strong support for the Satyashodhak movement, it illustrated the appeals of Aryanism.

It is important to stress, then, that Phule had to engage in debate and even polemic with nonbrahmans as well as brahmans. He mocked the claim to 'maratha' status, tried to redefine kshatriya as applying to all the original inhabitants, both peasants and warriors. He refers in his writing disdainfully to 'educated sudras' being influenced by brahmanism. This all-round conflict was reflected also in Phule's actions and it had an impact on his personal life. His educational efforts had already resulted in his being forced to live separately from his parents. One of the most important events in this respect occurred in 1864. As a provocative action, he proclaimed an 'orphanage' for the children of brahman widows; this was the first of its kind in India, a practical response to a situation that was made clear in the writings of a reformist like Lokahitawadi (Gopal Hari Deshmukh). Lokahitawadi had written of the pitiful state of brahman widows, not only made victims of orthodoxy and humiliation, but also often a prey for the men of the family. Phule's action was thus provocative, and caused an uproar among the brahman community; but worse followed when he actually adopted the child of one of the brahman widows, the boy who became his heir, Yashwant. For this, the family was boycotted by the mali community, and indeed, even into the 1920s Phule was attacked by leading mali spokesmen who were followers of the Tilak school.

With all of this, however, the Satyashodhak Samaj grabbed people's imagination, and remained the paradigmatic organization for nonbrahmans. It had a modest spread during Phule's lifetime, but even then included villages as well as cities like Pune and Mumbai. After his death in 1910, it was Phule's radical movement, not Bhalekar's compromising organization, that was revived and spread throughout the state.

The Indian Form of Slavery

From the beginning, Phule's efforts had one clear goal—the annihilation of caste; and one major enemy—the brahmans. His analysis of brahman power, however, included not only the themes of historical origin and process, but also an analysis of the present-day situation, with an overall critique of colonial power structures. The first version of this could be seen in *Gulamgiri*, his first major book and a hard-hitting polemic, published in 1873 and written in dialogue form as an orientation to mass communication. It gave something of a historical–mythological analysis of caste, and in doing so picked up the 'Aryan theory' that had emerged out of the British–Indian confrontation and collaboration.

In the fifteenth to seventeenth centuries, as we have seen, the radical sants preached the ecstasy of devotional bhakti freeing them from brahmanic ritualism and laid the foundations for new values of equality and rationality which challenged priestly dominance and caste hierarchy. However, the radical sants themselves did not and could not achieve the use of reason, that is, give a socio-historical analysis of caste. They could not even control the history of their own movement. It was only with the British that the 'plunge into history' could take place, when the historical and social worlds opened up before the newly educated groups in India. The shift from kaliyuga to colonial yuga was also a shift from an ahistorical cyclical vision of time and cosmology to a historical, creative one in which human rather than divine agency was predominant. Industrialism, of course, turned this into 'clock time', emphasizing precision and work discipline, but historical time was also a gift of knowledge. Mass-based but unlettered groups like the Kartabhajas had not seen this, but those who could gain some grasp of the new weapon of historical thinking, a new social scientific outlook, could do so. Phule thus aspired not simply to the ecstasy of devotionalism and escape from the life of caste and ritual, but also to the reason of analyzing and understanding history.

It was the missionaries who first communicated many of the new themes to the masses. They engaged in debates with brahmans, and they brought these debates out of narrow Sanskrit-dominated circles into a more mass audience. (Phule's first literary effort records such a debate, featuring a missionary challenging a brahman pandit.) They took up themes pioneered by the great European 'Indologists' and linked them with the new ethnographical studies of the varying caste groups in India. To these they brought the 'Aryan–non-Aryan' themes, which interpreted the caste system in terms of a great and ancient racial divide between conquering invading vedic Aryan peoples and indigenous inhabitants of the subcontinent. Thus we find, for instance, George Briggs not only writing on the chamars (1920), but also communicating and exchanging ideas with various groups of them.

Missionary efforts also had from the very beginning focused on language; they sought to record the language of the people because they needed it for communication; they translated the Bible and wrote scriptural texts. In the case of Marathi, the most famous and still the best Marathi–English dictionary is that by Molesworth, and the story of the dictionary, recounted in a later introduction, is an intriguing one. The earliest Marathi dictionary, we are informed, defined Marathi 'as the language spoken by Deshastha Brahmans in and around Pune'. Molesworth, who had the very modern idea that a dictionary should not prescribe but record the language as it was spoken, had a constant fight with his pandit informants. The pandits wanted to throw out all *desi* and Persian words, and use anything derived from Sanskrit. The final dictionary was somewhat of a compromise – in fact, the imposition of sanskritic words and forms is an ongoing process – and we can recognize a word as that of the bhakti literature when it is described as 'poetic, vulgar'. In the process, however, Marathi began to acquire a literary character.

The notion of an Aryan conquest was widely accepted—by missionaries, administrators and Indians themselves. Brahmans, whether in Bengal or Maharashtra, used it to emphasize the 'golden age' of the vedic Aryan period, before society was overwhelmed by indigenous decadence and by the exigencies caused by Muslim conquest. The British could simply see the Aryans as a spiritually gifted but otherwise inferior form of Europeans. Phule was a pioneer among the intellectuals coming from the masses when he took a different tack. In *Gulamgiri*, published in 1873, he turned the theory upside down, and wrote of the golden age in pre-Aryan India, with the Aryan invasion motivated by visions of this wealth and resulting in slavery.

Gulamgiri was an imaginative polemic, structured around the concept of avatars. These formed the various chapters and the main themes for his attack on brahmanic dominance. The idea of avatars was an all-pervasive notion in brahmanic Hinduism, used to reach out and win over the masses. Earlier radical sants like Kabir and Tukaram had expressed an unorthodox interpretation of the avatars, either rejecting the idea altogether or turning it around to make it an accusation against god himself. Phule attacked the avatars by historicizing the whole theory, ridiculing the mythology, while using it instead as metaphor for the varying forms of Aryan invasions. At the same time he incorporated the popular folk deities of Maharashtra, interpreting them as sardars of King Bali; thus Khandoba was a title given to a lord of a *khand* or area. Jotirao was a well-known sardar of the Kolhapur region, his fort located on the mountaintop where the temple is today. Here there was no mockery; these were taken as heroes. Greatest of all was their king, Bali—and Phule referred to the popular Marathi saying, *ida pida javo, Balica rajya yevo* ('Let sorrows and troubles go and the kingdom of Bali come'). Bali thus became for him the symbol of human achievement. The missionary influence was demonstrated by his reference to Christ as the 'Bali of the West'. Where most Europeans had seen Krishna as the equivalent and counter to Christ, and were followed by brahman theorists like Harishchandra making a reversal to claim priority for Krishna and Vishnu, Phule instead looked at the *asura* Bali as Christ. Bali figures at the centre of a long and somewhat puzzling brahmanic myth, killed despite his generosity by the deceitful brahman boy Waman.

Gulamgiri was written in dialogue form, as was true of most of Phule's writing with the exception of *Shetkaryaca Asud* (The Cultivator's Whipcord). Using raw and powerful language, he lost no chance to scorn and mock the 'Irani Aryabhats' who were seen as the enslavers of the masses. The first avatars, fish and tortoise, were said to represent invasion by sea. Then came the boar, apparently over land; then the direct confrontation with non-Aryans, as Aryans managed to win over some of them (Prahlad), and used deception to destroy the best of them, King Bali. Indeed, it was Bali Raja who provided the main symbol for Phule. Bali, remembered by the masses as an ideal king, who could make 'troubles and sorrows go', was for brahmanic theory a 'demon', upholder of *adharma* simply by the fact that he dared to violate his own demonic dharma to be a good king. Even the puranic stories (for translations, see Soifer 1991, 193–307) depicted Bali as a good king; it was simply that an asura was not supposed to be *dharmic*, and in being so, his kingdom rendered Indra and heaven unnecessary. The fact is even today Bali is remembered in Maharashtra; the symbol of Bali Raja has been used by massive farmers' organizations such as the Shetkari Sanghatana, anti-drought movements and others.[1]

A mixture of mythology and history, Phule's work had a strong appeal to many nonbrahman readers, but was scorned by the elite. A historian of the period, Sunthankar, expresses this condemnation, arguing that "Phule's reading of history and mythology was lacunary, mere imagination and unhistorical" (1993, 114). However, the intention was not so much to give a historical analysis – that Phule would do in his later *Shetkaryaca Asud* – but to mock the theory of avatars, which was a major theoretical prop for the mass appeal of brahmanism. This he did with devastating ridicule, giving great detail about the bodies of the presumed avatars, scorning the pretensions to many mouths, or describing the various varnas being born to parts of Brahma as requiring so many menstruating wombs that the god would have been drowned in blood. This was an 'empiricization' of the theory of avatars, bringing it down to earth with a vengeance. The purpose of stressing embodiment, of refusing a metaphorical approach and insisting on a literal one, was to ridicule, in the strongest language, the pretensions to divinity of brahmans and the stories they used to back it up.

That Phule was writing not only for Indians but also to educate the British about the caste realities of India is shown by his including an English introduction. This made no reference to the notion of avatars (and neither did his later, truly historical

[1] In Kerala, folk songs celebrate the rule of King Mahabali (known also as Maveli)—the benevolent ruler who presided over a casteless, just society before the rule of the Chera kings from the eighth century. Today, Bali is remembered every year during what has come to be coopted as the Onam harvest festival. The brahmanical 'Aryan' version invokes the birth of the brahman dwarf-priest Wamana as the occasion for Onam.

work, *Shetkaryaca Asud*, though he continued to use the concept of Bali Raja). This should remind us that the 'construction of caste', or rather the construction of consciousness about caste, was at least a three-way process in British India—including the colonial rulers, the Indian upper-caste elite, and members of the 'lower' castes who were also continually putting forward their own views on the system. Both elite and mass spokesmen endorsed the 'Aryan' theory of caste, linking it to ancient racial conquest, but they took very different points of view on this. The elite saw themselves as linked to Europeans, found their golden age in the vedic period, and stressed the decadence of the indigenous people. Phule was to evolve a theory whose golden age was pre-vedic, based on the indigenous non-Aryans and destroyed by Aryan invasions. The parallel was striking, and it was in a way presaged by the Kartabhaja emphasis on bhakti origins in contrast to the Brahmo emphasis on vedic origins.

Gulamgiri (Slavery) was a hard-hitting, single-minded and pointed expression of a 'non-Aryan' theory, and presaged what was to become a major and continuing theme of dalit-bahujan analysis. The elite dropped its interpretation of Aryans and non-Aryans around the 1930s, probably in reaction to the fact that emerging dalit movements (and nonbrahman movements in south India) were taking it up on a massive scale. 'Aryan' continued to be a symbol of superiority for them, but now their stress was on the argument that Aryans had originated in India itself, that they were the builders of the newly discovered Indus civilization. This remains a major theme of hindutva ideology today, while a 'non-Aryan' identity and 'remembering the kingdom of Bali' have retained their appeal for the dalit-bahujans.

Caste and Class Exploitation under British Rule

If *Gulamgiri* was the bold, pointed presentation of Phule's attack on brahmanic exploitation, in his second major work,

Shetkaryaca Asud, this exploitation was analyzed. Phule now put his nonbrahmanic polemic in the context of a full-scale political–economic analysis. The book, though short, ranged over world history; Phule referred not only to the history of humans in India, but also to Rome, Scotland, America, Julius Caesar, Benjamin Franklin—a variety of 'names' that were entering the historical consciousness of people around him. It was as if he wanted to appropriate the growing mass of world wisdom for the sudra–ati-sudra peasants whose exploitation he wanted to explicate and alleviate.

The context was the increasing economic and political assertion of the elite. By the early 1880s the elite was beginning to generate social movements, attacking British colonialism and seeking mass support: the swadeshi movement was birthing.

Phule endorsed much of the nationalist economic critique of colonialism, but did so with a good deal more colour than most elite treatises. He gave the British credit for their enterprise and industriousness in the conquest of India, but saw this turning into exploitation. Though *Asud* began with a detailed description of brahmanic exploitation through festivals, rituals and religion, it went on to an elaboration of colonial exploitation. The loss of service under native rulers, the loss of livelihood by weavers and other artisans was described in colourful detail, with reference to "attractive liquor of different flavours and taste, bread, biscuits, sweets, butter, halwa, pickles, needles of all sizes, knives, axes, sewing machines, bellows, stoves, brightly coloured glass goods, thread, rope, cloth, shawls, gloves, socks, pants, hats, sticks, umbrellas, brass, copper, iron plates, keys" (1991, 269).[2] Finally, Phule offered a rather mocking version of the 'drain theory':

[2] All citations of Phule used in this chapter and elsewhere are from the unpublished translations by Gail Omvedt and Bharat Patankar of the *Mahatma Phule Samagra Wangmay* edited by Y.D. Phadke (1991).

> Since the Laxmi of today cannot get food for the stomach or clothes for her body in the farmers' houses, she has wearied of it all and gone in full daylight to the house of her oceanic father; and as her English brothers from beyond the sea have thrown away their indolence and strive after industry according to her wishes, and keep their estate properly, giving equal respect to the young and aged women in the house, she (Laxmi) has become their slave and collects whatever wealth they want from the conquered sudra farmers. (310)

The colonial bureaucracy came in for the greatest criticism. The forest department had become a huge land-grabber and had reached "such a pinnacle of power that the poor, helpless, paralyzed farmers have an inch of ground left on earth for their goats to even inhale the wind of the fields" (chapter 2); the irrigation department gave huge loans to foreign 'moneylenders' but failed to provide water on time for farming. Unbearable tax burdens made the life of the peasantry practically impossible. Finally, the bureaucracy was attacked in general terms for 'extravagant pay and pensions' of the government employees, money taken out of taxes levied on the peasantry. The Europeans themselves came in for heavy criticism in this work, being charged with indolence, neglecting their duties in order to go hunting during the day and wandering with their *memsahibs*; they turn over most of the office work to brahman subordinates, giving them a free hand in rule. Phule even mocked their stumbling and badly pronounced Marathi.

Phule, however, was quick to stress that the bureaucracy has two faces: it is both British and brahman. The *aishya-aaraami* or 'lazy and indolent' white bureaucrats were described as dependent on the lower-level *dhurt arya-bhat* or 'cunning Aryan brahman' black bureaucrats, who found ample field for exploitation, weaving a web of power that ranges from bureaucracy to village-level services, from religion to the courts. In the end, then, in Phule's view British rule had only consolidated brahmanic power.

'Indolence' yielded ground to energetic 'cunning' in fashioning the exploitation of the sudra–ati-sudra peasantry.[3]

Following this, Phule gave his overall view of human history, beginning from the origin of planets and the original paradise-like situation of humans on the earth. Human nature, he tells us, is built on intelligence and oriented to change; human society is thus one that evolves throughout history:

> Now, if we observe the process of nature, it will be seen that aside from knowledge, humans and all other animals are basically alike in their nature. Animals need food, sleep and sexual intercourse; they raise their young, protect themselves from their enemies and understand nothing aside from belching after they have eaten and since there is not a speck of change in this constant behaviour of theirs, there is no upheaval or basic change in their original condition. However, the marvellous specialty in the nature of human beings is intelligence. With its help, they have won superiority over all the fish, animals, birds, insects and other creatures; and with this intelligence they have invented the system of writing to put their thoughts down on paper. (Chapter 5)

In historical evolution, after an earlier period of what amounted to primitive communism, a lyrical praise of nature and early human naivete and love, gradually change occurred. Land began to be settled and agriculture began; houses were built. At first 'police' arose only for guarding settlements from wild animals; and the first disputes ended with one of the disputing parties migrating. However, with the increase in population this was no longer possible and battles begin. Government and the state arose in the process of settling disputes, armies got formed. On the one hand, the tendency to peaceful production continued; on the other, some became marauders and rulers.

[3] In his *akhands* – poems written in the same meter as Tuka's abhangs – Phule describes indolence as a major sin or failing, the opposite of 'industriousness'.

But with a solution of a kind of federalism, peace was restored, prosperity grew. Then came the greatest of marauders, who were inhabitants of the lands beyond the Indus region, who envied the prosperity of the lands of India—and so began the process of Aryan conquest. A murderous ravaging of the continent and its people and protectors (above all King Bali) takes place, and the newly victorious Aryans form a religious fraud to consolidate their rule, denying the right of education and knowledge to the defeated sudra–ati-sudras. The most strongly resistant of these – Phule derived the term *mahar*, the largest dalit community of Maharashtra, from the word *maha-ari* or 'the great enemy' – were enslaved, the others became effectively serfs. Both were the bonded labourers of brahman rule, but there was a distinction between dalits (ex-untouchables) and sudras.

This was an important version of a historical materialism, one that looked dialectically in analyzing historical trends, but which focused on violence and conquest rather than changes in the forces of production. There was an almost spiral process of evolution, each advance bringing forth a brahmanic reaction, a regression and re-imposition of slavery that led in turn to conquest and new openings, new resistance. Aryan religious slavery was countered by efforts by Buddha and his contemporaries to bring a message of freedom; after these efforts were met with forcible repression and cooptation, the Muslims appeared to conquer India due to their great spirit and to the weakness of a brahman-enslaved India. As we have seen earlier, Phule's view of the role of Islam in India was a positive one: he was an admirer of Mohammed, and argued that even forcible conversion had a liberatory effect on the oppressed masses. But this liberating role declined when the Muslim rulers sank into indolence, preferring the luxurious life of the harem. Following them the British, a nation made powerful by industriousness and by its republican form of government (*Asud* had a section on the Romans originating this but losing it to the imperial Caesar and his followers), conquered India and brought also the possibility of liberation. However, this was again countered by brahmans grabbing positions of power and the British preferring to make an alliance with them. In the case of both the British and the Muslims, the indolence of the top rulers is seen as providing an opportunity for the immediate exploiters to continue their enslavement of the masses.

Asud concludes with recommendations to the British—primary schools throughout the villages with teachers drawn from the peasantry, 'reservation' in the services, and cutting down the pay of the higher members of the bureaucracy. All of this is in the context of his warning against *swadeshi*:

> [T]hese days these stalwarts of purity have been hiding their sword of religion, with all the ritual weapons that cut the throats of all the creatures of God, under the guise of being great lovers of swadeshi... and have been telling the frolicsome promising offspring of sudras, Parsis and Muslims through their books, newspapers, sabhas and similar methods that they should put aside all grumbling about the hierarchies and distinctions in the country and become united. (1991, 125)

In warning his sudra–ati-sudra peasantry against the rising nationalism of the elite, Phule began his most protracted debate.

Educating the Farmers

Phule was the first to stress education, indeed mass education, as the key to the uplift of the oppressed masses. He noted in the English introduction to *Gulamgiri* that the old forms of slavery had ended. But brahmans refused to acknowledge their past role: "Even the educated Brahman who knows his exact position and how he has come by it, will not condescend to acknowledge the errors of his forefathers and willingly forego the long cherished false notions of his own superiority" (Phule, 125). He was referring to the smugness he clearly found in Pune society, even among the most 'progressive' reformers. Then he accused the government of being responsible, in focusing on higher education and neglecting the education of the masses – in spite of the fact that almost all the revenues of the state were drawn from the labour of the peasantry. The result of brahman monopoly of higher education was the monopoly of higher offices under the British themselves in the government administration.

Thus his remedies for the exploitation he described centred on education. Was India falling behind in meeting the competition of foreign goods? The solution was not autarchy; this would cut off the country and deprive the masses themselves of needed inspiration and cultural exchange, but rather education of peasants and artisans so that they could learn industrial skills. Schools should not be run by brahman teachers, because these scorned the children they taught – Phule was perhaps remembering his own experience of having a village brahman advise his father not to educate him – but rather by teachers drawn from the sudra–ati-sudras who would teach both reading and writing, and useful skills.

Similarly, when Phule proposed a form of 'reservation' or affirmative action in the concluding chapter of *Asud*, he also linked it to the role of education:

> In reality, until the children of farmers become capable of taking charge of the government administration, brahmans should not be given governmental positions beyond the proportion of their caste, and the remaining governmental posts should be given to Muslims or British people in India. Unless this is done they (the brahmans) will not stop obstructing the education of the farmers. (1991, 320)

It is striking that the most famous slogan, one which opens *Shetkaryaca Asud*, is *Vidyavina mati geli, mativina niti geli, nitivina gati geli, gativina vitt gele, vittavina shudra khacle.* 'Without education wisdom was lost; without wisdom morals were lost; without morals development was lost; without development wealth was lost, without wealth the sudras were ruined.' In *Asud*, education was also seen as the alternative to swadeshi. Education would provide knowledge and technological education help raise the production levels of India.

The importance of education was defined by the fact that ignorance was the main obstacle to mass control; it was the ignorance enforced by brahmans that had kept the masses enslaved after their conquest, and the removal of this was the key to liberation. Here, between the ecstasy offered by bhakti and the reason that had previously been the province of brahmans, Phule was choosing reason: it was knowledge or jnana in its modern form that had been lacking.

The Universal Religion

Phule's final book, posthumously published, was *Sarvajanik Satyadharma Pustak*—The Book of the Universal Religion of Truth. It was primarily a presentation of an alternative, monotheistic religion of compassion. At the same time, it had a political thrust, and was a major intervention in the ongoing debate about the Indian nation. Religiously, what Phule had to say was simple. There was a severe critique of Hinduism:

> Jotirao Govindrao Phule: ....If the creator of all that is on earth and the solar system is one, then why has the empty vanity of national and religious chauvinism spread so widely, creating enmity among the people of so many countries on the earth? In the same way, if all the rivers of all the countries on the earth meet in the oceans, how can we say that one river in one country among them is a holy river? This very holy river never hesitates to carry even the excrement and urine of dogs in its belly to the ocean.
>
> Balwantrao: And similarly, why are some people on this earth considered to be ultra-holy, given respect as Bhoodevatas and treated as superior?

Jotirao: Since all human beings on the surface of the earth are alike in bodily form and intelligence, how can some be said to be holy by birth? Since they all live and die like one another, don't they all have the same capacity for good and evil? (1991, 441)

This set the tone. There was a critique and with it an assertion of equality among human beings, a fervent monotheism, and an ethical orientation. Sections of the book dealt with nearly all subjects—proper worship, ethical behaviour, the superiority of women (because they were caretakers of humans from childhood, they lacked the lust and aggressiveness of men, and what woman brought home one husband after another?), and critiqued notions such as dharma and fate. It severely attacked the immorality and improbability of the stories of Rama and Krishna. Years later, a manuscript of Ambedkar on "Riddles of Rama and Krishna," in much more reasonable but equally scornful language, would lead to oppositional demonstrations calling for its banning—this did not happen, since dalits could mobilize equally. *Sarvajanik Satyadharma Pustak* provided simple rituals for weddings and funerals, and attacked the notion of caste with the same 'Aryan theory'-based explanation that Phule had used in the past.

Phule had nothing but praise for both Islam and Christianity. He praised the 'religious heroic Muslims' and gave a remarkable acceptance of 'forced conversions' which had erased caste differences among those led to the mosque.

> The Muslims, destroying the carved stone images of the cunning Arya Bhats, forcibly enslaved them and brought the sudras and ati-sudras in great numbers out of their clutches and made them Muslims, including them in the Muslim religion. Not only this, but they established interdining and intermarraige with them and gave them all equal rights. They made them all as happy as themselves and forced the Arya Bhats to see all this. (1991, 491)

Phule described Christ as the great 'Yashwant', man of truth, the Bali Raja of the West. He ethically gave a central place to the 'great sacred sentence'—'Do unto others as you would have others do unto you.'

Throughout Phule used the term 'creator' to apply to god. This was a concept of religious monotheism and ethical behaviour based not on Indian tradition, not on Buddhism which Phule admired but knew little about, but rather on borrowings from Islam and Christianity. Like these religions, Phule too felt the need for a decisive 'Book' that would be open to everyone – there is a great deal of mockery of the secrecy of the vedas in phule – and he expressed his admiration for both religions.

Nation and Community

Phule had a tendency to put all of his thinking into each of his writings, and *Pustak* was no exception; it also contained the culmination of his critique of elite-led nationalism. The period of the 1880s onwards was one of the formation of nationalistic institutions, culminating in 1885 with the Indian National Congress. Around this was built a theory that identified India as a nation, largely built on a religious identity. This was a theme explicitly stressed by people like Savarkar, implicitly by almost all the leading Congress figures, who drew on the 'reformism' of leaders like Rammohan Roy to stress the 'ancient greatness' of the land.

M.G. Ranade, considered Maharashtra's greatest liberal, is a major example. At the Lahore session of the National Social Conference in 1893 he noted "two articles of my creed. This race of ours is the chosen race. This country of ours is the true land of promise. It was not for nothing that God has showered his choicest blessings on this ancient land of Aryavarta" (cited in Sunthankar 1993, 154). In describing these ancient glories, Ranade pitched his effort at both an all-India and a Maharashtrian audience. His writing of *The Rise of the Maratha*

Power in 1900 was a major attempt in this direction. It was in many ways a masterpiece of a 'progressive' Hindu interpretation. Knowing that the vedas and ancient Aryan glories would have little mass appeal, he focused on Shivaji and began with the bhakti movement, but interpreted them from a brahmanic point of view. Bhakti in Maharashtra, he argued, had brought the essential truth of the vedas to the masses and provided an all-encompassing national unity. In doing so, Ranade identified in fact with the orthodox Ramdas, seeing Ramdas as the guru of Shivaji. And along with this 'Hinduistic' interpretation, there was also an anti-Muslim thrust that was similar to that of the writings of overt 'Hindu nationalists' like Savarakar. Throughout the book he refers to Muslim 'excesses' and 'bigotry and fanatic cruelty', and sees the lack of Urdu in Maharashtra as a boon for people's languages. He contrasts the rise of Marathas with 'Mohammedan confusion': it is almost impossible, in his view, for any Muslim-led regime (or even Sikh-led regime) to be truly nationalistic. The very beginning of the book states:

> Anyone who sees no distinction between the great leaders who helped in the work of building up the Maratha Confederacy and the careers of Hyder and Tipu in Mysore, of Nizam-ul-mulk at Hyderabad...Ranjitsingh in the Punjab...will never be able to occupy the correct standpoint of vision from which this history must be study.... It is the history of the formation of a true Indian Nationality, raising its head high above the troubled waters of Mohammedan confusion. It was this force behind which supported the efforts of the leaders and enabled them to dream as a possibility the establishment of a central Hindu padshahi or Empire at Delhi.... (Ranade 1990, 1–5)

The fact that Tipu Sultan was the last major Indian force to stand against British power, that he sought an India-wide alliance that was refused by the Peshwa regime (in effect betraying the dream that Shivaji represented) was ignored. Ranade thus identified Shivaji with the Peshwas, amalgamating all equally into a 'nationalistic' Maratha power, and distinguishes this from even the most nationalistic of Muslim regimes. With such an interpretation, pro-brahman and anti-Muslim attitudes were built into the national movement from the beginning. More than Tilak, more than Savarkar, it was liberals like Ranade who represented the subtle but pervasive form of 'Hindu nationalism' in the Indian independence movement.

The Rise of the Maratha Power was thus an important political–theoretical coup, an important indicator of the ongoing power of brahman interpretation of history. It represented a culminating point in the creation of a new, Hindu-oriented national consciousness in Maharashtra, tying in regional (linguistic–national) pride, focusing on Shivaji and the theme of Hindu *swaraj*. It brought in, through Shivaji, the major caste-ethnic group, the Marathas. If 'Hindi–Hindu–Hindustan' proved to be a powerful ideological theme in north India, 'Marathi–Maratha–Hindustan' worked in the Marathi-speaking areas. The elite was constructing, as part of brahmanic Hinduism, the link between ethnicity and religion, to constitute the 'nation'. Finally, it tied the bhakti movement to the developing, brahmanic Maratha regional nationalism, amalgamating Ramdas and Tukaram—the orthodox and the radical sants.

Phule contested every link of this developing elite thesis. He did so by dealing at a theoretical level with the relationship between individual and nation, and at a sociological level in dealing with the conditions of nationality in India.

The theoretical points were later made more didactically by Ambedkar, who argued in the "Philosophy of Hinduism" that the major difference between 'antique society' and modern society was that in the first the individual was subordinate to the community while in the modern period the individual and justice became the guiding criteria. Modernization was thus a 'revolution' that put the individual at the forefront:

> At one end of the Revolution was the antique society with its religious ideal in which the end was Society. At the other end of the Revolution is the modern Society with its religious ideal in which the end is the individual. To put the same fact in terms of the norm it can be said that the norm or the criterion for judging right and wrong in the Antique Society was utility while the norm or criterion for judging right and wrong in the modern society is justice. (1987, vol 3, 22)

He went on to argue that the major religious difference between the 'modern' and the 'antique' society was that in ancient society god was viewed as a tribal deity, as a true kind of father of the people. In modernity, god becomes universalized, not tied into any one nation or ethnic group, a true father of humanity, only now much more metaphorically.

Phule anticipated these themes in *Pustak*. Overall, his focus was on the individual and his relation to god, a universalistic relation. The nation or community was to be judged by individual and universalistic morality, not vice versa. The universal – *sarvajanik* – was the main theme.

His critique of brahmanic Hinduism is harsher and more detailed here. The figures of Rama and Krishna are attacked, with the same kind of bawdy scornful description as was used in *Gulamgiri*, suggesting the unreality and ridiculousness of how they are conceived. The lack of morality is emphasized. Phule gives here alternative ceremonies (for marriage, death and other occasions) and suggests prayers and ways of worshipping god whom he calls *nirmik*—the creator.

It is in this work that an explicit criticism can be found both of the Pune Sarvajanik Sabha and the Congress. In an extended dialogue, Phule asked whether the Sarvajanik Sabha has any members from the various sudra castes and communities, which he names in detail, and on being told that not even five percent can be found, he argued that such an organization could never be considered truly sarvajanik or public/universal. In regard to the Congress, he declared:

> Due to the false self-interested religion of the Aryans, the cunning Arya Bhat-Brahmans consider the ignorant Shudras to be inferior; the ignorant Shudras consider the ignorant Mahars to be inferior; and the ignorant Mahars consider the ignorant Mangs to be inferior. As a result not only do the ultra-pure Arya Bhat-Brahmans consider the Ati-Shudras inferior, but since marriage and social relations are forbidden among them all, naturally their various customs, eating habits, and rituals don't match each other. How can such a conglomerate of 18 grains be united to become a 'nation' of integrated people? (1991, 494)

A nation, then, for Phule had to be built on the development of the individual and an abolition of social hierarchies, an equality which would allow the feeling of commonness (*ekmey lok* is the term he uses) to develop. Caste and brahman domination in India resulted in the lack of this commonality, this community, and without it no true integrated nation could be achieved.

Towards a New Kingdom of Bali

Phule thus had a multifaceted critique of brahmanism and its main supporters, the British. He gave an economic analysis of exploitation and a social interpretation of history. He demythologized the avatar theory, linking it to a metaphorical interpretation of Aryan conquest. And he made Bali Raja, already recognized in popular tradition, a symbol of the oppressed peasantry.

He insisted, in a clear moralistic way, on freedom and equality defining the relationship between human beings. This is seen in many ways in his presentation of an ideal family, which is not bound together by a particular religion but allows scope for all:

> [I]n the many religious books written by great Men of Truth on this globe according to their own understanding there is something or another of truth. In fact if some human woman

> in any family read the enlightened religious books she could choose whichever religion suited her fancy and her husband in the same family could read the old and new contracts and choose according to his fancy, if he wanted to be Christian and the daughter in his family wanted to become Muslim after reading the Koran it should be possible. And the son in the same family should be able after reading the Sarvajanik Satyadharma Book according to his own choice could become a Satyadharmi; and all of this together, mother and father, son and daughter could carry on their daily affairs without scorning or hating any religion and all of these should be able, as the children made by the Creator of all understand that they are of his (the Creator's) family and behave towards each other with love and sweetness. (523)

This depiction of a modern multicultural society expressed the moral foundations of secularism. Notably, Phule did not in this count 'Hinduism' as a true religion; it was, according to him, *krutim*, *banavat*—artificial and constructed.

Phule's Bali Rajya, Kingdom of Bali, existed primarily in the past. He did not visualize the future kingdom of Bali; he also did not envision Indian independence. This may be partly connected with his lack of knowledge of industrialism and the industrial revolution. Living in Pune, which was then primarily an administrative and cultural centre, he was quite aware of the market and of commerce, but he had no personal knowledge of factory production. The textile industry was only just beginning in Bombay, Ahmedabad and a few other places at the time. When he wrote, for instance, in *Shetkaryaca Asud*, that the "power of learning helped the artisans and the skilled Americans in industry to go ahead of the manufacturers in all the countries of Europe" (1991, 504), he was clearly aware of the role of knowledge and invention in manufacturing, but this was evidently as far as it went. He had referred to the multitude of products coming into India from Europe and impoverishing local artisans through their inability to compete, but of the background of factory production he apparently knew nothing. Thus he referred to roads, transport, and the telegraph, but little beyond that.

Nevertheless, as far as technology went, this, along with education, was crucial to his vision of a new Indian society. The children of peasants and artisans were to be educated—both in their own skills and in skills of reading and writing. Phule's poetry in addition made it clear that knowledge of Marathi, English, and Persian (at that time, still a very important language of administration, culture and exchange with other parts of the world) were to be taught. Technology was to be applied to agriculture; again, without much direct knowledge of modern technologies, he insisted on carefully applied irrigation given in careful measure to all the land. Exhibitions and import of animals for breeding should also be encouraged. And, of course, programmes of affirmative action – later to be called 'reservation' in India – were recommended to ensure that the doors of both educational institutions and employment were open to the children of sudra–ati-sudras. Finally, to tame the government bureaucracy, Phule called for reduction in the 'excessive pays and pensions' of government bureaucrats, exempting the lowest categories from this.

Phule thus laid the foundations for envisioning a utopia of independent India, one that looked to the remembrance and re-creation in modern form of the Kingdom of Bali. In the context of colonial rule, he made his concrete suggestions to move in this direction, including an emphasis on technological development, reservation, and the provision of literary and scientific education for all.

viii

Iyothee Thass
The Buddhist Utopia

We'll set fire to the divisions of caste,
we'll debate philosophical questions in the market place,
we'll have dealings with despised households.
We'll go around in different paths –
So dance, snake, dance!

(Pambatti Cittar, cited by Kailaspathy 1987, 391)

The Tamil country, in south India, was the site of awakenings and debates like those that unfolded in western India. Here too the brahman elite found a new accommodation with colonialism through the mastery of the new English education; however, they were challenged from relatively early by a strong, landlords-based, nonbrahman yet privileged-caste group, who formulated their 'non-Aryan' identity as a Dravidian one. At the same time, a dalit-based movement issued an even more fundamental challenge, identifying not with ancient Tamils but rather with Buddhist forerunners. Tamilnadu also gave birth to one of the famous anticaste radicals of the twentieth century, Periyar E.V. Ramasamy. This, then, was a complex process of formulating anticaste ideals, analysis and social visions.

From ancient times Tamilnadu had had a distinct identity. The Greeks knew it as *Damila* or *Damida*, south of what they called the *Dakkan*, which itself meant 'south'. The incursion of Aryans and vedic ideas came rather later in Tamilnadu; the earliest Sangam literature – though there is some debate about its dating – describes a warrior society not much touched by brahmanism. The *kavya* literature that followed this, as well as the hallowed *Kural* of Thiruvalluvar, were influenced by Buddhism and Jainism, and there is good evidence that these samana faiths found a strong base in the south. Kanchi, for example, was a major Buddhist centre though Asoka himself had never conquered the far south.

The brahmanic revival came around the sixth and seventh centuries with the Pallavas and the Cholas. It was marked by the preaching of advaita by the Sankaracharya, by fierce debates with Buddhists and Jains – debates that could end in the slaughter of the defeated – and by the development of a bhakti that was taken as a counter to the samana religions (see Nilakantha Sastri 1975, 1963). Later legends had it that the bhakti sants were from all castes, with Nandanar, a paraiya, counted as one of them. The equalitarian impulse that was in bhakti was fairly quickly overwhelmed by a re-established orthodoxy, both among Vaishnavites and Saivites (Stein 1980, 81–101). Temples and land management remained under the control of brahmans and elite, landed nonbrahmans such as vellalas. The latter often used the more orthodox Saivite trends to assert their social and religious dominance. Indeed, the Nandanar legend itself shows the hold of orthodoxy: he is depicted as allowed to enter the temple only after going through fire and being revealed as a brahman. (See also Karen Prentiss on Nandanar in Zelliot and Mokashi-Punekar 2005, 109–119.) Vellalas, considered 'high' caste (*sat-sudras*), claimed also an aristocratic position and scholarship in Saivite lore.

There were, however, heterodox radical forms of Saivism that had similarities in their equalitarianism to the bhakti of the north and the West. While this appeared as Virasaivism in the Telugu and Kannada areas, in the far south the Siddha tradition – related to the Nath-yogis – was the main carrier of this radicalism. This was a heterodox version of Saivism, unlike the more orthodox high-caste based Saiva Siddhanta. Its propagators, including Sivavakkiyar, Pambatti Cittar and the semi-legendary Kapilar, rejected caste, brahmanism, the authority of the vedas and shastras, idol worship and all the rituals expected of orthodox Hindus. Their poetry, written in the colloquial language of the people, stood as a challenge to mainstream tradition in both form and content. Some of these, recorded in the nineteenth century by missionaries, expressed in stark form their aspirations:

O Brahmans, listen to me!
In all this blessed land
there is but one great caste,
one tribe and brotherhood.
One God doth dwell above,
and he hath made us one
in birth and frame and tongue.

(Cited in Gover 2002, 169)

The Siddha frequently used the word *sivam*, meaning 'the good', rather than the term *Siva* referring to the god—a usage seen also in Tukaram (for instance, *Tuka dekhe jivi siv, he tar tyace anubhav*, meaning 'Tuka sees the good in life, this is his experience'). Some went so far as to reject the notion of rebirth:

Milk does not return to the udder,
likewise butter can never become buttermilk.
The sound of the conch does not exist once it is broken;
the blown flower, the fallen fruit do not go back to the tree:
The dead are never born again, never!

(Cited in Kailaspathy 1987, 401)

The Siddha tradition was linked in Tamilnadu to an indigenous system of medicine, and in spite of the powerful brahmanic hegemony in the region, survived as a subaltern vision among the subordinated castes. Among these were sections of paraiyas, and it was a Siddha doctor of medicine, Iyothee Thass, who was to become the most powerful spokesman for a renewed historical vision of liberation, and, before Ambedkar, the reviver of the ancient religion of Buddhism.

Colonialism and Dalits

Phule had been a leader of all the oppressed sections of society, and in particular had sought to unify dalits and 'bahujans', whom he termed as 'sudras and ati-sudras. But he was not dalit, and could benefit from a modest bit of prosperity that some of the middle-caste malis had. As he recognized, the dalits were much worse off.

Yet even the outcastes of the system could generate movements from very early in the colonial period. Those groups who did so were the large untouchable, field-labouring castes of India; in the drier regions these were often also small landholders. These included the mahars of Maharashtra, the chamars of north India, and the paraiyas of Tamilnadu. The paraiyas had been, in 'feudal' times, near slaves for the brahman and nonbrahman landlords of the rich rice-fields of coastal Tamilnadu, but in the drier areas they were often small farmers themselves. It was from this group, and from a small subcaste, the valluvans, who were priests and ritual specialists, that Iyothee Thass emerged.

The early, relatively more progressive period of colonialism up to about the middle of the nineteenth century provided significant scope for dalit mobility, so much that it has been described by David Washbrook as 'the golden age of the paraiyas'. The paraiyas in the south, similar to mahars of Maharashtra (which included Ambedkar's father) gained entry into the army and into British service, often working as butlers in their households, as servants, cooks, stable-hands. From the small income they thus gathered, they managed to increase their landholding. In Coimbatore, just as in Nagpur, they played an important role in the new textile factories that were being built, consolidating their position as mill-hands. In the south, in addition to mill work, dalits migrated and became plantation labourers and field workers in places as far-ranging as South Africa, Fiji, Mauritius and Southeast Asia. These south Indian dalits were the typical 'coolies' of colonialism and served as a heavily exploited labour force not only in Tamilnadu but also overseas, in Burma and Sri Lanka. However, for a period they experienced some prosperity and mobility. Their position was perhaps strongest in the dry northern districts of Tamilnadu surrounding Madras city, where the wealthy rice fields and their servitude to brahman control were lacking.

Dalits were searching for alternatives in a variety of ways. One was an association with Christianity, linking up with sections of missionaries who were making appeals to dalits. The early missionary–ethnographer of Tamil castes, Abbe Dubois, had described the paraiyas as terribly discriminated against and exploited, but also showed a revulsion towards the brutality of their existence, arguing that it left them open to all kinds of vice. "Their habits of uncleanliness are disgusting. Their huts, a mass of filth and alive with insects and vermin, are even more loathsome than their persons" (1996: 55). Dubois had a fascination for the brahmans and upper sudras (vellalas and others); it was perhaps natural that he should see the paraiyas' existence as a low one. Even those who gave their energy to working with them sometimes reacted strongly against the brutal living conditions of most of the dalits by describing them as low, unclean and often drunken. Thus, for example, Briggs writes of the chamars, "His quarters abound in all kinds of abominable filth. His foul mode of living is proverbial" (1990, 20). However, in the eighteenth and nineteenth century the paraiyas, and indeed dalits everywhere, were on the move. Missionaries sometimes fed this assertion, often documented it, but sometimes, as in the case of the paraiyas, they missed it.

Tamil Elite Discourse

From the nineteenth century onwards, the elites in Tamilnadu, like in Maharashtra, formulated a version of nationalist affirmation that included a conceptualization of themselves as Hindus. The Tamil variant of this was in the context of the rising themes of Dravidianism—an identity that was emerging in different ways, normally from nonbrahmans and dalits. Tamil versions of nationalism had to reconcile the vedic golden age with the themes of ancient Tamils, as the Sangam period of a unique poetry was being recovered. Here, rather than Aryanism a claim to indigenous status emerged as the Dravidian mystique was created. The basic strategy that emerged was to glorify Sangam period literature, but to reconcile it with a vedic heritage—with the sage Agastya, for example, taken as a creator of Tamil in a kind of parallel to Panini, but seen as a brahman immigrant from the north. The mixture of Aryan and Dravidian was stressed, for instance with the vedic elements appearing also in the Sangam period. The period of Buddhist and Jain hegemony in the early decades of the first millennium was seen as a 'dark age', a black interregnum before the return of brahmanic hegemony with the Pallavas and Cholas. These, with their temple sculpture, their Sanskrit and Tamil scholarship and poetry, were glorified as representing the culmination of Tamil culture. Finally, Saivism was taken as the main southern, Tamil religious identity. This, however, as we shall see, tended to exclude the subordinated castes.

The 'Hindu renaissance' that took place, pioneered not only by brahmans but even more by high-caste nonbrahman intellectuals, mostly vellalas, often focused on Saivism. In 1840–41 an Association for the Philosophy of the Four Vedas was organized in Madras, inspired by the Brahmo Samaj and led by former Christians who had renounced their conversions (Hudson 1992, 31). This aggressively responded to missionaries, and an atmosphere of charges and countercharges ensued with various publications and public speeches. One of the most successful writers and polemicists of this Saivite revival was a Sri Lanka Tamil, Arumuga Navalar (1822–79). He argued that Saivism was genuinely monotheistic, that it had everything that Christians claimed for their religion, without the various 'superstitions', and that it was a national *dharma* of the Tamils. Initially he drew parallels with biblical stories, linking Old Testament ritual injunctions with the ceremonies of Saivism, arguing that temple worship in the Bible and that in Saivism was not very different.

This fed into an assertion of pride in Tamil identity, a glorification of the Tamil language, a romanticization of the millennia-old culture of the Tamils. But there was little of social reform in it; little mention of caste. Women were given the southern version of the *pativrata* image, with devotion to the husband symbolized by the heroine Kannagi, who tore off her left breast and cursed the city of Madurai in revenge for the unjust killing of her husband by the king.

Tamil Buddhism

Subalterns challenged the elite in terms of identity, and often played a leading role, with the earliest radical anticaste movement in Tamilnadu being led by a dalit. Pandit Iyothee Thass (1845–1914) was a Tamil Siddha physician. Even as a young man, his search was religious and national, but from the particular viewpoint of the oppressed castes. He interacted with the political leaders who were part of the Congress movement, but he was not drawn to Saivism or to their reformism. His own first attempt at a kind of religious revivalism was the founding of an Advaidananada Sabha in 1870, oriented to the advaita tradition as a way of undermining caste. Since this was played up as a 'unity' of being, the subaltern castes could place hope in it that the unity of human beings was included; later, Sree Narayana Guru of Kerala would pioneer an anticaste version of advaita. In contrast to the Kerala group, however, Iyothee Thass became disillusioned with this.

In 1891–92 came a corresponding disillusionment with the Indian National Congress. This began to climax when his petition for support on removal of caste disabilities drew no response from the Congress in its 1891 Nagpur session. Then, in 1892 he raised the issue of temple entry with the Madras Mahajana Sabha. Iyothee Thass argued with simple logic: "We have heard that God and temples are common for all castes of the world. If that is so, why can't people of this community, following Vaishnava or Saivite traditions, be allowed to enter Vishnu or Siva temples?" He was appealing in the bhakti tradition, and perhaps using some of the logic given at the time by missionary arguments. But it was not convincing to the educated elite, who – as Iyothee Thass described it later – shouted their rejection: "For your community we have given gods like Madurai Veeran, Katteri and Karuppannan; and gods like Siva and Vishnu have nothing to do with you!" (2001, 152). Indeed, there was clear 'religious' segregation of gods in orthodox Tamilnadu. (In Maharashtra too, the folk gods were often quite different, only tenuously identified with brahmanic deities: Jotiba, Khandoba, Vithoba, Naikba, etc.) There was a tendency however to change this. The Saivite revival, somewhat like Brahmoism in Bengal, was indeed not coping with or challenging caste in any way.

The exclusion was clear, and this motivated a deeper search by

Iyothee Thass. Neither the revived Saivism nor classical advaita were willing to challenge caste and varna hierarchy. By the latter quarter of the nineteenth century, in contrast to Phule's time when hardly anything was known of Indian Buddhism, a good deal of pioneering work in the discovery of Buddhism in India had been done. Iyothee Thass, who felt the need for a spiritual and philosophical foundation for the modern quest for equality, began to look towards Buddhism. In 1898 he and his friends met with Sir Henry Olcott of the Theosophical Society—not to investigate theosophy, but with a request to meet Ceylonese Buddhist leaders. This led to a voyage to Ceylon, when Iyothee Thass went with two companions in July 1898 to Colombo and they were given the Panch Shila as a form of initiation by one of the Sinhalese Buddhist leaders.

Thus began Tamil Buddhism. It was interpreted by Iyothee Thass not as 'conversion' but as reversion—a return home. He argued that Indian dalits were originally Buddhists from the time of Emperor Asoka, and they had been degraded for their attachment to the faith and thrust into a state of slavery. Thus, they told the Sri Lanka Buddhists, they were hoping simply to recover their original faith. Iyothee Thass argued that in fact the Sakya paraiyas (a subcaste) were descended from Buddha's Sakya clan; his organization was called the Sakya Buddhist Society. The term 'Sakya' retains an appeal for Tamil dalits even today. The movement grew, not only in Tamilnadu but also in areas where the dalit Tamil diaspora was strong—in Burma, South Africa, Sri Lanka, among coal miners in Bihar and gold mine workers in the nearby Kolar district in Karnataka. The paraiyas formed the base, but a significant number of men and women from other castes also joined the 'noncaste Tamil Buddhists'. It evolved a totalistic way of life for its members, celebrating traditional festivals but giving them a Buddhist interpretation, providing religious solace, providing meals for all, including the poor as a concluding feature of its weekly services. Organizations grew, and the movement eventually changed its name to the South Indian Buddhist Association.

From 1907 Iyothee Thass published a weekly, *Oru Paisa Tamilan* (One Penny Tamilan) and then simply as *Tamilan*. He also gave summaries in this of his booklets which were published from time to time. These outlined the history of the subcontinent from his point of view. Let us now turn to the philosophy and vision of Tamil Buddhism.

Interpreting the Past, Looking toward the Future

The interpretation of the past as the origin of their present slavery and the hope of their future resurgence was an important aspect of the movement. It laid the foundations of a strong identity for Tamil Buddhism. Iyothee Thass resembled Phule in emphasizing an early indigenous society of peace and plenty, disrupted by Aryan incursions. However, his analysis of the mechanisms of the Aryan conquest was quite different. Phule had stressed violence and conquest in his interpretation of history: the Aryans were driven by greed and could defeat the indigenous people due to their mastery of weapons; it was only after the conquest that they established their mental hold over the minds of the conquered by keeping them ignorant, depriving them of knowledge and education, and weaving a spell of religion. (This, in fact, had some parallels with classical historical materialism.) In contrast, Iyothee Thass emphasized infiltration, and apparently dated this to a much later period. He also sought to appropriate (or re-appropriate) most of the 'valued' symbols of traditional society.

The original inhabitants of India, he argued, had been Buddhists; the 'vedas' were their rules of moral conduct. Their great and wise men were known as brahmans. When the invaders came, the *mlecchas*, they conquered not by the force of arms but by stealth and cunning. They appropriated the name 'brahman' for themselves; they claimed that the vedas were their holy books—and they gradually spread the ideology of caste and birth ascription. They did not emerge at the zenith of society through military achievement, but through infiltration, through taking over the names and symbols of the indigenous people, through sowing seeds of dissension, through fabrication. Their conquest was one of ideas—nearly all baneful, oppressive ideas. Using scholarship in Sanskrit and Pali – in contrast to Phule's reliance on the discoveries by Europeans of the Aryans and their dating of Aryan incursions – Iyothee Thass dated the 'takeover' rather late; at one point, 1200 years earlier—reflecting the period when brahmanism came to hegemony in Tamil society. Thus he was, in many ways, looking at the events from a distinctly Tamil point of view.

Yet, there were striking similarities. Just as Phule had seen the mahars as the greatest foe of the Aryans (only in a military sense), Iyothee Thass saw the dalits as the greatest Buddhist resisters of the infiltration. Both also placed an interesting emphasis on an 'etiology' of words that would reveal meanings that supported an antibrahmanical interpretation.

Though Iyothee Thass' form of expression was not as harsh as Phule's, he was equally particular about language. He never referred to the dalits as 'paraiyas', or by more 'modern' terms such as 'panchama' or 'adi-dravida' or in terms of any caste name. Rather he identified them as 'noncaste Tamils' or 'Tamil Buddhists'. Caste, he thus argued, was never fully accepted by the subaltern masses, but the use of names indicated an acceptance of brahmanic Hinduism:

> The term *Panchama* is generally used to refer to *Parayars, Chakkiliars, Kuravars, Villiars,* etc. This term as well as these caste-names are correctly applied only to those who are connected to Hindu religion and worship Hindu gods but not applicable to

> Buddhists. Relying on Hindu religion, those who agree that they are indeed panchamas or paraiyas, will be accepted (by the caste Hindus) neither in the dancing nor dumping yard. (Cited in Aloysius 1998, 152–53)

Similarly he interpreted the term *paarppan* (used for brahman) as a reference to the originally Buddhist 'seers', arguing that the 'Aryan-Brahmans' had appropriated this term from the original Buddhist inhabitants. This was also close to the original Buddhist definition of brahman as a wise and moral person.

Buddhism was interpreted as an equalitarian, rational religion. Just as Phule had absorbed the folk deities of Maharashtra as 'subedars' and underlings of his politically conceived King Bali, so Iyothee Thass interpreted the popular folk gods and goddesses of Tamilnadu as great and good men and women of the Buddhist past, famous for their healing or other benefits. Simple ceremonies were adapted to bind the community together. Membership emphasized the *pancha silam*, the five moral principles, rather than the 'three refuges', and the definition of a Buddhist was given as "all those who declare in the assembly of the Association to renounce idol worship, ritualism and caste discrimination and take Pancha Silam" (cited in Aloysius 1998, 97). Years later, Ambedkar would follow much the same path in reinterpreting Buddhism for the modern world.

Analyzing Colonialism and Brahman Collaboration

The period of Tamil Buddhism and the publication of *Tamilan* coincided with the swadeshi movement, the first great upsurge of Indian nationalism provoked first by the proposed partition of Bengal. Phule had challenged the swadeshi philosophy at the time of its beginnings (1870s and 1880s). Iyothee Thass also took on the movement. The pages of *Tamilan* are filled with mockery of the swadeshiites – he refused to describe them as nationalists – and the falsity of their proclamations of love for India.

As was common with most of the intellectuals of the period (even those in the Indian National Congress) British rule was viewed as largely beneficent. Whereas the more orthodox supporters stressed the maintenance of law and order and some developmental policies, Iyothee Thass focused on the undermining of caste differences and bringing unity to the country. The nationalists, in contrast, were seen as frauds in their claims to represent a national unity. As he wrote in October 1908:

> It is sheer injustice to clamour that driving away the British government of such heroism and ideals [as to save all kinds of people during famines] men of no heroism or ideals should rule...If we seriously analyze the enmities of religious divisions, caste divisions and language divisions and consider deeply the political strategies and administrative tactics required to bring about unity among these, we would realize that the present rulers – the British – are like father and mother to us, they are our moral deities, and they are our friends in need, and we would look for means of stabilizing their rule and following their ideals and character and conducting our own affairs accordingly. (Cited in Aloysius 1998, 67)

However, British rule had its flaws in that the British also yielded to brahman cunning. Iyothee Thass noted that in the early period of colonial rule, it was the so-called paraiya who had entered first into the army, into the hospital service and even administration. They had worked clearing jungles and deserts, laying roads, shedding their blood in the service of defence and in developing the country. They worked in hospitals where brahmans first remained aloof due to their hesitation to touch the sick of the subordinated castes. It was only later, in the realization of how prosperity could come through the new professions, that brahmans and other privileged castes entered and displaced the 'noncaste Dravidians' (Iyothee Thass 2001, 61–62). In this way, the dominance of brahmans under colonialism was seen as an emerging reality, reflecting the jealousy and self-interest of brahmans and the compromising tendencies of imperialism. Thus, colonial exploitation was for Iyothee Thass, as for Phule, one of collaboration between a British and a brahman elite.

Brahmans gradually took up English education, and Iyothee Thass described the process with a colourful sarcasm:

> As a result of some earlier good deeds, the British rule having appeared, these brahmanar have rolled up and thrown away all the Vedas, Puranas, Smrutis and Bhashyams devised for making a living; and learning now Vedas of high court jobs, Smritis of revenue board employment, Upanishads of Akbari office jobs and Bhashyams of municipal office employment, are in prosperous living. (Iyothee Thass 2001, 31)

This led to a description of the role of government officials in the exploitation of dalits. He described, in terms similar to Phule, the chain of influence occupied by the brahmans in the administration, beginning with the displacement of a dalit farmer by a conniving local brahman landlord:

> If this man [the displaced dalit farmer] takes his complaint to the Collector, he sends it down to the Tehsildar for enquiry; the tehsildar starts the enquiry with the munsif and the kanakkan; and since the munsif and the kanakkan are in collusion with the parppan, by making some technical-bureaucratic excuses tie up the affair in complicity and combining together drive the paraiyan out of the land. (2001, 27–28)

The backwardness of agriculture under colonialism was seen as part of unproductive landlordism; this itself was a result of casteism because brahmans refused to handle the plough or engage themselves in manual labour and relied on the labour of the field paraiya for these services. In turn, the paraiya who did the actual work had no control over land and was prevented by all kinds of manipulation and force from winning or maintaining it. Thus brahman landlords would own hundreds of acres of land without cultivating it, and still claim adjacent land belonging to the dalit poor, appropriating it through their influence with government administrators.

Iyothee Thass also developed a processual critique of Christianity similar to his depiction of the stages of colonialism. Recognizing the attractiveness that missionary doctrine had for dalits, he argued that it was these who turned first to Christianity, entering the church as part of a movement for liberation. But later, the missionaries themselves became oriented to privileged-caste Hindus and compromised with caste to seek respectability. Thus casteism gradually became re-instituted in the church, and dalits were forced to sit separately in churches which had once been theirs; positions such as pastors, catechists and priests were reserved for privileged caste converts. Thus he remained critical of Christianity:

> Building churches in the midst of cheris [dalit areas] and grabbing the resources of the poor to your heart's content without any mercy, you leave them to beg. Not only this, you have included their enemies who have been suppressing them for a thousand and five hundred years, who hold fast to caste discriminations. (2001, 90)

Today, dalit Christians are demanding their rights, building a separate movement. A century earlier, it is clear that the indifference to caste discrimination within the church was a major factor for leaders like Iyothee Thass to reject Christianity.

The Buddhist Commonwealth

Phule had phrased his ideal society with the metaphor of 'Bali's kingdom', projecting a visualized past golden age as a metaphor for an egalitarian future. Similarly, Iyothee Thass's attention began with the interpretation of past history of India and an analysis of the present. Few of the subaltern spokesmen were interested in 'independence' as such; it did not until the 1920s become a forthcoming reality for most of them. Iyothee Thass' prescriptions thus focused on the existing society, stressing education and a religion of rationality and morality, but he did not develop any detailed depiction of a future society. Rather, he sought to organize the sociocultural life of the subalterns, mostly dalits but people from other castes also, who followed 'South Indian Buddhism'.

One of the most important members of the South Indian Buddhist Society, Laxmi Narasu (1861–1934), however, did live to project a more detailed picture of a forthcoming society. Narasu was a science professor in Madras, a convert from a nonbrahman caste, and one of the most important interpreters and writers on Buddhism in English. He had become, along with Iyothee Thass and M. Singaravelu (later regarded as the founder of Indian communism) a member of the Mahabodhi Society branch in Madras started by the Sri Lankan Angarika Dharmapala in 1890, but Narasu differed from orthodox Theravada Buddhism in many ways, including a rejection of the importance of bhikkus and a rejection of the idea of reincarnation. He was proficient not only in English, Telugu and Tamil, but also in French, Sanskrit and Pali. His writings include *The Essence of Buddhism* (1907), *A Study of Caste* (1922), a manuscript entitled "Religion of the Modern Buddhist" (recently discovered and published) and numerous others.

Writing in the early 1920s, he made a critique of British colonialism that was very similar to that of Phule. Its objectives were not to spread western culture, but to exploit it for the benefit of Britain; and in fact 'the Hinduizing movement' (here he quoted Risley) had spread by the improvement of communication, while railways had merely extended the area within which caste prejudices remained. Brahmans retained their prestige, and there was no incentive for intercaste marriages. "The subtle political wisdom of the Anglo-Indian officials has not failed to perceive in the caste system a reason for the immobility of Hindu society and an advantage for bringing the people to obedience and therefore for ruling the country" (1988, 107). The worst failure was in the lack of mass education; Narasu pointed out that India had a lower percentage of population in primary schools than any other country, while only a slightly smaller percentage than England of people with university education (108–09).

He nevertheless rejected the national movement for much the same reason that Phule had: "The spirit of intransigent division which is characteristic of caste has not only rendered impossible all superior organization, but it has also sunk the Hindus into a state of intellectual immobility.... The spirit of caste is inimical, not only to the growth of national unity but also to the emancipation of the individual" (113). Caste was condemned in the strongest terms for rendering social cohesion impossible and leaving India open to become the prey of conquerors.

Thus an ideal society must include an educational system that would free the mind from shackles and enable all to realize their capabilities. There should be a fundamental equalitarianism in an equality of opportunities, in which success would be determined by talent and energy and not the accidents of birth. Referring to the "feud between capital and labour," he argued that this had not been ended by caste; rather it had made it impossible for workers in a factory to unite to improve their status. He argued for a cooperative system, with "the acceptance of joint responsibility both by the labour and the capitalist for the efficient conduct of industry." This required giving labour a share in the management of industry, with production oriented to necessaries and consumer goods for the majority; rather than "control of the means of production in the hands of a few" (126). Finally, he criticized the "spirit of nationality" as a "justification of the will to power and possession." Rather than a world of separate nations, the goal should be the development of the whole human race (158–59).

In his *Religion of the Modern Buddhist*, published posthumously (2002), he summarizes the main features of what he considered rational Buddhism, as contrasted with the Buddhism of the monks. The work is pervaded by admiration for modern science, seen as a crucial characteristic of humanity much as Phule had seen science and technology (inventiveness) as part of what it meant to be human. Thus, like Phule, but in much less poetic, more sober language, Narasu also gave an account of the formation of the stars and planets and the evolution of humanity. Here he extended his depiction of an ideal society as being based on morality including a very modified individualism, a rejection of the 'amoral individualism' characteristic of capitalism and an affirmation of cooperation.

> For [the Buddhist] the problem of government is not so much the location of power as the administration of human service. Buddhism, therefore, preaches the gospel of a commonwealth sustained by the spirit of loving kindness and the passion of humanity.... It will be a great cooperative association, in which all are partners not only in temporary and perishable things subservient only to animal and political existence, but also in a great fellowship inclusive of all science, all art, every virtue and all perfection. Such a commonwealth will infuse self-respect in all its citizens and will be looked upon with reverence by them. It can afford to be the sole capitalist, thus eliminating all the evils of modern industrialism and capitalism. (174–75)

Narasu condemned capitalism, but also did not explicitly call for a socialist alternative. However, the terms he used, such as 'commonwealth', implied some kind of common ownership. The only 'capitalist', that is manager, would be the collective. In contrast to this cooperation, which according to modern

Buddhism was the natural condition of humans, modern capitalist industrialism was engrossed in "unscrupulous and merciless struggle [as] the supreme object of human effort" (292). This fosters and culminates in militarism and war. The 'conquest of nature' – that is the purpose of industry – is lost with capitalism, whose parts engage in efforts to conquer one another. Thus, while avoiding the language of the social ownership of the means of production, while not engaging explicitly with historical materialism, Narasu speaks of 'organized cooperation', of the abolition of the division of labour. Caste is definitely negated, and not in the gandhian way of 'equal respect' for all tasks. Instead, the distasteful tasks of society should be undertaken by rotation; only in this way can everyone realize their heritage of freedom and equality.

This is obviously a very different vision from that of gandhism. It is not industrialism as such that is rejected but rather unbridled competition. The conquest of nature, the achievement of human advance that is part of this process, are all praised, but they have to have a basis of morality, the morality of *saddharma*. This is a position more akin to that of Nehru—a disdain for competition and commercialization. Where it differs is in the explicit renunciation of caste and refusal to valorize traditional caste and kinship as having some qualities of the desired cooperation. A comparison with the vision put forward in Nehru's *Discovery of India*, where he praises the 'old Brahman ideal of service', makes this clear.

Conclusion

Iyothee Thass' reconstructed Buddhism was a good deal more successful than Phule's *sarvajanik satyadharma* (universal religion of truth) and remained a crucial definer of identity and community for Tamil dalits until the 1930s. Subsequently it began to fade away, as political processes and conflicts became sharper and nationalism grew. The marxists moved in to make a new appeal to the oppressed, an appeal which neglected their caste identity but stressed their poverty and exploitation; it could not but have some impact, and it weakened the Buddhist movement. Other forces, the Indian National Congress, Ambedkar's powerful political organizing, and finally the Dravidian movement itself, also intervened. Thus, Tamil Buddhism did not last. Nevertheless, it was a forerunner of what was later to be Ambedkar's more powerful and lasting Buddhist revival in India.

It also illustrated the way in which dalits themselves, independently of bahujan leaders such as Phule but in a similar way, were analyzing their history and identity. In the Buddhist identity and in the myth of a golden Buddhist past, the Tamil dalits under Iyothee Thass found a new path to liberation, and as the movement grew, it also began to come to grips with the modern world, and through intellectuals such as Laxmi Narasu, formulated a new model of a 'commonwealth', a Buddhist commonwealth, which would guide their actions and express their hopes. Narasu's modified socialism also indicated the direction in which they would be doing so.

ix

Ramabai Women in the Kingdom of God

Phule and his Satyashodhak Samaj, Iyothee Thass and his Sakya Buddhists both imagined a utopia which now can be seen in more concrete, historical terms. It was, however, a woman who can be credited with being the first to try to create this as a living community: Ramabai, known as 'Pandita' due to her learning in the ancient texts of brahmanic Hinduism, who chose Christianity as a result of her disillusionment with this learning, and a feminist and activist all her life.

The Dilemmas of Indian Christians

Christian religious identity in India today is discussed in terms of 'conversion', a term which has come to mean a choice of religion representing the 'Other', forsaking an indigenous, inherited system of belief. It implies an alienation from a larger community (usually seen as a 'nation') of birth. This is a meaning deriving from the definition of Indian nationhood and identity in terms of a constructed 'Hinduism'. However, the simple concept of 'conversion' does not fit the various patterns seen among those who chose what often seemed to be the most 'alien' of religions—Christianity.

Two patterns can be identified in regard to 'becoming Christian' in colonial India. These can be related to caste and class. Among elite educated converts, affiliation with Christianity appears as one of individual choice and a grappling with 'Hinduism'; it also frequently involved social and economic hardship. Among the subaltern castes, there was more often a collective affiliation which had liberatory socioeconomic as well as spiritual implications.

Thus, for example, numerous educated Indians, as individuals, chose some form of following Christ but often without feeling that they were becoming part of a non-Indian, already-defined community. Many were very 'questionable' (from the orthodox Christian standpoint) adherents of Christianity. There was often no clear boundary between 'Christian' and 'non-Christian' in the colonial context. There was instead a gradation between those who never identified as sectarian Christians and were never baptized and yet honoured Christ in a special way – with Phule and Keshab Chandra Sen of Bengal at one end of the spectrum – to those baptized 'converts' such as Pandita Ramabai who never accepted church orthodoxy and changed denominational affiliation frequently.

These individual Christians, often from privileged castes, took up their new faith in varying forms, often in debate not only with the increasingly aggressive Hindu spokesmen but also with various existing church authorities and missionaries who were not only preaching to them but attempting to control the definition of faith. The fact that missionaries themselves varied in national and sectarian identities also had an impact.

Converts were often forced to be individual in their movement to a different faith because of heavy family opposition to their rejection of the rituals and practices of brahmanical Hindu orthopraxy. The opposition shown to Phule was symptomatic: he was identified as 'reverend Phule' – though, in fact, he never converted – and his mali caste-mates viewed him for a long time as a traitor. The variations in individual orientations were related to the variations in the degree to which defined Indian Christians were dependent on, or clung to, a new community. Where kin and caste opposition was strong, the person would become, in a genuine sense, a social convert, linked to a community with strong foreign links which provided what his old family and kin did not—belongingness, acceptance, life support structures. Where the opposition was minimal – which was usually linked to the degree to which the Christian believer continued to accept traditional social practices, including those of caste – he or she tended to be more eclectic in approach.

An important example of the latter was Vengal Chakkarai, a Tamil whom M.S.S. Pandian describes as a 'nationalist Christian', who saw himself as someone reconciling Hinduism and Christianity. "Hinduism has never been to me a prison-house from which I sought an escape…I did not, and could not think, nor do I so now, that the burden was laid on me to destroy my Hindu religious heritage" (quoted in Pandian 2003, 5360). In describing his conversion process, he wrote, "The image of the Lord grew in my mind slowly, while the figures of my Hindu bhakti retreated into the shadows without being dismissed as either phantoms of a troubled imagination or delusions of the Evil One…" There were no "violent upheavals of psychological conversion with which the records of the Indian Christian converts are so full" (5359). Chakkarai tried to interpret Christianity as the zenith of Hindu bhakti, and emphasized the need for the ecstatic devotionalism and emotion of bhakti in its use.

A continuing attachment to his Hindu identity remained an option for Chakkarai because his family did not, in fact, outcaste him; he wrote of their tolerance and even the relative indifference of the subcaste association to his conversion. This may well have been related to the fact that he did not violate caste restrictions. Where a new convert did so, he would be more likely to be isolated from his former caste community. His family did not easily follow him; a moving autobiography of Laxmibai Tilak, the wife of one of the most famous Maharashtrian brahman converts, Narayan Waman Tilak, tells of her agonizing over her husband in breaking caste restrictions—and the emotional meaning of the process when she finally accepted Christian universalism of brotherhood (Tilak 1998).

The subaltern castes and communities faced a different situation. The incentive to religious change was heightened because of the low status assigned to them within the brahmanic framework. In addition, they could view the existing Christian community in India – a mixed one of foreign missionaries and their Indian counterparts – as relatively economically better off. A different framework, an entirely new religion, thus could have a mass appeal on spiritual as well as economic grounds. For kin and family, breaking caste restrictions was often not the extreme personal step it was felt to be by the dwija castes (though the significance of such restrictions for the subaltern should not be neglected either, considering the degree to which they have been maintained in many churches). Thus, when missionaries spoke of conversions as 'mass movements' around the end of the nineteenth century, they were not so much referring to huge numbers as to the fact that people joined in groups—subordinated groups seeking a new kind of life, looking for new patrons and allies who could aid them in the search for social and economic freedom, looking also for a new meaning that was not ascribed by the traditional forms of what was being now seen as 'folk Hinduism'. This was conversion as a liberatory movement.

Conversion thus had different meanings from different social perspectives. Yet for most privileged castes, and increasingly for others as well, it was coming to be seen as an affiliation to a different faith, one not of India. Christians were coming to be viewed as belonging to a British-linked 'alien' faith, as somehow having left the faith and thus the people of their birth. The 'nation' was increasingly imagined as Hindu, in the complex process in which the high and ancient vedic antecedents provided a framework to absorb all kinds of disparate elements—including bhakti, seen now as a 'Hindu' answer to Islam or Christianity, not as a unique religious movement. In this process of defining 'Hinduism', individual Christians and Muslims were seen as only questionably part of the nation. Their own self-definition as nationalist or Hindu now made no difference. Even those such as Vengal Chakkarai who wanted to be a 'Christian Hindu' and a nationalist found themselves rejected by the majority. All this took place as part of a process in which, by the second quarter of the twentieth century Mohandas Gandhi was playing a major role, through his position as 'voice of the nation', as a protector of Hinduism from the threat of conversion. His was a position that did not differ in principle from Savarkar's definition of a Hindu as one "who considered India as his fatherland (*pitrubhumi*) and holy land (*punyabhumi*)." When Gandhi opposed Ambedkar's conversion announcement, on the grounds that untouchables should reform 'their own religion', the same implicit meaning was there.

The issue posed in the Gandhi–Ambedkar debate on conversion in 1935–36 was whether religion of one's birth was to be contested and reformed but not forsaken, or whether it was a matter of choice. For Ambedkar, who saw caste as the main source of his oppression, and caste, in turn, as an inevitable outgrowth of Hinduism, the rejection of Hinduism was necessary. Radicalism in politics – the establishment of a separate identity for dalits – went with radicalism in religion, the rejection of a false community. Nevertheless, Ambedkar, and before him Iyothee Thass, continued to define affiliation with Buddhism not so much as conversion as one of 'return' to an original dalit identity, emphasizing that 'untouchables' had historically been originally Buddhists. Thus dalits in Maharashtra today speak not so much of *dharmantar*, change of religion, as *dhamma diksha,* taking on the vows of religion, implying a new religious identity where they had been denied on before. However, there was also an implicit acceptance in Ambedkar that Christianity and Islam were alien, something made explicit when he said once in a discussion with another antibrahman convert that choosing Buddhism was like moving to a different room in a house, whereas the choosing of Christianity would be moving to a different house (cited in Aloysius, introduction to Dharmateertha 2004, iv-vi).

Thus, in many ways, the choosing of a Christian identity – following Christ, the acceptance of baptism – however defined, appeared the most radical of the various breaks with the growing hegemonic Hindu nationalism.

Among the most famous and important of the new Christians was Pandita Ramabai. In many ways she represented a combination of the two paths outlined above. She was of the most privileged caste by birth; her new faith involved a conscious rejection of Hinduism as she understood it (and she had studied it more thoroughly than most of its proponents), and she acted as a strong individual throughout her life. Yet her being a woman led her to share some of the characteristics of subaltern caste converts. Women as a group were marginalized by brahmanic Hinduism, and this in fact was what she stressed as her main motive for rejecting it. Thus her choice of Christianity was, for her, part of a life dedicated to a feminist cause, and she was ready to lead other groups of women to such a choice. She was perhaps the first 'autonomous feminist' of the new era of colonial modernity, and she acted throughout with a priority of saving Indian women from exploitation.

Wandering India, Encountering Women

Pandita Ramabai (1858–1922) was the daughter of a chitpavan brahman, Anant Shastri Dongre, a Sanskrit scholar who had been inspired by the example of the wife of Baji Rao Peshwa to educate his own wife. Ramabai's mother was his second wife, who he married as a widower. He was, as Uma Chakravarty (1998) has pointed out, a reformist brahman very different from the educated liberal elite brahmans: "a very orthodox Hindu and strictly adhering to caste and other religious rites," as Ramabai herself defined him. Rather than taking to modern professions or government employment, he made his living in the way considered prestigious and traditional for brahmans—wandering, teaching, running ashrams. The only variation from orthodoxy was in his education of women, though in taking the help of his wife in running the ashram he was also following an ancient tradition, the third of the four *ashramas* or stages of life, semi-retirement in the forests but with one's partner.

When he taught this second wife Sanskrit and the dharmashastras, he was threatened with excommunication by his caste fellows in the neighborhood. He contested their opposition in terms of the scriptures, quoting chapter and verse, and continued his innovations. It was his wife, in turn, who educated their infant daughter Ramabai. Then came a famine, and both parents died. Rama and her brother were forced by the hostility of their neighbors to leave their home, and traveled by foot across the country for six years. During this period,

> we had a good opportunity of seeing the sufferings of Hindu women and were much touched by their sorrows…it was the

> same in the Madras Presidency, Bombay Presidency, Punjab, the North-west Province, Bengal, Assam, etc. This made us think much of how it was possible to improve the condition of women and raise them out of their degradation...In the towns and villages we often addressed large audiences of people and urged upon them the education of the women and children. (Ramabai 1977, 17)

The lecturing and wandering was the beginning of what was to be a nomadic life for Ramabai, until her final settling in her utopian community outside of Pune. It gave her an insight into the life of the poor and rural people of the country, and at the same time provided a unique training in public speaking. After this, the tours on the lecture circuits in the US would seem a minor discomfort. It was as a result of these experiences of wandering throughout India that she was led to dedicate herself to reforming the position of women, a reform that took a revolutionary turn.

After a period of wandering she arrived in Calcutta, and what Chakravarty has described as the "halcyon days of Ramabai's public life" began. She became an icon for the new progressive Bengalis; taken up and patronized as a woman who could be considered "a living embodiment of their perceptions of ancient Indian womanhood" (Chakravarty 1998, 307). Again, when she was asked to speak, her training as a speaker on the 'village circuit' proved quite transferable to the Calcutta elite.

However, when Keshab Chandra Sen, the ideologue of the Brahmo Samaj, suggested to Ramabai that she read the vedas and the upanishads – the philosophical texts of ancient Hinduism and the focus of the Brahmo reformers' ardent hopes – the role of a woman as spokesperson for the glory of the vedic age and the new reformist monotheism resulted in contradictions. Sen must have thought she would be a good teacher of philosophy. But the opposite happened. The more she read and reflected on her experiences, the more she was exposed to the subtle patriarchy of the bhadralok reformist Bengalis, the more she began to feel that the problem was with 'Hinduism' itself. What she had seen in popular denigration of women and their inferior status throughout India, she realized, were connected increasingly with the teachings of the ancient sacred literature. The vedas and upanishads did not, for her, counteract the more crude expressions of the dharmasastras. As Ramabai later testified, it was crucial to her conversion that

> there were only two things on which all these books, the Dharma Shastras, the sacred epics, the Puranas and the modern poets, the popular preachers of the present day and orthodox high-caste men, were agreed: that women of high and low caste as a class, were bad, very bad, worse than demons, as unholy as untruth.... (Cited in Kosambi 1992, 33)

Her objections, then, were to the treatment of women. She did not, however, have a similar reaction to caste. Though she herself always refused to discriminate on the basis of caste, she did not see it for a long time as a major evil. Here she took her general approach from liberal brahmans. *The High-Caste Hindu Woman*, written during her trip to the US and as a means of financing it, takes a bland view of caste, one that is worth citing as the main 'liberal' view of the time, shared by all from the Brahmos to the Arya Samaj founder Dayanand Saraswati to Gandhi:

> Without doubt, 'caste' originated in the economical division of labour. The most talented and intelligent portion of the Aryan Hindus became, as was natural, the governing body of the entire race. They, in their wisdom, saw the necessity of dividing society, and subsequently set each portion apart to undertake certain duties which might promote the welfare of the nation. (Ramabai 1981, 3)

Ramabai then went on to describe the duties of the various varnas, remarking only about the sudras that "the fourth, or servile caste...was made up of all those not included in the preceding three castes." She also expressed the typical reformist belief in arguing that "in ancient times persons were assigned to each of the four castes according to their individual capacity and merit, independent of the accident of birth." Only later, she wrote, did caste become an article of faith, determined by birth and with customs forbidding intermarriage. She noted that not only did the Muslims accept the custom, but the million-plus Catholic converts "are more or less ruled by caste" (4–5). This work, which sought to describe Indian society from the perspective of its oppression of women, did not at the time show the same kind of fury about caste oppression.

Even as she absorbed the reformist views on caste, her Calcutta life was coming to an end. She had married again—defying convention and marrying a man of the sudra varna, a friend of her brother. However, when her husband died after six months, she was left as a widow with a small girl child and the problem of supporting herself. This she could not do in Calcutta; so she decided to return to Pune, where she had an invitation from the liberal brahman reformers.

One factor stands out in this story of her early life: Rama could become a powerful woman, spokesperson, leader and organizer almost entirely because of the death of nearly all the significant men in her life. Left without her parents' protection, she gained experience by wandering throughout India. Then her brother died; and then her husband—now there was no home to be absorbed into, no sheltering dependence. Had they lived, she would likely have been more the 'typical' woman—strong-minded within the family, active but not breaking its confines, not wandering on her own path. Forced into freedom, she increasingly acted as a free, autonomous woman, choosing her own religion, organizing other women, seeking the kingdom of god and founding her own utopian community in the process.

The Arya Mahila Sabha and Arya Men

Calcutta could no longer be a useful arena for action; she was after all nearly a native Maharashtrian. Ramabai had an invitation from Pune, from the group of social reformers active around M.G. Ranade and R.G. Bhandarkar, who promised their support. She took it up. By this time she had articulated her aim in life: setting up institutions for Indian widows. She began with general organizing, forming the Arya Mahila Sabha in 1882 and establishing branches throughout the Pune–Mumbai region. The name itself indicates an appeal to elite woman and the elite influence on her own thinking.

These were, however, strongly feminist. "It was believed that the Pandita only exhorted women to free themselves from the tyranny of women" (Chakravarti 1998, 313). This was a conservative reaction, but quite likely the liberal brahmans were not so enthusiastic once they experienced her growing rejection of many of their beliefs in the vedic golden age. It is unclear how much response there was. Most women still remained within the confines of the family. There were a few individual fighters, though the ones that stand out today were from more subaltern backgrounds. There was Tarabai Shinde, whose husband was a supporter of Phule and yet thoroughly patriarchal, driving her to write an early and hard-hitting book *Stri Purush Tulna*, Comparison of Men and Women (see O'Hanlon 1994, for a translation). And there was Rakmabai, from a subaltern but educated and progressive background, married off as a child but refusing (with the support of her father) to join her husband as his wife, fighting her case through the British courts (Chandra 1994 details the case and its implications).

Rakmabai became, for a time, the president of the Arya Mahila Sabha, and Ramabai followed her case throughout, though it climaxed much later. The Mahila Sabha, for the moment, barely survived. There was also no sign of any support forthcoming for a widows' institution. Ramabai began to react against the Pune progressives also, and fixed a determination of going to England, thinking now of seeking British support for her widows' home.

At the same time the disillusionment with elite liberalism and brahmanic tradition began to lead her away from Hinduism altogether. Bhakti could have little appeal for her; by the nineteenth century it was becoming fully established within the framework of orthodoxy. On the other side, the various Christian missionaries in Pune began to woo her. While her initial hopes were mainly to gain support for her work with women, once in England, settled and in contact with the sisters of the Wantage home, she drew closer to Christianity. On 25 September 1883 she accepted baptism. From this period she began to sign her name as Mary Rama—a symbol of dual identity, affirming the old along with the new.

Her baptism aroused a storm once word got to Pune. She was fiercely attacked by the conservatives, and criticized by the liberals. The only person who came to her defence was Phule, whose new periodical *Satsar* took up the cause of radical women, defending vigorously both Ramabai and Tarabai Shinde. *Satsar 1* (1885) was written as a dialogue between a 'Brahman' (alternately spelt 'Brahmo' since Phule identifies the Brahmo Samaj with a Brahman Samaj) and a 'Shudra', who begins by saying:

> I did not think that the lectures that Pandita Ramabai gave endorsing the Hindu religion when she came to Pune were very great...However, once she went to England and could compare the Christian and Hindu religions, didn't she see the mulishness and partisanship of Hindu religion and condemn it and accept Christianity? (Phule 1991, 353)

The Brahmo tries to hedge and deny the conversion: "It appears from her letters home that she is now doing a careful investigation of the Brahmo religion." Phule then goes on to attack the Brahmo Samaj, the history of 'Arya Brahmans' and caste differences. In *Satsar 2*, written in October of 1885, he again praised Ramabai, giving her credit for the education of women.

> These days, in the regime of the English, due to the efforts of Pandita Ramabai so many great learned men from the Arya Brahmans have become ashamed and in order to absolve their rishi anscestors of guilt, have begun to make their weak and helpless women educated like themselves. (Phule 1991, 372)

Phule's hope was that women's education would lead to a further rejection of brahmanism, that once privileged caste women became aware of the deception of sacred literature they would become like Ramabai, and "smash all the puraniks in the temples and force them to run away bawling." English education, though, was controlled enough in India and the processes of cooption sufficiently powerful that the majority of brahman women became content with the higher status of their caste within a reformed family structure.

Contesting Christianity

Ramabai went to England with the idea of raising support for her work with women. Her contacts were with Anglicans, and she lived in the Wantage mission, working as a teacher. But even after becoming baptized she was not ready to accept the authority of church authorities, even when they were women she loved and respected. Her conflicts began on two fronts—one social, the other religious.

The social issue was over her teaching men. The Wantage authorities tried to prevent this, arguing that it was against Hindu concepts of women's social and religious place. Ramabai did not so much question why they were trying to enforce these as contest their argument that they understood India. Referring to her wide experience, she said:

> I have not addressed only mixed audiences but most of them… [were] purely composed of men. It did not seem to take away my influence with my country people, and why it should be so now, I cannot see. I am not anxious to give lessons to young men, but I am anxious to do away with all kinds of prejudices that deprive women in India of her proper place in society. (1977, 60)

The fact that mission concerns here actually would reinforce Hindu patriarchy went unstated.

The second issue was theological. Ramabai found herself disagreeing with one of the most fundamental Christian doctrines, that of the Trinity, as espoused by the Catholic Athanasian Creed. She used the Bible for her justification. She would accept, she said, the Bible as an authority, but not what some fourth or fifth century church elders had said about the Bible. "I take it for granted that St. John's Gospel is authentic. So is the whole Bible; all I want you to do is prove the deity of Christ by reasonable explained words of the Bible." Her mentors had a difficult time combating her learning. They argued that it was due to Hindu notions, but in part she was refusing to see 'Hinduism' in Christianity—she identified the notion of the incarnation with the Hindu doctrine of avatars (136–38).

This uncomfortable situation, which included an ongoing conflict over the rearing of her daughter Manorama, was partially ended when Ramabai went to the US from England in 1886. Her excuse was an invitation to attend the graduation ceremony of Anandibai Joshi, a cousin and the first Indian woman to travel to the US to become a doctor. Anandibai's health was not good – she was to die in America – but this was not Ramabai's only reason for going. Her main motivation was to contact various church groups and women's welfare groups in a fundraising campaign for her long-held dream of a widows' home. Her host, Dr Rachel Bodley, was dean of the Women's Medical College in Philadelphia, but Ramabai did not intend to remain dependent on her either. She used her visit to embark on an extensive lecture tour, going throughout the country, talking to all kinds of groups. She ended with setting up a committee, and not willing to have a 'sectarian' religious body organize the work, she gave it under control of a Unitarian group but with representation from different denominations. This was the American Association.

Her letters from America give remarkable descriptions of much of the country. It is noteworthy, however, that she gave very little detail about the people she encountered. Her exceptions are equally noteworthy. She refers during her passage to a North American Indian youth who "worshipped the Great Spirit according to his national custom" at Niagra, throwing his ornaments into the stream one by one (174). She later praised the spirit of the Japanese during a visit there. She was clearly showing an interest in the nonwhite people of the world, now coming into their own.

Most of all, Ramabai met Harriet Tubman in Auburn, New York. Tubman was the famous ex-slave known as 'Grandmother Moses' because, after escaping herself, she had gone back and led over 300 people to freedom. Ramabai told her story in a long letter to Manorama, and described her:

> Harriet still works. She has a little house of her own, where she and her husband live and work together for their own people. I saw some orphan children and old people unable to work for themselves who are taken care of and supported by good old Harriet.... Harriet is very large and strong. She hugged me like a bear and shook me by the hand until my poor little hand ached! (208)

Ramabai identified with Harriet Tubman more than any other woman she met. As it developed later, America had clearly inspired her with notions of freedom—when she finally set up a large widows' home in Kedgaon, outside of Pune, she named it Mukti Sadan, meaning the 'Abode of Freedom'. Her publication, the *Mukti* periodical, had a large picture of 'a cracked bell' on the cover, undoubtedly the Liberty Bell of Philadelphia, together with a quotation from Isaiah: "The Lord hath anointed Me to preach Good tidings unto the meek and hath sent Me to bind up the broken-hearted, to proclaim liberty to the captives, and the opening of prison to them that are bound." Just as poets like William Blake were imagining 'Jerusalem' being built in England, Ramabai was determined to create a new Jerusalem – a women's community – in India.

The 'Abode of Freedom'

Ramabai's lecturing, fundraising and organization-building had always had one goal: the liberation of Indian women. Specifically it was to raise resources for a widows' home, a community of living and liberation. She had been on 'lecture circuits' since her childhood, and she had also used her writing to raise funds. She found her greatest audience in the US, proving to be a successful and energetic lecturer and fundraiser. However, on returning to Pune, having set up a committee and amassed the funds for it, she found herself engrossed in new battles with the Indian reformist elite—and with the British rulers.

Ramabai had, as a matter of course, taken part in nationalist activities. She addressed one Congress session in 1889 at Pune, challenging the men in her speech to include more women in the organization. There was not, it seems, a great deal of enthusiasm: only eleven men were present during the speech (Chakravarty 1998, 318). She had also, it is clear, strong nationalistic responses to the efforts of foreigners – whether British officials or fellow Christians – to control her actions.

British complicity in atrocities against women aroused her greatest fury. The case of Rakmabai preoccupied her while in England, and she was angry at the colonial state for its judicial complicity in enforcing brahmanic regulations.

> What strikes me is the remarkable indifference shown by the English in executing this promise when it comes between themselves and their own interests in India. But they wash their hands and prove their innocence to the world for not protecting the defenceless woman's person.... I wonder if such outrageous acts of the English Government will be excused by heaven.... The English would have allowed even the Suttee rite to take place...for were not for the good Christian missionaries who protested against it seventy years ago flatly replied by the East India Company's servants that they dare not interfere with the religious customs of the natives? Had it not been for Raja Rammohan Roy...the English would have winked at the widow-burning even in these days, just as they do not at many an inhuman custom. (177–78)

This was only an expression of opinion from abroad; she could do little activiely. But in Pune in 1897 she came into conflict with the British over their management of famine relief. She wrote a letter to the *Bombay Guardian* criticizing the plague measures, giving details about a girl who had been forcibly taken to the camp and then abducted by a watchman. The furore created by the letter aroused a discussion in the British parliament, and Ramabai continued to press her accusations (Chakravarty, 1998, 338). The Bombay Government harshly dismissed the charges, without bothering to institute an inquiry. A furious Ramabai repeated the charges, attacking the governor himself. Her Anglican missionary friends differed with her on this, and even her good friend and 'Ajibai', Sister Geraldine, described her letter as 'childish, sensational and seditious' (!), hinting that the it had fostered an atmosphere which had played a role in a murder of two officials by a brahman terrorist (the letter is given in Ramabai 1977, 348). It is clear that Ramabai had no good opinion of British rule, though she attacked it openly only in terms of her feminist concerns.

Ramabai's conflicts with the Indian reformist elite also had to do with her increasingly popular women's home. These were related to worldwide structures of patriarchy, for in providing the funding, the American Association had given control to a managing committee in India largely made up of reformist brahmans. These tended to impose strict rules upon admitting girls and against allowing conversion. Ramabai, however, was insisting on autonomy. She objected to the trust that foreigners placed in elite reformers, criticizing them much as Phule had done, though in very different language:

> I beg of my Western sisters not to be satisfied with looking on the outside beauty of the grand philosophies, and not to be charmed with hearing the long and interesting discourses of our educated men, but to open the trap-doors of the great monuments of ancient Hindu intellectuals, and enter into the dark cellars where they will see the real workings of the philosophies which they admire so much. (1977, 312)

This was in an account of an Indian tour undertaken in 1894, where she examined the Taj Mahal, but insisted on looking at the prison where out-of-favour members of the harem were kept; going to Banaras, Jagannathpuri, Gaya, Allahabad and other 'strongholds of Hinduism and seats of sacred learning' where the oppression of women was the concrete meaning of the 'sublime' philosophies. She relentlessly hammered home the theme, attacking the hypocrisy of educated men who could give such great orations without practising them. And, she continued her fight for autonomy.

Her widows' home in Pune aroused a storm, particularly when conversions took place. Yet, even when it was out of favour with the male elite, widows still came, and the wives of the same elite sometimes brought widowed girls without asking their husbands. One such incident occurred with Ramabai Ranade, wife of M.G. Ranade, bringing a relative. After many cruelties and beatings, wrote Pandita Ramabai, "at last all the neighbours, even the orthodox old ladies who are no friends of reform, came to Mrs Ranade in force and requested her to take the young widow to the Sharada Sadan" (277). Ramabai told all these stories to her American supporters. Then, when famines occurred, she aroused more reaction by going out to the affected areas and bringing in refugees herself. She praised her young widows for their warmth in welcoming the destitute girl widows, their delight when a baby was included, and their generosity in giving up small amounts of money in their possession for famine work.

With such convincing examples, Ramabai could win over her American committee who, in Sister Geraldine's account, "refused to sanction the rules with which the Advisory Board desired to restrict the liberty of the Pandita and left the matter of religious intercourse with the pupils entirely to Ramabai's honour and discretion" (1977, 297). The chairman of the committee, Judith Andrews, came over to investigate and to help. Finally, in 1894, the centre of activity was moved outside of Pune. Ramabai bought a hundred acres of land in Kedgaon, a village about forty miles from Pune, and established a whole set of institutions. The main theme was *mukti*; the main home for widows was Mukti Sadan, 'the abode of freedom'. This realization of a dream could be interpreted both as 'salvation' and as 'freedom', and Ramabai had it both ways.

The Mukti Sadan represented an attempt to set up something of an ideal women's community, a 'new Jerusalem' in India. Girls did everything in it—from weaving, dairy farming, cooking, gardening and farming, to running a printing press. Dedgaon had thousands of orange, lime and mango trees, a portion of irrigated land, and most of its food requirements were home-grown. The printing press published various writings, including a journal, all centred on the theme of mukti.

By the time of the famine, there was enough infrastructure to accommodate nearly 2,000 women and girls. There were sixteen paid teachers from outside, with other help coming from some eighty five of the residents who took on varying responsibilities as teachers, matrons and industrial workers. Sister Geraldine, who described the establishment, also commented on Ramabai's love of nature: "She is a child of the forest and an enthusiastic lover of flowers.... She had laid down good paths and planted palms and other graceful trees, shrubs and flowers" (Ramabai 1977, 362–63).

As Chakravarty notes, "by integrating widows into society, Ramabai was reconceptualising widowhood and womanhood in a way that most male reformers could never think of" (1998, 328). The reformers' solution was, ideally, remarriage—reintegrating women into the existing patriarchal structures. When a widows' home was first set up in Pune, by D. K. Karve, it continued to observe caste distinctions, refusing to admit nonbrahman widows. Mukti Sadan not only ignored caste distinctions, it rejected gender discrimination as well in trying to train women in all the areas of subsistence and profitable production. The mark of the Enlightenment anticaste reformers was in their vision of an anticaste, anticlass utopia; Ramabai not only added gender to this, but was the first to attempt to put the vision into practice in a real but utopian community.

X

Periyar
Imagining Tamilnadu

> Better than transforming this country into a Hindu country, Hindustan, what is wrong with changing it into Dravidastan, or if the Brahmans could not tolerate this name, into Pakistan, a different name but embodying the same Dravidian ideology?.... I am not an agent of Islam nor do I preach Islam...But in order to kill the devilish, dangerous and cruel snake of Brahmanism and Hinduism or at east to escape from the effect of its poison, this is the antidote.
>
> —Periyar, in a speech on 18 March 1947

Periyar's statement about Islam in 1947 captured some of the complex currents that were pervading India at the time of its independence. Remarkably, he expressed attraction towards Pakistan and not towards the marxist utopia, 'socialism'. This was, in fact, an example of the dilemmas of the anticaste movement of the time, of the confrontation that many of its leaders (in particular, Periyar and Ambedkar) were having with marxism and Indian leftists, and, in a very different way, with that powerful and near-hegemonic ideological force of nationalism—gandhism.

By the 1940s dalit-bahujan intellectuals were confronting new issues, most notably that of the actual shaping of the future they envisaged and the ways of creating it. In the nineteenth and early twentieth centuries, their preoccupation – and that of their brahmanic opponents – had been different, that of analyzing their present exploitation and relating it to the past history of India and the current situation as a British colony. But now independence was round the corner, and the utopia had to be brought down to earth or remain a fantasy.

It was a period of struggling ideologies as well as classes and ethno-religious groups. Among the most important of the new ideologies was marxism, which grew powerfully in India from the 1920s, and influencing nonbrahman as well as brahman intellectuals. Many of the later generation followers of Phule were influenced by marxism, most notably Dinkarrao Javalkar, whose last books before his untimely death – *Krantice Ranshing* and *Shetkari Hindustan* bear this influence (see Javalkar 1984, 273–340). In Tamilnadu, a large number of Self-Respect activists were drawn to it, with consequences we shall see.

This was not so true, however, of Periyar himself. He was preoccupied with the question of brahmanic religious dominance—not religion as the 'opium of the people' as preached by marxists and seen as requiring a thoroughly 'materialistic' outlook, which in India meant too often accepting an implicit Hindu identity based on continual ties with family and broader kin. Rather, Periyar contested specifically with the constructed religion which he saw as representing a conquering Aryan–Brahman minority and the major factor in the exploitation of the masses of Dravidians. And Islam to him was an alternative—not least because it was putting forward a concrete vision of a future society. For it was 'Pakistan' that had a much more powerful mass appeal to the Muslim community of its time than the vague marxist utopia did for the majority of even working-class

Indians. It was thus that the alternatives before the people were being posed as Pakistan versus Hindustan. Periyar, somewhat similarly, saw Islam as the powerful alternative to 'Hinduism'. As he put it in defence of his 1947 appeal:

> The Shudra-label will not go by merely consigning the Vedas, Shastras, Puranas and Itihasa to fire. It will not go by demolishing temples and breaking up idols...The Shudra-tag will not go by merely calling oneself Dravidian. In today's context it will not go even if you declare that you are not a Hindu...what is possible within our own lifetime is to move away from the Hindu religion. If we do so move away, in today's context, we need a name to declare who we are and that is to be created anew... what is wrong or the difficulty in declaring that I have embraced a religion, a religion which has already achieved influence and currency, that has been established and accepted by all thinking persons and which genuinely and rightfully embodies our own philosophy and religion of social equalitarianism. (2004, 13–14)

This was in fact a well-argued position. Brahmanism was so cunning, argued Periyar, that it could absorb 'materialism' or 'atheism'—*nastik*, after all, meant in the sanskritic tradition not someone who denied the existence of god, but someone who denied the authority of brahmans and the vedas. This meant it was not enough for a person to say simply that he/she was not a believer, or even 'not a Hindu'; the only solution was an alternative, powerful religion.

As Aloysius argues in his introduction to Periyar's writings on Islam (2004, 5–9), Periyar was never actually the crude or simple atheist he is often pictured as. He himself was not a believer, but he was clearly attracted by Islam's equalitarianism; he referred to the original meaning of the term as 'peace, submission' when he made his arguments. When he wrote about membership in the Self-Respect movement, he made it clear that anyone who followed a clear religion out of his own conviction could be a member.

Periyar, then, was one of the two major intellectuals of the post-1920 period who was grappling with all the conflicting ideological and political trends of the time. Continuously in struggle, looking for a political outlet, he had no 'natural' caste base like Ambedkar; he did not have the education or the English to operate on a national scale, but he was the 'grand old man' of Tamilnadu politics.

The Rise of Nonbrahmanism in Tamilnadu

In Maharashtra, after Phule the nonbrahman movement had grown, and the Satyasdhodhak Samaj had a revival between 1910 and 1920, but many aspects of Phule's radicalism were lost. The firm effort to include untouchables was retained, the village orientation remained central to Satyashodhak organizing, the involvement of all castes could be seen—but 'anti-Aryanism' tended to fade in the presence of a renewed effort to regain a 'kshatriya' identity. With this, the critique of brahmanism weakened. The harbinger of this had been the Maharajah of Kolhapur, himself one of the greatest anticaste, anti-untouchability champions. It was his fight to win vedic rights for his personal and family rituals that set off a battle with the brahmans of Maharashtra. This resulted in his becoming the great champion of nonbrahmanism. He was staunch in this, fighting untouchability, fighting caste pride in many ways in his own household; he was the first to institute a reservation policy in public service in 1902 when he issued a government order to recruit only nonbrahmans in his state service. Yet the desire to be considered a kshatriya meant accepting many brahmanic norms; it meant accepting sanskritic rituals, and it gave sanction to all the similar efforts going on throughout the Marathi-speaking areas whereby 'Marathas' and those of similar caste were encouraged to consider themselves kshatriyas (and hence Aryans), use the Gayatri mantra, use *vedokta* rituals and so forth. It is not accidentally that Shahu Maharaj himself joined the Arya Samaj, though he gave his support to the more radical Satyashodhak Samaj. The later generation of militant nonbrahmans, notably Keshavrao Jedhe and Dinkarrao Javalkar in Pune, fought militantly on the streets and in the courts, but continued to emphasize a maratha and kshatriya identity. Subsequently, Ambedkar would tell these young marathas that "you are against brahmans but not brahmanism; we are against brahmanism." The Satyashodhak movement of Phule thus got transformed into the nonbrahman movement (see Omvedt 1976, for a survey).

In Tamilnadu, the situation was different. Here the kshatriya identity was made practically impossible by the longstanding belief among both brahmans and nonbrahmans that privileged caste, nonbrahman Tamils were, at best, *sat-sudras* or 'true sudras'. At the same time, the Dravidian indigenous identity was formulated with enough emotional appeal to rule out the charm of Aryanism. Iyothee Thass' Buddhist movement had built on this, and had carried it forward with a strong historical analysis linked to the interests of the strong but hitherto despised paraiyas, the largest dalit caste in the region. In Tamilnadu, there was much more political force behind attacking an Aryan identity; though this did not necessarily always get expressed in radical form.

The political movement of nonbrahmans, arising in the twentieth century, by and large ignored Iyothee Thass. It had a far different social base, among the urban, educated middle class, and in the rural areas among a nonbrahman landowning semi-aristocracy. Its first expression, the South Indian Liberal Federation gave rise to the Justice Party which won the first provincial elections that gave some kind of power to Indians in 1920. The aims of the Justice Party emphasized development, education, proportional representation and the curtailing of brahman religious power. Once in power, it passed government orders to increase the proportion of posts held by nonbrahmans, including initial recruitment and promotion; this was the first effort to fight the monopoly of brahmans in government administration. It also brought in progressive legislation on intermarriage, franchise, educational facilities for 'weaker sections', abolition of the devadasi system, throwing open temples to untouchables, and bringing temple administration under state control. It promoted primary education by introducing free and compulsory education in about eighteen of twenty-five municipalities by 1925, and a scheme to feed deprived children in school was a harbinger of free lunch policies pioneered in Tamilnadu after independence. It paid special attention to the spread of education among adi dravidas (as dalits were coming to be known—despite Iyothee Thass' efforts), ensuring that management would forfeit grants if such students were denied entry.

Where the Justice Party failed was in rousing strong mass support – its limited social base hampered this; it never took up issues of land relations or problems of the working class – and in framing its efforts in a broad vision with mass appeal. Here, perhaps, its separation from the efforts of the Buddhists (documented in Chapter 8) and from the all-around cultural, religious as well as social and political needs of dalits was a major limiting factor. The remedy was to come from a different direction—from a small town in western Tamilnadu.

Building Self-Resepct

Erode, the home of Periyar, was a small town in a drought-ridden area of Tamilnadu. E.V. Ramasamy Naicker, born in a well-to-do merchant family, had no claims to culture or education, having left school after the age of ten to join his father's business. His memories of caste from childhood come from his school, not home: he went to a private school in a subaltern caste locality, was told to drink water only from a 'high caste' teacher living nearby. Their treatment of Ramasamy – not allowing him to sip from the cup – was perceived as harassment and he gradually broke the rule. His religious-minded family eventually put him in a public school, then stopped his education altogether—much as Phule's had been stopped in his village (2005, 63–66). Only in Periyar's case there was no mission college and encouragement to allow him to continue.

After his marriage in 1898 to thirteen-year old Nagammal, he undertook a pilgrimage in 1904 which took him north to Calcutta, Puri and Kashi—a trip that confirmed his rejection of Hinduism. This appears to have been a formative experience, somewhat like Ramabai's youthful lecture tour through Indian villages. Just as Ramabai experienced the pain of women, so Periyar experienced, again, the pain of being considered a sudra, and the corruptions of religious orthodoxy and holy places. As Geetha and Rajadurai put it, "Periyar, it seems, was refused food at many a choultry because he was not a Brahman and he took to living off the food offered to dead ancestors by those who came to perform funeral rites on the banks of the Ganga. Periyar discovered to his horror that men and women freely indulged in drinking and meat eating and debauchery in Kashi..." (1998, 306). He himself took to offering prayers at the temple without the customary purifying bath.

He joined the Indian National Congress in 1919, not the Justice Party, for he was attracted by the initial progressiveness that Gandhi seemed to symbolize. His first major public foray in the anticaste issue was when he joined the Vaikom satyagraha in 1924. The satyagraha had the limited aim of opening up a road adjoining a temple for the ezhavas, a sudra caste in Kerala. He returned as the 'hero of Vaikom'. Later, he continually sought to bring up issues of caste within the Congress. In 1920 he presided over a separate session of nonbrahmans at the twenty-sixth provincial session of the Congress, which adopted resolutions demanding the reservation of constituencies and government posts for nonbrahmans. But orthodox Congress leaders were not ready to let 'Justicite' politics into the party, and the resolutions were not allowed to be taken up in the open session by the Congress president, Srinivas Iyengar. In the 1924 session, where he was made Tamilnadu president, he again emphasized the need for proportional representation. Again, his proposed resolution on the subject was not allowed in the open session. He walked out of the Congress with his supporters, saying:

> If we attain swaraj, it must be a swaraj for all the people. Today, there is growing fear in the minds of the people that swaraj would be Brahman raj in toto. We must create confidence in people. Every community should be cordial to others. We must ensure that every community is safe and prosperous. Today, crores of people are in a pitiable state. They are dumb. The only way is to give legitimate representation to all the communities. (Cited in Mani 2005, 322)

Following his walkout, Periyar formed the Self-Respect Movement—a broad sociocultural movement of the oppressed. It could have been modeled after Phule's Satyashodhak Samaj, except that there is no evidence that Periyar knew much about Phule. Later, reminiscing on it, he noted, "The cause and effect theory is accepted by the wise world. The human being seeks the season for everything. He has begun to conduct research of nature. A life of ignorance is considered as a slave's life. This is the doctrine of the Self-Respect Movement. Before doing any thing, one should think whether it is right or wrong, see the causes, analyze things, do research and respect the truth" (Periyar 2005, 69). In essence, this was the 'Satyashodhak' credo.

The Self-Respect Movement shared the Satyashodhak critique of 'Hinduism'. This is seen most often as a critique of religion as such, citing his most famous statement. "There is no God. There is no god at all. He who created god is a fool. He who propagates god is a rogue. He who worships god is a barbarian." This was part of an address to the Rationalist Association in 1971 (Periyar 2005, 222), and the focus was almost entirely on brahmanic Hinduism. Periyar was occasionally admiring of Christianity and Islam, seeing them as less inherently superstitious. The critique of brahmanism, of priestly superstition and of the sanskritic scriptures, of festivals, rituals and temples, was the core; though Self-Respecters also criticized the hierarchical practices, including patriarchal ones, found in Christianity and Islam. In criticizing brahmanic ritual, Self-Respecters called for a boycott of brahman priests at nonbrahman weddings, and organizing marriages of their own with a simple contractual ritual. In several marriages women served as priests.

Critiques of the sacred texts of Hinduism, especially of the puranas – including the Ramayana, at a time when Gandhi was speaking of India as a future Ram Rajya – emphasized its lack of morality by citing the attacks on Shambuka and the treatment of Sita. Just as Phule had interpreted the avatars as stages in the conquest of India, Periyar also referred to them as moments in the Aryan–Dravidian conflict (Geetha and Rajadurai 1998, 340). This heralded a mass anticaste movement in the 1920s that spilled over to the streets. In Pune, young nonbrahmans at the time, surging into the tumult of the public Ganpati festival – begun originally by Tilak as a way of linking the masses to Hinduism – attacked brahmans with bawdy songs in their 'Chhatrapati Mela'. Around the same time Ambedkar was writing "The Riddles of Rama and Krishna", but this remained as an unpublished manuscript. The Self-Respect Movement also took their critique to the streets, with attacks on idols, garlanding images of Rama with shoes, and breaking statues of Ganesha. More than in Maharashtra they attacked the basic symbols of the Hinduism being constructed and defended by the elite. They began a long period of debates with the Saivite trends, especially activists like Gurusamy who attended Saivite conferences, arguing with their positions (345–46).

The varna system which assigned the identity of 'sudra' to nonbrahmans was harshly criticized. As the Self-Respecters put it, the term 'sudra' denoted 'son of a slave'—and referred to the quality of *tamas* (darkness and ignorance) which was supposed to dominate them (342). In accepting this label, the sudras were accepting their own degradation.

Marxists and Self-Respecters

For most of its early existence, the Self-Respect Movement acted as a pressure group trying to influence the Justice Party. In the 1930s, however, this changed briefly. Militant young men and women were attracted to the movement; many of these were also attracted to marxism, one of whose important standard-bearers in Tamilnadu was M. Singaravelu Chettiar, who was also connected with the Buddhist movement. This involved a new kind of politicization—beginning with pressures to form a 'self-respect party' and then to move directly to communism.

In August 1934 a new paper, *Samadharmam*, was launched. While the term 'samadharma' was taken as a synonym for socialism, its definition was innocuous enough:

> The term 'samadharma' which today is resonant throughout the world is used in each nation and by people professing different religions and belonging to different castes with an emphasis peculiar to their context. However, we wish to explain the exact sense in which we use the word. We hold that people in all walks of life must exist in equality and eschew differences based on birth and we wish to see humankind lead a life free from worry and discontent [so] we have begun *Samadharmam*. (Cited in Geetha and Rajadurai 1998, 454)

The context makes it clear that the word was being used as a translation for socialism; however, the definition is cautious. In fact, along with articles on Russia, Lenin, the New Economic

Policy and other socialistic issues, *Samadharmam* carried many antibrahmanic articles by P. Jeevanandam and others. These young militants sought to radicalize the movement in a class direction. Jeevanandam, among others, argued against a compromise of any type. For instance, he objected to such decisions as inviting Somasundra Bharathy, a Saivite scholar and Congressman, to preside over an untouchability abolition conference and sought to disrupt his address. This was generalized by Singaravelu into objections to associating with the rich in general (449–52).

Self-Respecters by and large used the term *samadharma* differently than it was used by Singaravelu. The latter described its use for socialism as distinct to the Tamil country, but argued that since Buddha had used the term dharma to refer to things, *samadharma* should be interpreted as 'ownership of property in common'. Laxmi Narasu sought to give it Buddhist credentials, here he was putting forward his rather different vision of a 'Buddhist commonwealth'.

During 1933–34 as they tried to bring socialism to the Self-Respect Movement through the concept of *samadharma*, the young militants propagandized against the Justice Party. They began to put forward proposals for a Self-Respect League or Samadharma Party of South India. There was an initial meeting held in Erode to decide on a future plan of action for Self-Respecters after Periyar's return from a tour of Europe and the Soviet Union. After a long debate, a Self-Respect Samadharma Party was decided upon to function as the movement's legislative wing. Periyar, at this juncture, was using class rhetoric, arguing that the socialism of the Self-Respecters could not possibly anger anyone except "those who lived off the labour of others, the capitalists, parasites, zamindars, kings and maharajas" (443–44). The programme decided at Erode included adult suffrage, security of service and minimum wage to workers in public and private utility services, the removal of all caste distinctions (by removing caste titles from public records and making the retention of these a disability to hold any kind of public service), 'municipalization' of housing, transport, milk and medical services, and the repeal of "irrational safeguards for the private enjoyment of public utilities and for harmful religious and caste practices and habits in order to free the masses from their degrading religious and caste superstitions and habits and improve." Its 'aims and ideals' included cancellation of national debts, public ownership of railways, banks, shipping and transport services, and agricultural lands (529–30).

This also, however, awakened opposition; the movement was riven by debates on the usefulness of a socialist agenda—and on the recruitment efforts of those turning to communism. While the programme was mild enough, the 'aims and ideals' appeared to be something of an imposition. S. Ramanathan, who had not been present at Erode, objected to the decisions, arguing that they reflected only a section of Self-Respecters who had appeared as a well-knit group; he did not feel they were consistent with the ideals of the movement, objecting especially to the decision to contest elections. Singaravelu's response did not really answer these. Ramanathan had written on Lenin and translated his articles, and attempted to apply the analysis to Hindu society, interpreting this as a 'class–caste system' in which brahmans were at the top but the actual oppressors were often the peasant and trading castes; the dalits in turn were seen as something of a revolutionary vanguard (447–48). Periyar too made a similar effort, writing in 1931 in his journal *Kudi Arasu*, in relation to Bhagat Singh's socialism, that "just as notions of high and low [castes] have to be abolished for untouchability to be destroyed, so must the division of society into capitalists and labourers be ended for the abolition of poverty" (463–44).

Social radicalism, however, was in a sense extracted from the

Self-Respect Movement came to an end on its own. It was not simply that the Samadharma Self-Respect Party was a nonstarter—the movement was more apt as a pressure group. In 1937, on the eve of the elections, Jeevanandam, S. Vallatharasu and others joined the Congress. Geetha and Rajadurai remark that "this desertion by the young samadharmists is in a sense inexplicable" because they were submitting themselves to a leadership which they had earlier denounced (459). But it was not 'inexplicable'; it was a result of the communist initiative. After 1937, the Communist Party decided to throw its support to the socialists within the Congress as part of an 'anti-imperialist united front'; V.D. Ghate, the Mumbai leader, had even made a special trip to Tamilnadu for this purpose. Jeevanandam now came out clearly arguing that the primary contradiction in Hindu society was between the rich and the poor. The general effect of the growth of marxism, therefore, seen both in Maharashtra where some young nonbrahman leaders left the support of Ambedkar, and in Tamilnadu, was to draw many militant youth away from the anticaste movement, and to propagate a rather mechanical form of class analysis. In response, the Self-Respect Movement gave up its effort to combine class and caste, and turned to efforts to develop a more adequate analysis of caste itself, using some of the language of socialism, but refuting its basic propositions. However, it was in some crucial senses weakened by the loss of the energy of the young militants.

The generally negative effects of marxism on the anticaste movement can be seen in regard to the man considered one of the brightest stars of the movement, the poet Kanaga Subburathinam or Bharatidasan, a name taken as a sign of his devotion to the Tamil nationalist poet Subramania Bharati. In 1928, Bharatidasan had joined the Self-Respect Movement, devoting himself to rationalism, urging Tamils to lead a life of purity and bravery. He critiqued untouchability, argued that the varna system had never existed in ancient Tamilnadu, supported intercaste marriages, and criticized the *Manusmriti*. However, he was gradually moving towards a traditional marxist position. By the 1930s his poetry stressed the exploitation of workers and farmers, and a basically marxist utopia. Thus in "Rise Up" he wrote:

Like a chaff in a harsh wind we'll harass
this world of strife, breeding castes, sects
and superstition, later we'll smash it
and we'll build a new world.
That united, enlightened world
we'll call the world of 'self-respect'.
See this, society! Follow our words,
and rise! Rise! Rise up!
What creates this evil that separates
those who would unite – religions, is it not?
We've got great learning, they say,
'we're merciful with great acts,' they say!
Ramanujan, Muhammed, Christ,
speaking of the ancient ghosts they know not.
Their ignorance that brings war in this world!
Go forward, society! With our principles!

(2005, #52)

In fact, blaming 'religion' in general, discussing 'caste' in the abstract along with 'sects' and 'superstition' was far from the goals that the Self-Respecters had set themselves. Bharatidasan thus moved from dependence on the Congress to dependence on marxism. All religions were, in the marxist manner, criticised in the same way.

Marxism in India was expressing its socialist utopia, and inspiring poets to write of the affluent society based on workers, without religion, without dogmas and superstitions, without all the 'ancient ghosts'. Yet it absorbed nothing of the already-existing vision that had been put forward since the fifteenth century radical sants—the vision of a classless *and casteless* society. In the specific context of brahmanic tradition, this was important, yet a terribly missed opportunity. Geetha and Rajadurai argue that "a radical economic and political agenda was consciously deferred and discarded by the Self-Respecters" (443)—yet equally a radical social and cultural agenda was deferred and discarded by the Left. In return, the bahujans and dalits sensed a betrayal of their vision. The marxist version of utopia was, in the Indian context, curiously empty.

Hindustan, Pakistan and Beyond

By the late 1930s, then, the anticaste movement was looking for a broader expression. The nationalist movement, dominated by the Congress – with the communists and socialists playing a supporting role – basically revolved around Gandhi and Nehru. Subhash Chandra Bose had offered something of a militant alternative, but Gandhi had carefully seen him excluded from power. Nehru's socioeconomic vision was based on a lukewarm socialism, with a good deal of Hindu nationalism lurking underneath. Gandhi's was nearly openly a Hindu nationalism; he idealized Ram Rajya and traditional village society and, as is well known, had supported the abolition of untouchability but not that of varna as a whole: this was the heart and soul of his debate with Ambedkar. The fact is that most of the Congress stood with Gandhi; and this in turn provoked the antagonism of 'non-Hindu' leaders like Jinnah and Ambedkar.

Two men played a major role in the formation of Pakistan: the poet and writer Muhammad Iqbal (1875–1938) and Muhammad Ali Jinnah (1876–1948). Jinnah, a brilliant lawyer from a modestly well-to-do Gujarati family, began as a secular nationalist and remained a secularist to the end of his life. If he was driven to take up the cause of Pakistan, it was to a large degree because the 'secular' Congress could not tolerate a Muslim leader, no matter how brilliant. Essentially the same situation was to drive Ambedkar into separatism: the Congress was in a crucial way a caste-Hindu organization. Like it happened with Ambedkar, Gandhi and Jinnah reacted against each other from their very first meeting (Wolpert 1984, 37–8)

It is Iqbal, however, who is considered the philosopher of Pakistan. He was a modernist in his interpretation of Islam, stressing evolution and dynamism: "Universe as well as life are involved in a process of continuous becoming; and man, who stands at the peak of evolution, can maintain, in himself and in the society to which he belongs, the momentum of this primeval movement by ever-new conquest of the forces of nature" (Ahmad 1967, 143). He argued in contradiction to the conservatives (which included Maulana Azad, the Congress Muslim leader), that the 'gates of *itjihad* (reason)' were not closed, and that humans had the right of interpretation of what it meant to create an Islamic society on earth. Whereas *ijma* or 'consensus' had been seen earlier as the exclusive privilege of the *ulama*, Iqbal saw it as a consensus arrived at through a parliamentary system of government in an Islamic state (154–55). Thus he welcomed the growth of democracy in Islamic states. He discussed and rejected communism, stressed the unity and universality of Islamic society, argued that the ownership of all land was in god, and man's duty was to produce wealth for the benefit of humanity (158–59). Iqbal's vision was world-encompassing; he represented the searching and forward-looking thrust of the Muslim world which was too often overwhelmed by defensiveness in reaction to western power. It is striking that the founding figures of Pakistan were more modernist than Congress Muslims.

In 1930, in a momentous presidential address to the Muslim League, Iqbal put forward a proposal for the creation of a separate state in India; in the course of which he said, "The religious order of Islam is organically related to the social order which it has created.... therefore, the construction of a polity on Indian national lines, if it means a displacement of the Islamic principles of society, is simply unthinkable to a Muslim" (160). Thus he argued that the emotional and psychological homogeneity needed to create a nation did not exist in India; neither the eclecticism of Akbar and the mystic syncretism of Kabir had succeeded in capturing the imagination of the masses; what had triumphed instead was the great religious divisions and the caste structure of Indian society (162). He saw a separate Muslim state not as a theocracy, which to him was fanaticism, but as a democracy.

In an exchange of letters with Jinnah in 1936–37 Iqbal pressed for the creation of a separate Muslim state, in northwest India and Bengal. He argued, regarding its form: "For Islam, the acceptance of social democracy in some suitable form and consistent with the legal principles of Islam is not a revolution but a return to the original purity of Islam" (cited in Ahmad, 163). Jinnah, in his introduction to this series of letters, stated that these arguments led him to the final view, which found expression in the 'Pakistan' resolution passed by the Muslim League in its 1940 session. Jinnah took it up, arguing in 1940 that "Hinduism and Islam represent two distinct and separate civilizations and, moreover, are as distinct from one another in origin, tradition and manner of life as are the nations of Europe" (166). A single nation dominated by a single parliament could only mean Hindu rule over the minority religious groups.

The final formulation of Pakistan came late. The term itself was coined by a group of students at Cambridge, who were considerably more Islamicist than either Iqbal or Jinnah; it referred mainly to northwest India and represented an anagram of 'Punjab, Afghanistan, Kashmir, Sindh' along with the term *pak* for 'pure'. Whatever its origin, and with often very vague connotations, it caught the imagination of the Muslim masses.

And, as we saw, it also caught the imagination of a few others, including Periyar. An alternative to both gandhism and the purely classless society of socialism, which seemed so distanced and marked by priviliged-caste disregard of their actual situation, it proved a powerful – and ominous – force. The future shape of Pakistan would not fit the early democratic dreams of Jinnah and Iqbal, while its formation provided a constant and useful enemy to the caste-based 'Hindu nationalists' of the subcontinent. But Pakistan, a failed nation, stimulated much of the visions of separatism that rose in India.

Imagining Dravidanadu

Periyar's ideology and vision developed with several aspects in this context of a persuasive marxism and a Pakistani movement endorsed by fervent Muslims.

One constant theme was his stress that brahmanism was a more dangerous enemy than capitalism. Indeed, he saw capitalism and the exploitation of labour as occurring within the caste framework created in the brahmanic social order. He once offered the definition: "I understand the antonym 'rich–poor' to mean one that exists between one who does not work with his hands for a living, that is, one who holds it sinful and wrong to labour thus, and considers it his right to not labour, and one who is condemned to work and who considers it his 'right' to work for another and who suffers physical distress on that account" (1934, cited in Geetha and Rajadurai 1998, 455). The implication here is that 'condemned to work' and considering labour 'sinful' were all aspects of traditional brahmanic thinking. In "Caste and the Wage Worker", written in 1940, he argued that caste divided labourers into high and low and preserved these divisions through elaborate rules of intermarriage and dining; weaver, blacksmith, agricultural labourer were all equally toilers but observed caste restrictions among themselves. Thus casteism created 'competitive envy among workers' that hampered any kind of unity.

When Periyar was elected president of the Justice Party while in prison in 1938–39, his presidential address was sent from prison and read out. In this, he discussed the relationship between priest-intellectuals (brahmans) and the nonbrahman rich. "Periyar argued that the caste order perpetuated itself by consigning a vast section of the populace to eternal shudrahood and unrelieved labour. To gather assent for this unequal social order, brahmans had, at all times, sought the help of the rich and powerful" (Geetha and Rajadurai 1998, 499–500).

Generally, according to Periyar and the Self-Respecters, economics was related to religion, interpreted within the framework of brahmanic Hinduism. A major example was the tremendous wealth of south Indian temples, which represented accumulation through unproductive religious activity. Periyar referred to brahmans as 'birth capitalists', those who sought to capitalize on a sacred birth. Deities in temples were referred to as 'stone capitalists' for being massive accumulators of wealth.

However, Periyar, and later Ambedkar, shared with marxism an insistence on economic development and progress. It was here that the critique of gandhism came in, with Periyar developing a full-fledged analysis of gandhian economics. The advocates of khadi, he argued, wanted to keep intact division of labour by caste in their fascination for traditional handicrafts. Gandhi's disdain for technology was romantic nostalgia for the past; in a society organized around varna, labour had no worth or dignity (436–37). Responding to the Congress' Wardha Plan for education, Periyar stressed that with machines and expanding technology, there was little future for a child schooled in his or her traditional caste occupation. At the same time he had a warning for marxists: the traditional notion of the 'worker' as someone who worked with machines and in capitalist production neglected these artisans, who were the dominant group in India but were not organized and were marked by their caste identity which linked occupation and birth. They were 'caste workers' or labourers by birth. Somewhat as Phule had argued much earlier, artisans needed to enhance skills their skills and mechanize the production processes. Technology was seen as a crucial human advantage: it would also help in overcoming the drudgery and tedium of life of artisans, and provide leisure. Gandhi's Wardha Plan was consciously rejected and Periyar put forward an alternative (438–39).

He saw an important role for the state in economic development. The 'action plan' submitted to the Justice Party in 1934 argued that industries for public needs and transport facilities should be run by government; religion should be a private matter (this was a different stress from what instead eventually developed, with the independent Indian state taking over temple management—thus making the state a religious head). Taxes should be minimized; government salaries reduced; additional powers should be given to local and municipal boards and cooperatives; the indebtedness of farmers must be resolved; prohibition and proportional representation must be implemented (525–26).

Behind all the discussion concerning the economics of independent India was a vision of the individual. Periyar, like Phule before him and Ambedkar in the same period, put the individual at the centre; in this respect they were among the great liberals of modern India. Whereas Phule had stressed 'truth-seeking' in the name of his organization, Periyar used the term 'self-respect'. The Tamil word for self-respect, *suyamariyathai*, was linked to the notion of a universal subject of history with natural inalienable rights; this was put into practice through the movement and various campaigns of scorn for the self-denying religion.

Where Periyar's movement was also unique among those of anticaste intellectuals as well as the general elite was that it was built around linguistic nationality themes. Periyar sought to give his movement a solid base by emphasizing that genuine Tamil culture had no room for caste; he did not, however, join the extreme pro-Tamilian ideologues. Under the impetus of the Pakistani movement he began to put forth a Dravidastan demand; he also tried to reconcile Tamil with the existence of other south Indian languages by emphasizing the federal nature of a proposed Dravida Nadu. The various provinces would be base on linguistic identity – Telugu, Kannada, Tamil, Malayalam – but would be united as Dravidam.

With Periyar, thus, there is a move towards a more concrete utopian vision. This remained unachieved. The withdrawal of marxist Self-Respecters from the movement weakened it; the nonbrahman Saivites remained the dominant force within the Dravidian movement as a whole. Periyar remained the 'grand old man' of the movement, respected and honoured within Tamilnadu, but increasingly disregarded as a politically ineffectual radical.

Periyar Today: Critique and Response

Obviously, the utopian dream of an casteless society has not been realized in Tamilnadu; it remains, in spite of all the movements, a part of India, where caste has considerable, if transformed, strength. Tamilnadu is a state with considerable economic progress and a strong administration (owing to the pre-independence policy of reservation which brought nonbrahmans into administrative as well as political power). Yet conflicts between dalits and OBCs remain severe, and many dalits are likely to feel that 'sudra rule' has not been to their benefit. In contrast to Maharashtra, where Phule is accepted widely by dalits as well as bahujans, Periyar is a contested icon.

One of the most extensive critiques of Periyar has been given by a dalit intellectual, Ravikumar, now an elected member of the legislative assembly in Tamilnadu. Ravikumar argues, citing Periyar's writings and speeches, that Periyar was anti-Muslim, that he clubbed dalits and Muslim with brahmans as 'non-Tamils,' that he derided dalit leaders, that he never initiated any direct struggle for dalits, and that he worked "solely for the cause of the non-Brahman, non-religious minority, non-dalit backward and upper castes" ("Periyar's Hindutva", *Outlook*, 3 September 2003). A more scholarly critique is offered by Narendra Subramaniam whose study *Ethnicity and Populist Mobilization* is in many ways a sustained attack on the Periyar era (1999, 101–121), including a subsection titled 'The Tamil Variant of Fascism?'. Subramaniam sees 'some features' of fascism in its discourse but absolves the Dravidian movement in terms of actions, noting Periyar's close personal relationships with many brahmans. He describes the organization of the movement as personalistic, patrimonial and hierarchical, noting that his supporters "without independent means, who worked on the party newspaper, were fed at Periyar's home, but had to sleep on sacks containing agricultural produce in the godown" (117n). On the other hand, Thirumaavalavan, the leader of the Viduthalai Chiruththaigal (Dalit Panthers) of Tamilnadu, hopes that the upsurge of parties like his "will turn the dreams of leaders like Periyar and Ambedkar into an impressive reality" (2000, 18) and praises Periyar as a firm believer in uprooting brahmanism to achieve social justice, and quotes with approval his saying that "if you spot a Brahman and a snake together, leave the snake, beat the Brahman!" (152–53). And scholars such as Geetha and Rajadurai (1998) and Aloysius (1998) endorse the existence and significance of a common tradition of the Tamil anticaste movement of the colonial period ranging from Iyothee Thass to Periyar.

The issues raised are important. It would clearly appear that

Periyar was concentrating his efforts on the nonbrahmans and lacked the broader vision of Phule in Maharashtra. On the other hand, Tamilnadu never had a leader with as broad a vision as Ambedkar, who knew well the faults of the nonbrahmans but nevertheless strove for an alliance.

This has to be seen in the context of two crucial theoretical questions: whether the main fight was against brahmanism and how to carry it on. The nonbrahman movement had argued that the main fight was against brahmanism. If this is true, even though Periyar fought primarily for nonbrahmans – and expressed his dissatisfaction with dalits getting reservations at independence but not 'other backward castes' – a defeat of brahmanism would be in the interests of dalits as well. However, Indian history is littered with concessions made, with nonbrahmans making gains, and becoming brahmanized. This was the fear expressed by dalits, who have argued that a blind fight which neglected their specific interests would do them little good in the end. The fight against brahmanism, from their point of view, had to be carried on always with the concerns of those most oppressed by brahmanism in mind. Thus the desire for autonomy was expressed also by Ambedkar though in very different circumstances (when he was the clear important leader, eclipsing any of the Maharashtrian nonbrahmans). Periyar has remained popular in Tamilnadu, and he remains a symbol of the fight against caste and brahmanism. Yet in many ways this struggle historically and politically has been incomplete, partly due to a failure to thoroughly associate dalit issues with it. The consequences remain today. This need not mean a rejection of Periyar, but a recognition of the incompleteness of the historical task of the nonbrahman–Dravidian movement and its causes is a prerequisite for moving ahead. Clearly the goal of achieving a caste-free Dravidanadu – or a Kingdom of Bali – requires unity of dalits and OBC nonbrahmans; it may also require the leadership of dalits.

xi
Ambedkar Prabuddha Bharat

As with Periyar, the period of active leadership of Dr B.R. Ambedkar comprised all the significant trends of late colonial India. In contrast to the founding era of Phule, industrialization was now a certainty, independence an impending reality, the currents of marxism, liberal nationalism, Hindu communalism, Muslim separatism and the question of Pakistan were live and mass-based. In contrast to Periyar, however, the stage on which Ambedkar acted was geographically much larger.

The most important recent analysis of his political strategy by Christophe Jaffrelot has stressed its pragmatism (2005, 6–7). As the leader of an oppressed and economically, educationally backward minority, Ambedkar had to cope with all the huge and more powerful political trends of the country. It was natural that he looked for allies, thought in terms of tactics, and made compromises. As he himself said, noting his periods of taking help from the British, "we cannot fight two enemies at once." Yet, looking at Ambedkar's politics only as pragmatic, and tactical, misses the importance of his underlying vision. He was preoccupied throughout with the issue of creating a just society, the opposite of the inequalitarian caste-ridden society he was familiar with, a vision he shared with the other anticaste thinkers examined here. His whole experience and the outlook that developed from it emphasized the stress on fighting brahmanism and destroying caste along with economic inequality. Besides grappling with economics and politics, Ambedkar spent much of his life searching for a rational religion – trying to combine what we have discussed as 'reason' and 'ecstasy' – and in the end he found it in Buddhism, a choice that was in a sense 'overdetermined'. This was in no way inconsistent with his economic and political thinking, and among his last writings were those that sought to unite economics, politics and religious-cultural vision.

Ambedkar was a trained economist, and a believer in industrialization as a crucial way of overcoming poverty and backwardness. He taught economics for most of his life, and in the 1920s published two important books on Indian economic history. He saw 'rapid economic growth' as solution to poverty; this was one of his concerns as he grappled with the issues of socialism and capitalism. However, the other important passion was the particular form of slavery suffered by dalits under the caste system. A rather massive set of unpublished writings document this, showing him struggling to comprehend the passages of Indian history and caste; here he wrote more as a sociologist. The vision of India that he put forward, consistently from the beginning but with greater force at the end of his life, was an all-around one, with economics, social life and 'religious' (or sacred) morality linked together, with the modern theme of 'liberty, equality and fraternity' founded in the ancient Indian tradition of Buddhism.

Economic Theory: The Linking Thread

In an earlier essay, I had outlined three seemingly disparate stages of Ambedkar's economic philosophy (Omvedt 1999, 276–77). In the 1920s, following his degrees in economics from New York and London, he published two works showing the marks of a standard liberal position flavoured with Indian nationalism. Later, as mass struggles grew in the 1930s, he drew closer to marxism in many ways, claiming in a speech that he shared a lot with marxist economic theory. In a speech to dalit railroad workers in 1938 at Manmad he stressed the need for fighting 'brahmanism and capitalism', a theme still persuasive to many dalits today. This heralded a kind of dualistic position, similar to arguments about 'class and race' or 'class and gender', which left marxism hegemonic in the discourse on economics. This stage reached its culmination with the publication of *States and Minorities* in March 1947, giving an apparent framework for the proposed Constitution, a framework that discussed 'state socialism' along with separate village settlements for dalits. However, the last stages of his life saw a return to a more pragmatic economic position, most marked in the 1952 programme for the Scheduled Caste Federation, talking of democracy more than of socialism and of industrialization as the solution for India's problems. This final 'economic Ambedkar' seemed to be envisioning a kind of welfare state, capitalist but avoiding the over-exploitation of workers. It was a kind of social democracy that in many ways was a return to his earliest famous teacher, John Dewey.

Jaffrelot argues that Ambedkar stressed the closeness with marxism at a time when he was working with the communists in the mass movement, and later moved back towards liberalism when it was clear that independence was at hand without any sign of a marxist revolution. It is clear that Ambedkar was a tactician, familiar with movement language and in a sense indulging in it—in context. However, Ambedkar was indeed fascinated with but at the same time repelled by marxism, and the development of his thinking had a logic of its own. Like the dalit-bahujan intellectuals since the time of the radical sants, he had a vision underlying his programmes and tactics.

Throughout, in many ways, one can see a preoccupation with the role of the state in promoting development. In his analysis of colonial rule, both in *The Problem of the Rupee* (1923) and *The Evolution of Provincial Finance in British India* (1925) (in Ambedkar 1989, vol. 6). Ambedkar had been critical of British colonial policy. British fiscal policy impoverished India: "While the land tax prevented the prosperity of agricultural industry, the customs taxes hampered the manufacturers of the country. There were internal customs and external customs, and both were equally injurious to trade and industry" (75). It was clear, he noted, that the British government was running India in the interests of British manufacturers. In the case of the rupee problem, he also more or less agreed with Indian businessmen in supporting a devaluation of the rupee, in contrast to the British bureaucracy that wanted a high rupee to support a pound value of pensions and salaries (see the discussion in Omvedt 1994, 231–34).

It is noteworthy, however, that even here he did not limit his critique of British colonialism to the economic issue, even in this economic study. Exploitation was not only economic but social. But, the British government, he wrote,

> could not sympathize with the living forces operating in the Indian society, was not charged with its wants, its pains, its cravings and its desires, was inimical to its aspirations, did not advance Education, disfavoured Swadeshi and snapped at anything that smacked of nationalism....the Government of India dared not abolition the caste system, prescribe monogamy, alter the laws of succession, legalize intermarriage or venture to tax the tea planters. Progress involves interference with the existing code of social life and interference is likely to cause resistance. (1979, vol. 1, 233)

This, of course, suggested that he had hopes from an independent state, a genuinely democratic one that did represent (and seek to lead) popular opinion: that it would lead the way in social reform.

This gave him a commonality with the nationalists, though it was partly rhetorical; like other dalit-bahujan intellectual spokesmen he had opposed swadeshi. In *Bahishkrut Bharat* (a fortnightly Marathi paper he launched and edited in April 1927), an early editorial had criticized the movement from an economic standpoint: swadeshi would raise the price of commodities, so that helping capitalists would penalize consumers, especially those belonging to subordinated castes. Like others nonbrahman leaders, he too laid great stress on education.

What were his positions in the 1930s? In fact, he never wrote a theoretical support of socialism, though he had little reason to trust Indian capitalists. In his speeches, he used its rhetoric; he talked of 'capitalism and brahmanism', but always with some qualification. For instance, it was during the great peasant march to the Bombay Council Hall on 12 January 1938 that he made his statement about the closeness to marxism, and did so with "a few words to my communist friends":

> I have definitely read studiously more books on the Communist philosophy than all the Communist leaders here. However beautiful the Communist philosophy is in those books, still it has to be seen how useful it can be made in practice. The test of this philosophy has to be given in practice. And if work is done from that perspective, I feel that the labour and length of time needed to win success in Russia will not be so much in India. And so in regard to the toilers' class struggle, I feel the Communist philosophy to be closer to us. (*Janata*, 15 January 1938)

'Closer to us' is hardly an overwhelming theoretical and political endorsement, leave aside the caution about practice. The fact is that Ambedkar's critique of marxism and of the communsit movement was nearly continuous from the 1920s onward.

He had first written on the issue in 1929, at the time of

the communist-led great textile strike. This was actually the second strike, not so massive and popular as the first, with a weakened working class. And it was untouchable workers, who generally had lower-paid jobs and no village land to sustain them through long strikes, who suffered the most. Because of feelings about untouchability, dalits were excluded from the higher-paying weaving department, where thread that broke had to be held between the teeth. The mills were an important source of income, but the operation of caste inequalities here also was visible—and continued, it may be noted, up through independence. All of this could not help but condition his response to communism. In a *Bahishkrut Bharat* article on 27 September 1929, Ambedkar expressed his difference with the communist hope and expectation that revolution was at hand, that revolution was the only thing that could save the working class. In fact, Ambedkar argued, the working class was not ready; it did not understand the philosophy of the communists, and if workers realized that communists rejected religion, caste and nation, they would lose their base as such. He gave an example of the anger of maratha workers when communists had refused to have a picture of Shivaji in the union office. The great obstacle to revolution was the practice of caste and religious distinctions among the workers. "If Lenin had been born in India he would first eradicate casteism and untouchability from among workers, for without this they could get no concept of revolution."

The article was entitled, "First the Pillars, Then the Base", invoking the base–superstructure architectural model. This theme remained crucial to Ambedkar's critique of marxism. The theme was repeated at length during the 1930s agitations. It formed an important article in *Janata* in 1936, reprinted again on 19 April 1938 as "The Illlusion of the Communists and the Duty of the Untouchable Class". This elaborated his point in detail.

> But the base is not the building. On the basis of the economic relations a building is erected of religious, social and political institutions. This building has just as much truth (reality) as the base. If we want to change the base, then first the building that has been constructed on it has to be knocked down. In the same way, if we want to change the economic relations of society, then first the existing social, political and other institutions will have to be destroyed.

He went on to say that to build the strength of the working class, the mental hold of religious slavery would have to be destroyed. Thus the precondition of a united working-class struggle was the eradication of caste and untouchability. Further, he dissented from a later common theme of marxist–dalit rhetoric in arguing that capitalism would not be opposed to the eradication of caste as such, since freeing potential workers from caste restrictions would increase the labour supply (he used here the phrase 'reserve army of labour').

These were important differences. For Ambedkar, the theme of caste and untouchability was a major preoccupation, and he was increasingly inclined to stress the linkage with religion and culture, particularly since these were ignored by marxism. Marxism taught him a holistic point of view, but he needed to examine what marxism, because of its tendency to a mechanical materialism, neglected. This was done in his historical researches, resulting in two books – *The Untouchables: Who were they and Why they Became Untouchables* (1948), and *Who Were the Shudras* (1946) – and numerous unpublished and unfinished manuscripts.

Ambedkar as Minister

An additional factor possibly went into the making of Ambedkar's thinking on development, and that was his experience as minister under the British. In the early 1940s, partly under pressure from the British to firm up his backing as a leader of the 'untouchables', he had transformed the old Independent Labour Party (ILP) into the Scheduled Caste Federation (SCF). It was in one way a momentous change: the ILP had been limited in strength to Marathi-speaking areas, but it had drawn on some nonbrahman as well as dalit support (particularly in the Konkan, where land struggles led by a coalition of ambedkarite dalits and kunbi peasants had been going on since the early 1930s). He was now becoming a leader of all-India stature, but only of dalits; nonbrahmans continued to be drawn into the Congress (and socialist) political frameworks, except in Tamilnadu.

Ambedkar's talents were recognized and he joined the Viceroy's Executive Council holding the portfolios of Labour, Irrigation and Power between from 1942 and 1946. This was a formative period for the planning that was to become a feature of the Indian economy after independence, and here he played an important role. A major concern was for 'reconstruction' after the war destruction; but here, though the model was in many ways Europe, Ambedkar (and others) stressed that the goal was more than this; planning had to be for economic development and irrigation. As he argued in a speech of 25 October 1943, to the Reconstruction Policy Committee, industrialization was crucial for India:

> To my mind there can be no greater proof to show that India's agriculture has failed, and failed miserably, when it is as plain as anything that India which is engaged in producing nothing but food does not even produce sufficient food to feed its people.... The poverty in India...is entirely due to its being made dependent on agriculture. (Cited in Thorat 1998, 213)

The background, of course, was the terrible Bengal famine of 1943, when millions were dying for lack of food. But Ambedkar's thinking on this goes back to his earliest essays on agriculture as a student: he had always stressed that the problems of agriculture could be solved only through industrialization.

Thus, he was distressed by the fact that irrigation was, originally, thought of mainly in terms of flood control by most people. Agriculture, he stressed, needed water; more than this, irrigation should provide for electricity and water transport. Thus irrigation projects were 'multipurpose'. Also, because electricity was a provincial subject, there was a need to get beyond simply 'central' schemes. The remedy suggested was multiregional authorities, modelled somewhat on the Tennessee Valley project in the US (188). A central organisation – the Central Waterways, Irrigation and Navigation Commission – was also set up. Ambedkar was thus involved, at the beginning of the development of water policy, with several schemes: the Damodar Valley project, Hirakud project in Orissa, the Sone river project mainly in Bihar, and some of the Deccan rivers. He also stressed at times the necessity of sufficient water for agriculture (200–201): "Water is wealth. Water being the wealth of the people and its distribution being uncertain, the correct approach is not to complain against nature but to conserve water" (200).

In regard to electricity, he stressed its importance for industrialization, and emphasized the necessity of the central government having a role. State control or ownership was necessary. Addressing the Reconstruction Policy Committee on 2 February 1945, he stressed that "there are very few opponents of State ownership and State control who do not make an exception in the case of electricity" (223).

At the end of this period, Ambedkar produced his *States and Minorities* (1947), which, as the subtitle indicated, was a 'Memorandum on the Safeguards for the Scheduled Castes submitted to the Constituent Assembly on behalf of the All India Scheduled Castes Federation'. The idea of 'state socialism' may have been somewhat utopian, but it is clear that the operative factor for him, which remained throughout, was the emphasis on state responsibility, planning and control—and he played a crucial role in this during the seminal period just before independence.

From State Socialism to Buddhist Economics

In many ways, then, Ambedkar was in the 1940s living a life of political practice and theoretical work that went contrary to the marxist radicalism that had earlier affected him and which continued to be so powerful in India. It is surprising, then, that his expression of such radicalism should culminate in the late 1940s as a 'memorandum' regarding safeguards for Scheduled Castes in the forthcoming Constitution (*States and Minorities*). Here he laid out detailed proposals for a federation, and for the protection of Scheduled Castes from social and economic exploitation. This document included proposals for nationalization of industries: key industries should be owned by the state, and 'basic industries' (the difference was not defined) should be owned by the state and operated by the state or by corporations established by the state. The state should acquire property or subsisting rights in industries, insurance and agricultural land owned by individuals, with compensation to be paid. Agricultural land also should be nationalized and run as collective farms.

In discussing this, Ambedkar argued that state ownership was essential for rapid industrialization, and that 'fundamental rights' meant little to the unemployed. In a classic marxist argument, he disagreed with the assumption of constitutional lawyers that enactment of fundamental rights itself would guarantee liberty. Almost echoing Lenin, he wrote, "To whom and for whom is this liberty? Obviously this liberty is liberty to the landlords to increase rents, for capitalists to increase hours of work and reduce rate of wages...what is called liberty from the control of the State is another name for the dictatorship of the private employer" (1979, vol. 1, 410). He argued that 'state socialism' must be made a constitutional provision, beyond the power of the legislative body to change.

In this memorandum published in 1947, Ambedkar wrote in the introduction that "it was my hope that the Constituent Assembly would elect me to the States Committee. Evidently it has found men of superior calibre for the work. It may also be because I am one of those who are outside the tabernacle and therefore undesirable" (384). Just months, later, he was not only chosen to the Constituent Assembly but elected its chairman, and during the long course of its deliberations he made no attempt to implement the 'state socialist' provisions he had heralded in *States and Minorities*. Not only that, as Jaffrelot has argued in a detailed and excellent chapter on the Constituent Assembly, he used his powers more or less to fight both the gandhians and the socialists.

Instead, there was a clear shift in his economic position. By the time of the Scheduled Caste Federation election manifesto, he was openly expressing his pragmatism. The manifesto stated:

> For the purposes of increasing production, the Scheduled Castes Federation will not be bound by a dogma of any pattern. The pattern of industrial enterprise will be a manner regulated by the needs, the time and circumstances. Where national undertaking of an industry is possible and essential, the Scheduled Castes Federation will support national undertaking. Where private enterprise is possible and national undertaking not essential, private enterprise will be allowed. Looking at the intense poverty of the people of this country no other consideration except that of greater production and still greater production can be the primary and paramount condition. A pre-conceived pattern of industry can not be the primary or paramount consideration. The remedy again is more production and not the pattern of production. One reservation the Scheduled Castes Federation must however make. Any scheme of production must in the view of the Scheduled Caste Federation remain subject to one over-riding consideration – namely, that there should be no

> exploitation of the working classes. (Cited in Khairmode 1989, vol. 10, 156–57)

In addition, in regard to agriculture, Ambedkar argued for mechanization (with machinery to be supplied by the state on rent) and large farms; cultivatable waste was to be given to landless labourers where possible; otherwise afforestation was recommended.

A great deal of attention was paid to the question of resources; in implicit contrast to gandhism, Ambedkar was in favour of the salt tax and against prohibition, urging a heavy taxation on alcohol instead. Nationalization of insurance was seen as the most profitable source of funds, but it was stated that the SCF would not press for nationalization, but make insurance compulsory for state and private employees. Finally, in regard to alliances, the SCF wanted to work in cooperation with the OBCs (other nonbrahmans) and the tribal groups, but rejected alliances with both the Hindu nationalists on the one hand and the communists, on the other, because the Communist Party of India's (CPI) object was to "destroy individual freedom and parliamentary democracy and substitute dictatorship in its place" (Khairmode 1989, 167).

This, in one sense, was undeniably pragmatism. But it was also a dedication to democracy and liberty. Ambedkar was showing a strong reluctance to even mention socialism or public enterprise, though the concern about exploitation remained. It was a shift to pragmatism, to social democracy or welfare capitalism. What had intervened in the meantime? A heavy dose of experience of communist practice in India (where he had conflicts with the CPI over the 1952 elections from Bombay, since their 'natural' constituencies, where dalits were a central group in the working class, overlapped) and elsewhere (the communist takeover of Tibet). In addition, Ambedkar's growing interest in Buddhism, which provided him with an alternative vision, was also undoubtedly influencing his economic and social thinking.

Buddha and Karl Marx

Ambedkar's unpublished manuscripts – written during the 1940s, primarily, when he was grappling with the issues of Hinduism and caste – stress increasingly the role of Buddhism as the primary alternative force in Indian history. The history of India is "nothing but a history of a mortal conflict between Buddhism and Brahmanism," he had written in one of these essays, describing the ancient period as one of "revolution and counter-revolution" (1987, vol. 3, 267). Buddhism was also coming to be seen as an alternative to marxism in providing an overall vision, and a foundation for the values of economic development, rationality and (an always stressed value) 'liberty, equality, fraternity'. In one late essay, "Buddha and Karl Marx", he summed up his rejection of Marx, refuting the inevitability of scientific socialism and the main analysis of historical development (exploitation, ended by nationalization of private property) with the argument that the course of revolutionary developments in Russia had disproved these. But the 'residue of fire' remained, including the conflict of interest between classes and its base in private property, and hence the necessity for the abolition of private property, he accepted (1987, vol. 3, 443–44).

Gradually also Buddhism became the source of a model for creating a new society. In "Buddha and Karl Marx" he stresses both the Sangha as a 'communist' organization – voluntary in contrast to the violence that pervaded and corrupted marxism – and the role of the righteous king, the Buddhist *cakkavati* (ruler). He cites a sutta that describes the plight of a state that falls into decadence, decline and chaos because its king does not follow the advice of his monk advisors and act to remedy poverty.

Interestingly enough, he also stresses prosperity in this essay. Prosperity, the ending of poverty, had always been a value with him, and consequently he valued development and industrialization along with the marxists and the nehruvian socialists. In an early student essay on Bertrand Russell, he had criticized the theme of renunciation as characteristic of a 'pain economy' which had a low level of development. This was a rejection of gandhism before he had ever heard of Gandhi. Ambedkar returned to this theme in "Buddha and Karl Marx", arguing that this was a major difference between Buddhism and Christianity: Christianity glorified poverty, Buddhism did not.

> The first charge [made by communists] against Christianity was that they made people [value] other worldliness and made them suffer poverty in this world. As can be seen from quotations from Buddhism in the earlier part of this tract such a charge cannot be levied against Buddhism....to acquire wealth legitimately and justly, earn by great industry, amassed by strength of the arm and gained by the sweat of the brow is a great blessing. The householder makes himself happy and preserves himself full of happiness; also makes his parents, wife, and children, servants and labourers, friends and companions happy and cheerful and preserves them full of happiness (460–61).

He concludes by referring to the three revolutionary values—liberty, equality and fraternity:

> The French Revolution was welcomed because of this slogan. It failed to produce equality. We welcome the Russian Revolution because it aims to produce equality. But it cannot be too much emphasized that in producing equality, society cannot afford to sacrifice fraternity or liberty. It seems that the three can coexist only if one follows the way of the Buddha. (462)

Ambedkar's Buddhism, then, was to a large degree posed against marxist radicalism, and claimed to have the answers to forming and maintaining a just society. In his last book, written for the millions who followed him in taking *diksha* to Buddhism, *The Buddha and His Dhamma* (1956), he seemed to be presenting a socially radical Buddha—this-worldly, rationalistic, moralistic. In the introduction, he states the things that he cannot accept in the mainstream, canonical presentation of Buddhism—the notion that 'all is sorrow' (*dukha*), the other-worldly nature of the Sangha, the idea that the Buddha's 'going forth' was due to seeing a sick man, an old man and a dead man.

The way Ambedkar handles the latter shows his style. Borrowing a story from the Jatakas, he has Buddha leaving home to prevent a war over water starting between the Sakyas and a neighbouring tribe. After hearing that the tribes have made peace, Ambedkar then cites Buddha as saying:

> The problem of war is a problem of conflict. It is only part of a larger problem. This conflict is going on not only between kings and nations but between nobles and Brahmans, between householders, between [friends and family members]....The conflict between nations is occasional. But the conflict between classes is constant and perpetual. It is this which is the root of all suffering in the world.... I have to find a solution to the problem of social conflict (1992, vol. 11, 58).

This reflects the influence of marxism, though it is not really marxist (this would take 'class conflict' as not fundamental, but rather stress the exploitation and the role of the proletariat).

Ambedkar's Buddhism adds up to an emphasis on morality (he thus defines Buddhism as 'morality—sacred morality') and the achievement of a just society. "The Buddha...did not tell people that their aim in life should be to reach some imaginary heaven. The kingdom of righteousness lies on earth and is to be reached by man by righteous conduct" (283). And, following his first sermon, the five first disciples exclaim, "Never in the history of the world has salvation been conceived as the blessing of happiness to be attained by man in this life and on this earth by righteousness born out of his own efforts!" (131).

From the sociological point of view, Ambedkar argues that this type of religion is what society needs: Dhamma is fundamentally social, he tells us.

> Society has to choose one of the three alternatives. Society

> may choose not to have any Dhamma as an instrument of Government. For Dhamma is nothing if it is not an instrument of Government. This means Society chooses the road to anarchy. Secondly, Society may choose the police, i.e., dictatorship, as an instrument of Government. Thirdly, Society may choose Dhamma plus the Magistrate wherever people fail to observe the Dhamma. In anarchy and dictatorship liberty is lost. Only in the third liberty survives. Those who want liberty must therefore have Dhamma. (317)

This was indeed an empirical, social, this-worldly Buddhism.

There was, however, one flaw in Ambedkar's kingdom of righteousness and justice that he hoped to establish on earth through moral conduct—and that was his view of women. The original Buddhist view had considered women as inferior to men, requiring the Bhikkuni Sangha to be subordinate to the male Bhikshus. It was not the view of women as inherently lascivious and requiring male control that was seen in the *Manusmriti*; rather it was a kind of capitalist inequality in which 'women's place is in the home.' Ambedkar reproduced this, citing one of Buddha's 'Vinaya for girls' in which they are told that they should vow to give service:

> To whatsoever husband our parents shall give us...because of compassion for him we will rise up early, be the last to retire, be willing workers, order all things sweetly and be gentle voiced. Train yourselves thus, girls....[vow that] We will be deft and nimble at our husband's home-crafts, whether they be of wool or cotton....The money, corn, silver and gold that our husband brings home we will keep safe, watch and ward over it, and act as no robber, thief, carouser, wastrel therein. Train yourselves thus, girls. (466–67)

Ambedkar can be contrasted here with Pandita Ramabai: he was a supporter of women, in the sense that he fought strongly for their equal rights as a minister trying to guide the Hindu Code Bill through a contentious parliament. But his fight was against the strictures imposed by brahmanism; he did not see very much farther than the ideal of a nuclear family typical of capitalist society, in which the woman provided support and help to the principle earner and worker, the man. This was also a vision of ancient Buddhism, and it was modern for its time. Pandita Ramabai's vision of women went further: in her final ashram, Mukti Sadan, women did all kinds of work and maintained themselves. She herself had struggled as a staunch individual for the whole of her life – like Ambedkar, blaming brahmanical Hinduism – but also resisting the patriarchy and control efforts found in the Christianity she converted to. But conversely, while she herself was free from caste prejudice, she did not feel so deeply the strictures imposed by the hierarchy of casteism in the way that dalits and OBC spokespersons did.

Ambedkar, like many of the dalit-bahujan intellectuals formulating visions of a just world, had come to religion. But it was a special kind of religion, not an elite 'opium of the people', but an empirical and social religion. His interpretation of Buddhism could be called a 'liberation theology', if the term theology could be applicable; perhaps 'liberation cosmology' would be more apt. It encompassed themes of an economically just social order; it was not accidental that his essay "Buddha and Karl Marx" concluded with a reference to the great ideals of the French Revolution—liberty, equality and fraternity.

Ambedkar appears to us above all as a man of reason. His writings reveal a painstaking effort at logical thinking, at argument. Yet beneath this cool façade of reason was a strong element of passion. As reported, he was easy to anger, and he had much in his life to get angry at. He was passionate about his goals, passionate about the annihilation of caste. Ecstasy and reason, then, were combined in Ambedkar's vision of an enlightened India, *Prabuddha Bharat*—embodied in the name he gave to the last of the three newspapers he published in his lifetime.

xii

Conclusion
Seeking Begumpura

From Namdev, Kabir, Ravidas and Tukaram through Phule, Ramabai and Ambedkar, dalit-bahujan and many women intellectuals have evoked an ideal of a casteless, classless society, and have increasingly outlined its characteristics as a prosperous, democratic, socialist, development-oriented society. This study has traced the varying expressions of the ideal and the concrete forms in which it was envisaged.

In the form of utopian values they upheld, the anticaste intellectuals differed significantly from those who are taken today as nationalist leaders. As G. Aloysius (1997) has pointed out in describing a 'nationalism without a nation in India', Congress as well as Hindu Mahasabha leaders had aimed for 'cultural nationalism'—that is a transfer of power without a change in the basic culture (as they saw it) of the Indian people. In doing so, they explicitly or implicitly endorsed its brahmanic elements, and in doing so laid the foundations for a more virulent Hindutva. Gandhi's Ram Rajya symbolized the ambiguity of their vision: it was seen as an ideal state, but Gandhi had to neglect the actually written role of Ram (for instance, in his treatment of Sita and Shambuka), something he consistently sidelined. Nehru's ideal was a vague socialism, but he associated it with a managed economy, an updated version of what he saw as the traditional brahmanic ideal of service, taking the values of collectivity in family, caste and village as positive and somehow socialistic. This connected him ideologically with Gandhi, though in many respects his marxist emphasis on economic development puts him in the same camp as Ambedkar.

In contrast to the tendency of the elites to seek an independence ideal in the recreation of past values – located in an imagined vedic golden age, with many of them idealizing varnsashrama dharma, and without much change in the hegemonic structures of society – the subaltern intellectuals sought what Aloysius calls a 'political nationalism', that emphasized equality with solidarity. Theirs was a vision that sought the reconstruction of Indian society, the creation of a new society that would flourish under independence.

One of the earliest expressions of this search was Ravidas' poem "Begumpura"—depicting a city without sorrow, with no taxes or toil, no exploitation, no hierarchy, and freedom for all to walk anywhere. It is a city, not a village; there is no mention of a king or a temple; for a bhakti poet indeed no mention of god is unique. Its prosperity is also stressed. This was to remain a theme—the ideal, whether Begumpura or an imagined Pandhari, was a city of dancing, of merchants, of prosperity. Its anticaste vision may be contrasted with Gandhi's Ram Rajya which indeed focused on village India, with Ram as a supposedly ideal king. Ravidas, even in the fifteenth century, was more 'secular' and certainly more socialistic than Gandhi.

Independence

With independence, the creativity of dalit-bahujan intellectuals seemingly died away. Ambedkar died in 1956; he left behind a political party, a policy of a broad Left alliance, a new religion, and a heritage of pride. But the Republican party, though conceived of as a party for all the oppressed (and named after the US Republican Party, seen as the party of Lincoln and the ending of slavery), turned out to be only for dalits and more or less limited to being a powerful pressure group in Maharashtra. A later, greater effort by Kanshi Ram to recreate the alliance of dalits and OBCs with the Bahujan Samaj Party (BSP) has had limited success: for a time it seemed to arouse a thunder all over India. For some time it remained confined to Uttar Pradesh and the northern, chamar belt of the state—though Mayawati's resounding victory in the 2007 assembly elections brought new hope and new questioning, especially regarding the alliance with brahmans.

Dalit literature had emerged as a powerful voice of the oppressed—first in Maharashtra, later in other regional languages. But it has remained as a literature of protest, lacking the broad vision of the earlier 'Begumpura' intellectuals; and to a large degree its consumers, its audience, have been caste Hindus. When the Dalit Panther was formed in 1972 by some of the leading writers of Maharashtra, it emerged as a militant organization but quickly became split over 'marxism' versus 'ambedkarism', and died within a year. Much of the dalit movement in the following years appeared to be under the hegemony of the Left, and this sapped its creativity.

After 1990, with the new globalization, and propelled by the internet, a new dalit intelligentsia seized the opportunity to take their cause to the world arena, and in 2001 put caste on the agenda as a form of racism at the United Nations World Conference Against Racism in Durban, South Africa. This new form of mobilization has found it difficult to connect in an organic way with the dalit masses; it was too often based on

NGO activity rather than strong mass movements. Yet the many initiatives heralded the beginning of a new era. Dalits were aspiring to be a global force now, symbolized by the celebration of the 'Dalit goddess of English' by intellectual Chandra Bhan Prasad on the birth anniversary of – of all the available icons – Lord Macaulay (for introducing English education to India) on 25 October 2005. Looking a bit like the Statue of Liberty with a floppy hippy hat, the 'goddess' was standing on a computer, with book and pen in hand, springing from the map of India as if to move on to the world. Claims Prasad, who hosted the party, "English the Dalit Goddess is a world power today; it is about emancipation; it is a mass movement against the caste order. Over a century ago, Savitribai Phule, wife of social revolutionary Jotirao Phule, had written the same thing, saying in a poem that sudras and ati-sudras (dalits) now have the right to education; and through English, casteism can be destroyed and brahmanical teaching can be hurled away." But it remains to be seen how much the subaltern castes will be able to use the weapons of global connections, computer, and English skills.

The Waves of Creativity

In fact, the ups and downs of the emergence of anticaste intellectuals were probably not accidental. The two main eras of creativity were the fifteenth to seventeenth centuries – when the great poet-saints and 'wandering minstrels' known as leaders of the 'bhakti movement' sang their songs to arouse the people against priestly dominance and caste exclusiveness – and the colonial period. Both represented forms of globalization. In the first case, Muslim rule brought a wide commercialism and an era of order to the subcontinent, broke through the stagnation of brahmanic regionalized states, and brought a connection with global trends, both in terms of mysticism and broader stirrings of assertion. In the second case, it was British colonial rule that linked India to a wider heritage. These linkages, and the resources they offered, benefited the anticaste intellectuals who emerged to try to give a telling blow to ritualism and hierarchy.

Thus the bhakti poets made use of the openings provided by Muslim rule to reject the brahmanical elements of tradition. It is not accidental that Ravidas chose a largely Persian name for his "Begumpura", symbolizing both the end of sorrow and a feminine identity. Similarly, other bhakti poets rejected many of the brahmanic symbols – choosing Pandhari over Vaikuntha, often rejecting the avatar theory or turning it upside down, to hail the goodness of Bali, Sibi and the like. Even where names such as Rama were used by poets like Kabir, he made it clear that this was not the avatar 'Ramchandra' and at times combined 'Allah-Ram': "Every man and woman born are forms of you, so says Kabir: I'm Ram and Allah's foolish baby, he's my guru and my pir" (shabd 97).

Similarly, during the colonial period the initial response of the subaltern Kartabhajas was to hail the prosperity of the *kompani*, a king bringing wealth and prosperity from oversees. Intellectuals like Phule drew upon missionary research and propagandizing to help them provide a full-fledged theory of brahmanism, created by Aryans and maintained through keeping the masses in ignorance. And he turned the avatar theory on its head, again, to hail the *rakshasas* (connoting demons in Sanskrit) as defenders of the people and Bali Raja as the good king, both powerful and sacrificial. It is thus not unexpected that the 'Aryan theory' in reverse was claimed by the dalit movement in India as a whole—it provided a powerful metaphor for undermining brahmanic power.

These early eras of 'globalization' in many ways benefited the anticaste movement. Yet just as theorists today stress that globalization has both dangers and opportunities, so it did earlier. The ruling classes and ethnic groups during these early periods also were not interested in promoting mass welfare; outsiders themselves, they often made alliances with brahmans and worked to maintain caste. Muslims themselves absorbed much of caste hierarchy, defining their elite as *ashraf* – descendents of Turks and Persians, Sayyids and Shahs – and treating the subaltern caste converts as inferior. The British, in turn, in taking up caste were likely to identify with the brahmans the more distant Aryans. Both Muslim and British rule in many ways actually served to strengthen brahman dominance, for brahmans managed to monopolize education and the roads to bureaucratic service. In both cases, in spite of challenges from below, a brahmanic recuperation occurred: the bhakti movement was absorbed, and the anticaste intellectuals of the colonial period were deflected as the call for national independence took on a powerful aura. And with independence, most of the issues raised by subaltern groups were buried. The way affirmative action was handled was typical: through the policy of 'reservation' that absorbed all the rigidities of the public sector bureaucracy, renouncing any trust in broader policy decisions, and institutionalizing an ideological split between 'merit' and 'reservation' candidates. The 'global' forces have been used, in the end, more effectively by the elites, and rather than revolutionary moves towards abolition of caste, an updating and restructuring of caste inequality has occurred.

Reason and Ecstasy

Reason and ecstasy, *dnyan* and *bhakti or bhav*, have been the underlying themes of this book. They constitute the two main strands of the utopian vision: the joy taken in the consciousness of a promised land – a Begumpura, a kingdom of Bali, a Buddhist commonwealth, an enlightened India – and the analytical power that defines the contours of that land. Together, they make the road that leads to the promised land.

There is a difference, however, in their historical expression, which can be seen in India as well as elsewhere. In the early modern age, when the beginnings of economic progress, exploration and adventure gave birth to the utopian vision, there was still not the material basis to produce the wealth that underlies a prosperous utopia. This is the job of capitalism; but if capitalism develops the forces of production to lay the foundations for socialism, in its beginnings these foundations could only be sensed, not understood. Particularly in India, where brahmanism had deprived the dalit-bahuajns access to education, reserving *dnyan* for the elite, they could only concede a dreamlike ecstasy. As a result, in bhakti there was no analysis of the caste that constrained them, only a fervent celebration of the joy and solidarity that was found in the 'communion of saints'. Colonialism was welcomed in this mood, rather uncritically – by groups such as the Kartabhajas – as bringing with it a new prosperity.

Though colonialism in many ways solidified caste, it also provided openings for subaltern assertion. Among these were the research and tools of history that the dalits and bahujans could seize to analyze their situation. The first generation of anticaste intellectuals in the colonial period concentrated, then, on the historical past, on the causes of caste slavery. They found their utopia in a 'golden age' before the coming of the Aryans—whether defined as Buddhism by Iyothee Thass or as the land of Bali by Phule. This was in a sense projected into the future, but little was done to analyze the road to achieving it, other than developing a critique of elite nationalism and a tendency to place their hopes in the British. Some, notably Pandita Ramabai, made an effort to establish a utopian community.

It was the last colonial generation of anticaste intellectuals – in particular Ambedkar and Periyar – who were the ones to grapple with the actual contours of a realizable utopia. Major underlying causes for this new specificity were the coming of independence and the clear beginnings of industrialization: the first laid the political foundations, and the second the productive foundations, for the achievement of a prosperous, equalitarian sustainable society. In engaging in political struggle, the anticaste leaders formed parties whose programmes outlined a form of democratic socialism, sometimes verging on an extreme form of socialism (as in Ambedkar's 'state socialist' period), sometimes looking to pragmatism and democracy. However, their vision always sought to combine an end to caste along with the classless society.

Begumpura of a Globalized Society?

We are entering a new era of globalization, involving the transformation of 'imperialism' into 'Empire' in the terminology of Antonio Negri (Hardt and Negri 2000), which means in part that the old system of competing nation-states, each with their own set of colonies and dependencies, is being replaced by a more integrated international system. Capitalism is becoming disorganized at the national level and taking on the character of a global capitalist mode of production. New forms of production are becoming dominant, emphasizing communications technology and a greater penetration into the very bodies and lives of producers.

The question in this situation is whether the vision of the anticaste intellectuals can gain a new relevance. In some ways the situation for it may be more favourable than ever: as the relevance of nation-states subsides, and it becomes increasingly clear that the question is not one of going back to a 'nationalist' resistance to global and colonial domination but rather of overcoming capitalism itself to create a new global socialist society, the significance of the nationalist forms of liberation diminishes. Also, the relevance of nonclass forms of exploitation – such as gender, race, sexual orientation and caste – is being increasingly recognized; even the impact of 'dalit' is being felt to some degree at the world level.

But whether possibilities will be realized depends on a creative response from the subalterns. Dalits and bahujans themselves are only beginning to adjust to the new order, and the articulation of how to deal with it still remains caught within old shibboleths—either simple support of globalization without nuances, or an updating of the old Left paradigm of opposition to 'LPG' (liberalization, privatization and globalization). In this sense, Begumpura remains to be translated into a vision appropriate to the new era.

References

Abbot, Justin E. 1930. *Life of Tukaram: Translation from Mahipati's Bhaktalilamrita, Chapters 25–40.* New Delhi: Motilal Banarsidass, 1980.

Ahmad, Aziz. 1967. *Islamic Modernism in India and Pakistan: 1857–1964.* London: Oxford University Press.

Aitzaz Ahsan. 1997. *The Indus Saga and the Making of Pakistan.* Karachi: Oxford University Press.

Alavi, Seema, ed. 2002. *The Eighteenth Century in India.* New Delhi: Oxford University Press.

Aloysius, G. 2004. *Dalit-Subaltern Emergence in Religio-Cultural Subjectivity: Iyothee Thassar and Emancipatory Buddhism.* New Delhi: Critical Quest.

———. 1999. Caste in and above history. *Sociological Bulletin* 48 (1&2).

———. 1998. *Religion as Emancipatory Identity: A Buddhist Movement among the Tamils Under Colonialism.* New Delhi: New Age International.

———. 1997. *Nationalism without a Nation in India.* New Delhi: Oxford University Press.

Ali, Syed Asad. 2000. *Influence of Islam on Hindi Literature*. New Delhi: Idarah-i-Adabiyat-I Delhi.

Ambedkar, B.R. 1976–2004. *Dr. Babasaheb Ambedkar Writings and Speeches*. Ed. Vasant Moon. 17 vols. Mumbai: Government of Maharashtra.

———. 1974–76. *Dr. Babasaheb Ambedkaranci Bhashane*. Ed. M.K. Ganjare. 4 Vols. Nagpur: Ashok Prakashan.

Arangasamy, Palany. 1991. *Life and Works of Bharatidasan*. Thanjavur: Tamil University.

Armstrong, Karen. 1993. *A History of God: The 4,000 Year-Old Quest from Abraham to the Present*. New York: Vintage.

———. 1929. *Bahinabai: A Translation of Her Autobiography and Verses*. By Justin Abbott. Delhi: Motilal Banarsidass, 1985.

———. 1979. *Sant Bahenabainca Gatha va Samiksha* (The Songs of Bahenabai and an Analysis). Ed. Shalini Anant Javadekar. Pune: Dharmik va Sanskritic Prakashan Mandal.

———. 1998. *The Abhangs of Bahinabai*. Trans. Krishna P. Bahedur. New Delhi: Munshiram Manoharlal.

Bahirat, B.P. 1956. *The Philosophy of Jnanadeva, As Gleaned from the Amrtanubhava*. New Delhi: Motilal Banarsidass.

Bama. 2000. *Karukku*. Trans. from the Tamil by Lakshmi Holmstrom. Chennai: Macmillan

Bandyopadhyay, Sekhar. 1997. *Caste, Protest and Identity in Colonial India: The Namasudras of Bengal*. 1872–1947. London: Curzon.

Barnett, Richard, B. 2000. *Rethinking Early Modern India*. New Delhi: Manohar.

Basu, Swaraj. 2003. *Dynamics of a Caste Movement: The Rajbansis of North Bengal, 1910–1947*. New Delhi: Manohar.

Bayly, C.A. 1998. *Origins of Nationality in South Asia: Patriotism and Ethical Government in the Making of Modern India*. New Delhi: Oxford University Press.

Bayly, Susan. 1999. *Caste Society and Politics in India: From the Eighteenth Century to the Modern Age*. The New Cambridge History of India IV: 3. Cambridge: Cambridge University Press.

———. 1997. Caste and 'race' in colonial ethnography. In *The Concept of Race in South Asia* edited by Peter Robb. New Delhi: Oxford University Press.

Bellwinkel-Schempp, Maren. 2003. Pre-Ambedkar Buddhism in Uttar Pradesh. Paper presented at the IAHR Regional Conference on the Study of Religions in India, panel on Buddhism and Dalits. New Delhi, December.

———. 2002. Kabir Panthis in Kanpur: From sampradaya to dalit identity. In *Images of Kabir* edited by Monika Horstmann. New Delhi: Manohar.

Bezbarua, Lakshminath. 1968. *The Religion of Love and Devotion: Four Lectures on the Bhakti Movement of India*. Jorhat: Assam Sahitya Sabha.

Bhalekar, Krishnarao. 1877. *Baliba Patil*. Parbhani: Niramay Prakashan, 1998.

———. 1878 (?). *Krishnarao Bhalekar Samagra Vangmay: Satyashodhak Calvalitil Mahatma Phule yance Sahakari* (Collected Works of Krishnarao Bhalekar: Companion of Mahatma Phule in the Satyashodhak Movement). Ed. Sitaram Raykar. Pune: Mahatma Phule Samta Pratisthan Prakashan. 1998.

Bharatidasan, n.d. Poems translated by S. Blackburn, downloaded from www.apnaorg.com on 26 October 2005.

Briggs, George W. 1920. *The Chamars*. New Delhi: Low Price Publications, 1990.

———. 1938. *Gorakhnath and the Kanphata Yogis*. New Delhi: Motilal Banarsidass, 1982.

Bulog, Uradyn E. 1997. Mongols, Buddhism and modernity. *Bulletin of Concerned Asian Scholars* 29, 4.

Bulleh Shah. Trans. Suman Kashyap. Downloaded from www.apnaorg.com/suman/shah_poems/html on 15 September 2006.

Callewaert, Winand M., and Swapna Sharma. 2000. *The Hagiographies of Anantadas: The Bhakti Poets of North India*. Richmond: Curzon.

———., and Mukund Lath. 1989. *The Hindi Padavali of Namdev*. New Delhi: Motilal Banarsidass.

Chakravarty, Uma. 1998. *Rewriting History: The Life and Times of Pandita Ramabai*. New Delhi: Kali for Women.

Chandra, Sudhir. 1994. *The Oppressive Present: Literature and Social Consciousness in Colonial India*. New Delhi: Oxford University Press.

Chatterjee, Partha. 1993. *The Nation and its Fragments*. New Delhi: Oxford University Press.

———. 1988. Review of Satish Saberwal's *India: The Roots of Crisis*. *Contributions to Indian Sociology* 22, 1.

Chitre, Dilip. 2003. Tukanomics: Tukaram's view of money, wealth, value and human life. Paper at Tenth International Conference on Maharashtra: Culture and Society. Pune, 16-18 August.

———., trans. 1991. *Says Tuka: Selected Poetry of Tukaram*. New Delhi: Penguin.

Chokhamela. 1998. *Sant Chokhobance Abhang: Samiksha aani Samhita*. Ed. Ramesh Modi. Nagpur: Vijayi Prakashan.

———. 1987. *Sant Chokhamela Abhangvani*. Ed. M.S. Kanade and Bhalchandra Khandekar. Pune: Snehavardhan Publishing House.

Corbridge, Stuart, and John Harris. 2000. *Reinventing India: Liberalization, Hindu Nationalism and Popular Democracy*. Cambridge: Polity Press.

Dalmia, Vasudha. 2001. Forging community: The guru in a seventeenth century Vaisnava hagiography. In *Charisma and Canon: Essays in the Religious History of the Subcontinent* edited by Vasudha Dalmia, Angelika Malina and Martin Christof. New Delhi: Oxford University Press.

———. 1997. *The Nationalization of Hindu Tradition: Bharatendu Harischandra and Nineteenth Century Banaras*. New Delhi: Oxford University Press.

———. 1995. 'The only real religion of the Hindus': Vaisnava self-representation in the late eighteenth century. In *Representing Hinduism: The Construction of Religious Traditions and National Identity* edited by Vasudha Damia and Heinrich von Stietencron. New Delhi: Sage.

Dandekar, Ajay. 2003. In the name of pastoralism: The early medieval Maharashtra. In *Mobile and Marginalized Peoples: Perspectives from the Past* edited by Rudolf C. Heredia and Shereen F. Ratnagar. New Delhi: Manohar.

Dharwadker, Vinay, trans. 2003. *Kabir: The Weaver's Songs*. New Delhi: Penguin.

Deak, Dusan. 2005. Maharashtra sants and the Sufi tradition: Eknath,

Chand Bodhle and the Datta Sampradaya. *Deccan Studies* 3, 2.

———. 2001. The wandering minstrel. *The Hindu*, 23 September.

———. 1994. *The Cult of Vithoba*. Pune: Deccan College Postgraduate and Research Institute.

Devakala, D. 2005. *St. Thomas Dravidian Christianity and Iconography*. Chennai: Meipporul Publishers.

Deivanayagam, M. and D. Devakala, n.d. Origin of Hindu religion: Six-fold religion. http://www.geocities.com/Athens/Ithaca/1412/origin.html

Dharmatheertha, Swami. 2004. *No Freedom with Caste: The Menace of Hindu Imperialism*. Ed. G. Aloysius. New Delhi: Media House.

Dhere, R. C. 1984. *Shri Vitthal: Ek Mahasmanvay* (Shri Vitthal: A Great Confluence). Pune: Shri Vidya Prakashan.

Diehl, Anita. 1978. *E. V. Ramasami Naicker-Periyar: A Study of the Influence of a Personality in Contemporary South India*. Bombay: BI Publications.

Digby, Simon. 2003. The Sufi Shaikh as a source of authority in medieval India. In *India's Islamic Traditions* edited by Richard M. Eaton. New Delhi: Oxford University Press.

Dirks, Nicholas. 2002. *Castes of Mind: Colonialism and the Making of Modern India*. New Delhi: Permanent Black.

Dubois, Abbe J.A. 1906. *Hindu Manners, Customs and Ceremonies*. Trans. Henry K. Beauchamp. New Delhi: Asian Educational Services, 1996.

Eaton, Richard M. 2005. *A Social History of the Deccan, 1300–1700: Eight Indian Lives* (The New Cambridge History of India I–8). Cambridge: Cambridge University Press.

———. 2000. *Essays on Islam and Indian History*. New Delhi: Oxford University Press.

———. 1978. *Sufis of Bijapur 1300–1700: Social Roles of Sufis in Medieval India*. Princeton, New Jersey: Princeton University Press.

Engblom, Philip. 1987. Introduction to *Palkhi: An Indian Pilgrimage* by D.B. Mokashi. Trans. from the Marathi by Philip Engblom. Albany: SUNY Press.

Erande, Ashok Vishnupant. 1996. *Satyashodhak Mukundrao Patil*.

Ahmednagar: Sphurti Prakashan.

Ernst, Carl W. 2005. Situating Sufism and Yoga. *Journal of the Royal Asiatic Society*. Series 3: 15, 1

Eschmann, A. 1978. Mahima dharma: An autochthonous Hindu reform movement. In *The Cult of Jagannath and the Regional Tradition of Orissa* edited by Anncharlott Eschmann, Herman Kulke and G. Charu Tripathi. New Delhi: Manohar.

Ferguson, Harvie. 2000. *Modernity and Subjectivity*. Charlottesville: University Press of Virginia.

Fuller C.J., ed. 1997. *Caste Today*. New Delhi: Oxford University Press.

Gaikwad, Pradip, ed. 2000. *Kamgar Calval: Dr. Babasaheb Ambedkarnchi Niwadak Mashane va Lekh* (The Workers' Movement: Dr Babasaheb Ambedkar's Selected Speeches and Writings). Nagpur: Ksitij Publications.

Ganvir, Ratnakar, ed. *Mahad Samta Sangarsh* (The Mahad Struggle for Equality). Nagpur: Ratnamitra Prakashan

Gavaskar, Mahesh. 1999, Colonialism within colonialism: Phule's critique of brahman power. In *Dalits in Modern India: Visions and Values* edited by S.M. Michael. New Delhi: Vistaar.

Geetha, V. 2002. A Dangerous play with time: Brahmanism and the anxieties of history. Paper at the symposium 'Caste and Its Discontents: Rethinking the Nation'. A Symposium of the Southern Asian Institute, Columbia University, New York. 18 October.

———., and S.V. Rajadurai. 1998. *Towards a Non-Brahmin Millennium: From Iyothee Thass to Periyar*. Calcutta: Samya.

Gelders, Raf and William Derde. 2003. Mantras of anti-brahmanism: Colonial experience of Indian intellectuals. *Economic and Political Weekly*, 25 October.

Ghugare, Shivaprabha. 1983. *Renaissance in Western India: Karmaveer V.R. Shinde (1873–1944)*. Bombay: Himalaya Publishing House.

Glushkova, Irina. 2000. Norms and values in the varkari tradition. In *Intersections* edited by Meera Kosambi. New Delhi: Orient Longman.

Gooptu, Nandini. 1996. Caste and labour: Untouchable social movements in urban Uttar Pradesh in the early twentieth century.

In *Dalit Movements and the Meaning of Labour in India* edited by Peter Robb. New Delhi: Oxford University Press.

Gordon, Stewart. 1998. *The Marathas 1600–1818* (The New Cambridge History of India II.4). Cambridge: Cambridge University Press.

Gover, Charles. 1871. *Folk Songs of Southern India.* New Delhi: Rupa, 2002.

Government of Maharashtra. 1884. *Gazetteer of the Bombay Presidency: Vol. XX.* Sholapur, Bombay: Government Central Press (facsimile edition).

Guru, Sree Narayana. 1994. *The Song of the Self* (Atmopadesasathakam). Trans. from the Malayalam by K. Sreenivasan. Thiruvananthapuram: Jayasree Publications.

Habib, Irfan. 1987. *Caste and Money in Indian History*. Bombay: University of Bombay.

Hardgrave, Robert. 1969. *The Nadars of Tamil Nadu: The Political Culture of a Community in Change.* Berkeley: University of California Press.

Hardt, Michael and Antonio Negri. 2000. *Empire.* Cambridge, Mass.: Harvard University Press.

Hart, George L. 1995. Archetypes in classical Indian literature and beyond. *In Syllables of Sky: Studies in South Indian Civilization* edited by David Shulman. New Delhi: Oxford University Press.

Hawley, John Stratton. 2005. *Three Bhakti Voices: Mirabai, Surdas and Kabir in Their Times and Ours.* New Delhi: Oxford University Press.

Hawley, John Stratton and Mark Juergensmeyer. 1988. *Songs of the Saints of India.* Oxford University Press.

Hess, Linda. 1987. Kabir's rough rhetoric. In *The Sants: Studies in a Devotional Tradition of India* edited by Karine Schomer and W.H. McLeod. New Delhi: Motilal Banarsidass.

Horstmann, Monika, ed. 2002. *Images of Kabir.* New Delhi: Manohar

Hudson, D. Dennis. 1992. Arumuga Navalar and the Hindu renaissance among the Tamils. In *Religious Controversy in British India: Dialogues in South Asian Languages* edited by Kenneth W. Jones. Albany: SUNY Press.

Ikram, S.M. 1964. *Muslim Civilization in India.* Ed. Ainslee T. Embree. New York and London: Columbia University Press.

Irschick, Eugene. 1986. *Tamil Revivalism in 1930s*. Madras: Crea-A.

Iyothee Thass. 2001. "Selected Writings of Iyothee Thassar". Selected, translated, introduced and edited by G. Aloysius. Unpublished manuscript.

Jaffrelot, Christophe. 2005. *Dr Ambedkar and Untouchability: Fighting the Indian Caste System*. New York: Columbia University Press.

Jadhav, Ramesh. 2004. Krishnaji Arjun Keluskar's contribution to social thought in Maharashtra. In *Development in India: Anxieties and Alternative Paradigms, Essays in Honour of Professor S.N. Pawar* edited by R.B. Patil et al. Kolhapur.

Javale, B.G. 1999. *Pandharica Pandurang Bodhisatva Hota* (Pandurang of Pandhari was a Bodhisatva). Bid: Dolas Prakashan.

Javalkar, Dinkarrao. 1984. *Dinkarrao Javalkar Samagra Wangmay* (Collected Writings of Dinkarrao Javalkar). Ed. Y.D. Phadke. Pune: Vidya Prakashan.

Jnandev. 1997. *Shri Jnandev's Anubhavamrut: The Immortal Experience of Being*. Trans. from the Marathi by Dilip Chitre. New Delhi: Sahitya Akademi.

Joshi, Madhukar Ramdas. 2002. *Siddh Parampara ani Maharashtratil Sant* (The Siddha Tradition and the Sants of Maharasthra). Nagpur: Vijay Prakashan.

Kabir. 2003. *Kabir: The Weaver's Songs*. Trans. Vinay Dharwadker. New Delhi: Penguin.

———. 2003. *Kabir in Songs: The Muslical Tradition of a Great Religious Poet of India*. Trans. Linda Hess. New Delhi: Indian Council for Cultural Relations.

———. 2000. *The Millennium Kabir Vani: A Collection of Pads*. Winand M. Callewaert with Swapna Sharma and Dieter Tallieu. New Delhi: Manohar.

———. 1991. *Couplets from Kabir* (Kabir Dohe). Ed., Trans. and Comp. G.N. Das. Delhi: Motilal Banarsidass.

———. 1986. *The Bijak of Kabir*. Trans. Linda Hess and Shukdev Singh. New Delhi: Motilal Banarsidass.

———. 1977. *The Kabir Book: Forty-Four of the Ecstatic Poems of Kabir*. Trans. Robert Bly. Boston: Beacon Press.

———. 1997a. *Kabir Bijak*, Commentary Abhilash Das. Trans. Prem Prakash. Allahabad: Parakh Prakashak Kabir Sansthan.

———. 1915. *One Hundred Poems of Kabir*. Trans. Rabindranath Tagore with Evelyn Underhill. New Delhi: Macmillan, 1997.

Kailasapathy, K. 1987. The writings of the Tamil Siddhas. In *The Sants: Studies in a Devotional Tradition of India* edited by Karine Schomer and W.H. McLeod. New Delhi: Motilal Banarsidass.

Kaiwar, Vasant. 2005. Silences in postcolonial thought: The case of provincializing Europe. *Economic and Political Weekly*, 20 August.

Kamble, B.C., 1984–87. *Samagra Ambedkar-Charitra*. 8 Vols. (The Comprehensive Biography of Ambedkar). Mumbai.

Kanhopatra. n.d. Downloaded from http://www.geocities.com/sksearch/tukaram/kanhopatra.html on 20 January 2008.

Karashima, Noboru. 1997, The untouchable in Tamil inscriptions and other historical sources in Tamil Nadu. In *Caste System, Untouchability and the Depressed* edited by H. Kotani. New Delhi: Manohar.

Keer, Dhananjay. 1990. *Dr Ambedkar: Life and Mission*. Mumbai: Popular Prakashan.

———. 1974. *Mahatma Jotirao Phooley: Father of the Indian Social Revolution*. Bombay: Popular Prakashan.

Khairmode, C.B. 1959–1989. *Dr. Bhimrao Ramji Ambedkar*. 12 Vols. Pune: Sugawa.

Khare, R.S. 1984. *The Untouchable as Himself: Ideology, Identity and Pragmatism among the Lucknow Chamars*. Cambridge: Cambridge University Press.

Khan, Dominique-Sila. 2003. Muslim saints and Hindu rulers: The development of Sufi and Ismaili Mysticism in the Non-Muslim States of India. Downloaded from the website of The Institute of Ismaili Studies, http://www.iis.ac.uk/view_article.asp?ContentID=105018 on 10 January 2008.

Kopf, David. 1969. *British Orientalism and the Bengal Renaissance: The Dynamics of Indian Modernization, 1773–1835*. Berkeley: University of California Press.

Kosambi, D.D. 1975. *An Introduction to the Study of Indian History*. Second Rev. Edn. Bombay: Popular Prakashan.

Kosambi, Meera. 1992. Indian response to Christianity, church and colonialism: Case of Pandita Ramabai. *Economic and Political Weekly*, 31 October.

Kotani, H. 2000. Historical Formation of Hindu Identity in Relation to British Colonial Rule. In *Fusing Modernity: Appropriation of History and Political Mobilization in South Asia* edited by H. Kotani et al. Osaka: Japan Centre for Area Studies.

———. 1999. Kingship, state and local society in ritual functions: Maratha kingdom to Bombay government. In *Rituals as Popular Culture: Towards Historico-Anthropological Understanding of Indian Society* edited by Steering Committee of the Research Project: Institutions, Networks and Forces of Change in Contemporary South Asia.

———, ed. 1997. *Caste System, Untouchability and the Depressed.* New Delhi: Manohar.

Kurikilamkatt, James. 2005. *First Voyage of the Apostle Thomas to India.* Bangalore: Asian Trading Corporation.

Lach, Donald F. 1968. *India in the Eyes of Europe: The Sixteenth Century.* Chicago: University of Chicago Press.

Laine, James. 1998. Reflections on the meaning of *grhastha* in Maharashtrian culture. In *House and Home in Maharashtra* edited by Irina Gtlushkova and Anne Feldhaus. New Delhi: Oxford University Press.

———. 1996. Sivaji's mother. In *Images of Women in Maharashtrian Literature and Religion* edited by Anne Feldhaus. Albany: SUNY Press.

Latthe, A.B. 1924. *Memoirs of His Highness Shri Shahu Chhatrapati. Maharaja of Kolhapur.* Bombay: The Times Press.

Lele, Jayant. 1995. The political appropriation of bhakti: Hegemony and dominance in medieval Maharashtra. In his *Hindutva: The Emergence of the Right.* Madras: Earthworm Books.

Lorenzen, David, ed. 2004. *Religious Movements in South Asia 600–1800.* New Delhi: Oxford University Press.

———. 2002. Marco della Tomba and the Kabir-Panth. In *Images of Kabir* edited by Monika Horstmann. New Delhi: Manohar.

———. 1996. *Praises to a Formless God: Nirguni Texts from North India.* Albany: SUNY Press.

MacNicol, Nicol. 1926. *Pandita Ramabai: A Builder of Modern India.* Calcutta: Association Press.

Mahipati. 1933. *Bhaktavijaya* (Stories of Indian Saints). Trans. Justin E. Abbot and Narhar R. Godbole. New Delhi: Motilal Banarsidass, 1999.

Malik, Jamal. 2003. Muslim culture and reform in 18th century South Asia. *Journal of Royal Asiatic Society* 3: 13, 2.

Mali, Gajmal. 1996. *Gyanoba Krishnaji Sasane* (Biography of Gyanoba Krishnaji Sasane). Aurangabad: Rajmudra Prakashan.

Mallik, Basant Kumar. 2004. *Paradigms of Dissent and Protest: Social Movements in Eastern India (ca AD 1400–1700).* New Delhi: Manohar.

Mani, Braj Ranjan. 2005. *Debrahmanising History: Dominance and Resistance in Indian Society.* New Delhi: Manohar.

Mann, Gurinder Singh. 2001. *The Making of Sikh Scripture.* New Delhi: Oxford University Press.

Mannheim, Karl. 1936. *Ideology and Utopia: An Introduction to the Sociology of Knowledge.* Trans. from the German by Louis Wirth and Edward Shils. New York: Harvest Books.

McAdam, Doug, John D. McCarthy and Mayer N. Zald, eds. 1996. *Comparative Perspectives on Social Movements: Political Opportunities, Mobilizing Structures and Cultural Framings.* New York: Cambridge University Press.

Menon, Dilip. 2002. Religion and colonial modernity: Rethinking belief and identity. *Economic and Political Weekly*, 27 April.

Mira.1994. *Songs of Meera: In the Dark of the Heart.* Trans. Shama Futehally. New Delhi: HarperCollins.

———.1980. *The Devotional Poems of Mirabai.* Trans. A.J. Alston. New Delhi: Motilal Banarsidass.

Mishra, Vijay. 1999. *Devotional Poetics and the Indian Sublime.* Albany: SUNY Press.

Mohan, J. 2001. *History of Dalit Struggle for Freedom: Dravidian Parties and Dalit Uprise in Tamilnadu.* Pondicherry: Dhamma Institute of Social Sciences.

Moon, Vasant. 1987. *Madhyaprant-Varhadatil Dr. Ambedkarpurva Dalit Calval* (The Dalit Movement of Dr. Ambedkar in Madhya Pradesh and Vidarbha). Pune: Sugawa.

More, Sadanand. 2003. Sant Tukaram on money matters. Paper presented at the Tenth International Conference on Maharashtra: Culture and Society. Pune: 16–18 August.

———. 1996. *Tukaram Darshan*. Pune: Gaj Prakashan.

More, Thomas. 1516. T*he Best State of a Commonwealth and the New Island of Utopia*. In *The Complete Works of St Thomas More*, Vol. 4. Ed. Richard S. Sylvester. New Haven: Yale University Press. 1965.

Mukta, Parita. 1997. *Upholding the Common Life: The Community of Mirabai*. New Delhi: Oxford University Press.

Murugesan, K. and C.S. Subramanian. 1975. *Singaravelu: First Communist in South India*. New Delhi: People's Publishing House.

Namdev. 1999. *Sant Namdevance Abhanggaatha (*The Abhangs and Songs of Sant Namdev). Satara: Rashtriya Samiti.

———. 1989. *The Hindi Padavali of Namdev*. Ed. Winand M. Callewaert and Mukund Lath. New Delhi: Motilal Banarsidass.

Nanda, Meera. 2004. *Prophets Facing Backwards: Postmodernism, Science and Hindu Nationalism*. New Delhi: Permanent Black.

———. 2002. *Breaking the Spell of Dharma and Other Essays*. New Delhi: Three Essays Press.

Narasu P. Lakshmi. 1907. *The Essence of Buddhism*. New Delhi: Asian Educational Services, 1993.

———. 1905. *Religion of the Modern Buddhist*. Ed. G. Aloysius. New Delhi: Wordsmiths, 2002.

———. 1922. *A Study of Caste*. New Delhi: Asian Educational Services, 1988.

Norgaard, Richard. 1994. *Development Betrayed: The End of Progress and a Coevolutionary Revisioning of the Future*. New York: Routledge.

Novetzke, Christian Lee, 2005, The tongue makes a good book: History, religion, and performance in the Namdev tradition in Maharashtra. Ph.D. diss. abstract [forthcoming as a book]. www.sas.upenn.edu/~cln/Dissertation%20Abstract.htm

Oberschall, Anthony. 1993. *Social Movements: Ideologies, Interests and Identities.* New Brunswick and London: Transaction Publishers.

O'Hanlon, Rosalind. 1994. *A Comparison between Women and Men: Tarabai Shinde and the Critique of Gender Relations in Colonial India.* New Delhi: Oxford University Press.

———. 1985. *Caste, Conflict and Ideology: Mahatma Jotirao Phule and Low Caste Protest in Nineteenth-Century Western India.* Cambridge: Cambridge University Press.

———., and David Washbrook, 1991. History in transition: Approaches to the study of colonialism and culture in India. *History Workshop Journal* 32.

Omvedt, Gail. 2005. Perspectives of the anti-caste movements: Subaltern sociological visions. In *Understanding Indian Society: The Non-Brahmanic Perspective* edited by S.M. Dahiwale. New Delhi: Rawat Publications.

———. 2003. *Buddhism in India: Challenging Brahmanism and Caste.* New Delhi: Sage.

———., and Bharat Patankar. 2002. "Selected Writings of Mahatma Phule". Unpublished translation.

———. 1999. Dalits and economic policy: Contributions of Dr. B.R. Ambedkar. In *Dalits in Modern India; Vision and Values* edited by S.M. Michael. New Delhi: Sage.

———. 1994. *Dalits and the Democratic Revolution: Dr. Ambedkar and the Dalit Movement in Colonial India.* New Delhi: Sage.

———. 1976. *Cultural Revolt in a Colonial Society: The Non-Brahman Movement in Western India, 1873 to 1930.* Poona: Scientific Socialist Education Trust.

Oppert, Gustav. 1888. *The Original Inhabitants of Bharatvarsa or India.* New Delhi: Oriental Publishers, 1972.

Palany, Arangasamy. 1991. *Life and Works of Bharatidasan.* Thanjavur: Tamil University.

Palekar, Bhagvantrao. 1989. *'Jagrutikar' Bhagvantrao Paelkar Samagra Wangmay* (The Collected Writings of 'Jagrutikar' Bhagvantrao Palekar). Pune: Sugawa.

Palekar, Bhagvantrao. 1966. *Navya Manutla Maratha: "Jagruti" Patratil*

Nivadak Lekh (The Modern-Minded Maratha: Selected Writings from the *Jagruti* Paper). Baroda.

Pandharipande, Rajeshwari. 2000. Janabai: A woman saint of India. In *Women Saints in World Religions* (McGill Studies in the History of Religions) edited by Arvind Sharma. Albany: SUNY Press.

Pandian, M.S.S. 2003. Nation as nostalgia: Ambiguous spiritual journeys of Vengal Chakkarai. *Economic and Political Weekly*, 27 December.

———. 1995. Beyond colonial crumbs: Cambridge school, identity politics and Dravidian movement(s). *Economic and Political Weekly*, 25 February.

Pati, Biswamoy. 2001, Identity, hegemony, resistance: Conversions in Orissa, 1800–2000. *Economic and Political Weekly*, 3 November.

Patil, Mukundrao. 2001. *Dhaddhashastri Paranne*. Ahmednagar: Taravadi.

———. *Dinmitra Vicar-Kiran: DinMitratat Prasid Zhalele Nivadak Lekh*, Part 1, 1952. Part 2, 1956. Ahmednagar: Taravade.

Patil, Pandarinath Sitaram. 1927. *Mahatma Jotirao Phule Charitra* (Biography of Mahatma Jotirao Phule). Mumbai: Manovikas Prakashan, 2001.

Pennington, Brian K. 2005. *Was Hinduism Invented? Britons, Indians and the Colonial Construction of Religion*. New Delhi: Oxford University Press.

Petrievich, Carla. 2002. Making 'manly' poetry: The construction of Urdu's 'Golden Age'. In *Rethinking Early Modern India* edited by Richard Barnett. New Delhi: Manohar.

Phule, Jotirao. 2002. *Selected Writings of Jotirao Phule*. Ed., with annotations and introduction by G. P. Deshpande. New Delhi: LeftWord.

———. 1991. *Mahatma Phule Samagra Wangmay* (Mahatma Phule's Collected Writings). Ed. Y.D. Phadke. Mumbai: Maharashtra Rajya Sahitya ani Sanskriti Mandal.

Phule, Savritibai. 1988. *Savitribai Phule Samagra Wangmay*. Ed. M.G. Mali. Mumbai: Maharashtra Rajya Sahitya ani Sanskriti Mandal.

Pinch, William. 1996. *Peasants and Monks in British India*. New Delhi: Oxford University Press.

———. 1999. Devotion and the search for Nabhadas of Galta. In

Invoking the Past: The Uses of History in South Asia edited by Daud Ali. New Delhi: Oxford University Press.

Pollock, Sheldon. 1998. India in the vernacular millennium: Literary culture and polity, 1000–1500. *Daedalus* 127.

———. 2001. New intellectuals in seventeenth century India. *The Indian Economic and Social History Review* 38, 1.

Rajadurai, S.V. 1998. When memory dies... *Periyar Era*. September.

Rajaram, P. 1988. *The Justice Party: A Historical Perspective, 1917–1937*. Madras: Poompozhil Publishers.

Rajendran, N. 1994. *National Movement in Tamil Nadu, 1905–1914*. New Delhi: Oxford University Press.

Ramabai, Pandita. 1977. *The Letters and Correspondence of Pandita Ramabai*. Comp. Sister Geraldine. Ed. A.B. Shah. Bombay: Maharashtra State Board for Literature and Culture.

———. 1981. *The High-Caste Hindu Woman*. Bombay: Maharashtra State Board for Literature and Culture.

Ramamurtti, P. 1987. *The Freedom Struggle and the Dravidian Movement*. Hyderabad: Orient Longman.

Ramanujan, A.K. 1973. *Speaking of Siva*. New Delhi: Penguin.

Ramasamy, E.V. 'Periyar'. 2004. *Periyar on Islam*. Trans. and introduced by G. Aloysius. New Delhi: Critical Quest.

———. 2005. *Collected Works of Periyar EVR*. Comp. K. Veeramani. Chennai: Periyar Self-Respect Propaganda Institution

Ranade, M.G. 1900. *Rise of the Maratha Power*. New Delhi: Government of India, Publications Division, 1990.

Ravidas. 2001. *Holy Hymns and Miracles of Guru Ravidass Ji*. (Translations from the Punjabi of the Adi Granth.) Jalandhar: Shri Guru Ravidass Janam Asthan Public Charitable Trust.

———. 1988. In Hawley, John Straughton, and Mark Juergensmeyer. *Songs of the Saints of India*. New Delhi: Oxford University Press.

———. 2007. Downloaded from http://www.geocities.com/pritpal_bindra/s-014.html on 1 October, 2007.

Ravikumar. 2003. Periyar's hindutva. 3 September. Downloaded from www.outlookindia.com on 10 September 2003.

Rhys-Davids. T.W. 1917. *Buddhist India*. New Delhi: Motilal Banarsidass, 1997.

Richards, John. 1997. Early modern India and world history. *Journal of World History* 8, 2.

Roy, Rammohun. 1958. Selections. In *Sources of Indian Tradition* edited by William Theodore de Bary, Stephen N. Hay, Royal Weiler and Andrew Yarrow. New York: Columbia University Press.

Saberwal, Satish. 1987. *India: Roots of Crisis*. New Delhi: Oxford University Press.

———. 1988. Roots of crisis: A response to Partha Chatterjee. *Contributions to Indian Sociology* 22.

Saeed, Salman. 2001. The grand master: Baba Farid Shakar Ganj of Pak Pattan [AD 11733–1266]. Downloaded from http://www.the-south-asian.com/April2001/Sufis-wisdom%20against%20violence3.htm on 10 January 2008.

———. 2001. Bulleh Shah [1680-1758]. Downloaded from http://www.the-south-asian.com/April2001/Sufis-wisdom%20against%20violence5.htm on 10 January 2008.

Sahadevan, M. 1993. *Towards Social Justice and Nation-Making: A Study of Sahodaran Ayyappan*. Palakkad: Sophum.

Salunkhe, A. H. 1999. *Tukaramancha Sheti* (The Agriculture of Tukaram). Kolhapur: Express Publishing House.

———. 1997. *Vidrohi Tukaram* (Tukaram the Rebel). Pune: Gopal Mokashi.

Sarkar, Sumit. 2000. Identities and histories: Some lower-caste narratives from early 20th Century Bengal. In *Fussing Modernity: Appropriation of History and Political Mobilization in South Asia* edited by H. Kotani et al. Osaka: Japan Centre for Area Studies.

———. 1997. *Writing Social History*. New Delhi: Oxford University Press.

Sartori, Andrew. 2004. Emancipation as heteronomy: The crisis of liberalism in later nineteenth-century Bengal. *Journal of Historical Sociology* 17, 1.

Sastri, Nilakantha K.A. 1975. *A History of South India from Prehistoric Times to the Fall of Vijayanagar*. New Delhi: Oxford University Press.

———. 1963. *Development of Religion in South India*. Hyderabad: Orient Longman.

Schouten, J.P. 1995. *Revolution of the Mystics: On the Social Aspects of Virasaivism*. New Delhi: Motilal Banarsidass.

Schomer, Karine and W. H. McLeod, eds. 1987. *The Sants: Studies in a Devotional Tradition in India*. New Delhi: Motilal Banarsidass.

Searle-Chatterji, Mary. 1994. Caste, religion and other identities. In *Contextualising Caste: Post-Dumontian Approaches* edited by Mary Searle-Chatterjee and Ursula Sharma. Oxford: Blackwell.

Sellergren, Sarah. 1996. Janabai and Kanhopatra: A study of two women saints. In *Images of Women in Maharashtrian Literature and Religion* edited by Anne Feldhaus. Albany: SUNY Press.

Shah, Idris. 1964. *The Sufis*. New York: Anchor Books.

Shahu Maharaj. 1978. *Rajarshi Shahu Chhatrapati Papers*. Vol. I. 1884–1894 (Adoption to Installation). Ed. A.G. Pawar. Kolhapur: Shahu Research Institute, Shivaji University.

———. 1985. *Rajarshi Shahu Chhatrapati Papers*. Vol. III (1900–1905) (Vedokta Controversy). Ed. Vilas Sangave and B.D. Khane. Kolhapur: Shahu Research Institute, Shivaji University.

———. 1994. *Rajarshi Shahu Chhatrapati Papers*. Vol. VI (1910–1913) (Initiation of Social Economic Movement). Ed. Vilas Sangave. Kolhapur: Shahu Research Institute, Shivaji University.

Sharma, Krishna. 1987. *Bhakti and the Bhakti Movement: A New Perspective. A Study in the History of India*. New Delhi: Munshiram Manorharlal.

Shinde, Tarabai. 2000. *A Comparison Between Women and Men: Tarabai Shinde and the Critique of Gender Relations in Colonial India*. Trans. and Introduced by Rosalind O'Hanlon. New Delhi: Oxford University Press.

Shinde, Shripatrao. 1993. *Nivadak Vijayi Maratha* (Selections from *Vijayi Maratha* newspaper). Ed. Jaysinghrao Pawar and Ramesh Jadhav. Kolhapur: Vijaya Maratha Prakashan.

Shinde, Vitthal Ramji. 1991. *Mazhya Athvani va Anubhav* (My Memories and Experiences). Pune: Shubhda-Sarasvat Prakashan.

Shitre, N.D. 1995. *Mi Pahilele Satyashodhak: 'DinMitra' Kar Raosaheb Mukundrao Patil* (The Satyashodhak I have Known: Raosaheb

Mukundrao Patil of 'DinMitra'). Ahmednagar: Taravade.

Shukru, A. 1994. Caste: A personal perspective. In *Contextualising Caste: Post-Dumontian Approaches* edited by Mary Searle-Chatterjee and Ursula Sharma. Oxford: Blackwell.

Sikand, Yoginder. 2002. The Chishti Sufi saints of India. *Qalandar*, 12 May.

———. 2003, Re-imagining Sikh-Muslim relations in the light of the life of Baba Nanak. Downloaded from http://www.theamericanmuslim.org on 2 September 2006.

Singh, Shukdeo. 2002. The sants and the struggle against brahman dominance. In *Images of Kabir* edited by Monika Horstmann. New Delhi: Manohar.

Sivathamby, K. 1995. *Understanding the Dravidian Movement: Problems and Perspectives*. Madras: New Century Book House.

Smith, David. 2003. *Hinduism and Modernity*. Oxford: Blackwell.

Soifer, Deborah A. 2001. *The Myths of Narasimha and Vamana: Two Avatars in Cosmological Perspective*. Albany: SUNY Press.

Srivatsan, R. 2005. Native noses and nationalist zoos: Debates in colonial and early nationalist anthropology of castes and tribes. *Economic and Political Weekly*, 7 May.

Stein, Burton. 1980. *Peasant State and Society in Medieval South India*. New York: Oxford University Press.

Subrahmanyan, Sanjay. 2002. The window that was India: The place of South Asia in early modern history. Keynote address, 31st Annual Conference on South Asia, Madison, Wisconsin, 11 October.

———., ed. 1994. *Money and the Market in India, 1100–1700*. New Delhi: Oxford University Press.

———., ed. 1990. *Merchants, Markets and the State in Early Modern India*. New Delhi: Oxford University Press.

Subramaniam, Narendra. 1999. *Ethnicity and Populist Mobilization: Political Parties, Citizens and Democracy in South India*. New Delhi: Oxford University Press.

Sunthankar, B.R. 1993. *Maharashtra 1858–1920*. Bombay: Popular Book Depot.

Tavakoli-Targhi. 1998. Modernity, heterotopia, and homeless texts. *Comparative Studies of South Asia, Africa and the Middle East* XVIII: 2.

Taylor, Charles. 2002. Modern social imaginaries. *Public Culture* 14: 1.

Tilak, Laxmibai. 1998. *I Follow After: An Autobiography*. Trans. E. Josephine Inkster. New Delhi: Oxford University Press.

Thorat, S.K. 1998. *Ambedkar's Role in Economic Planning and Water Policy*. New Delhi: Shipra.

Thirumaavalavan, Thol. 2001. *Talisman. Extreme Emotions of Dalit Liberation*. Trans. from the Tamil by Meena Kandasamy. Kolkata: Samya.

Toulmin, Stephen. 1990. *Cosmopolis: The Hidden Agenda of Modernity*. New York: The Free Press.

Tukaram. 2000. *The Poems of Tukaram*. Translated and Re-arranged with Notes and Introduction by J. Nelson Fraser and K.B. Marathe. Delhi: Motilal Banarsidass.

———. 1991. *Says Tuka: Selected Poetry of Tukaram*. Trans. from the Marathi with an Introduction by Dilip Chitre. New Delhi: Penguin.

———. 1990. *Punha Tukaram* (Tukaram Once Again). Ed. Dilip Chitre. Mumbai: Popular Prakashan.

———. 1973. *Shri Tukarambavancya Abhangaci Gatha*. (Marathi collection of Tukaram's Abhangs.) Mumbai: Shaskiya Madhyavati Mudranalay.

Ugale, G. A. 2004. *Dnyanoday ani Mahatma Phule* (Dyanoday and Mahatma Phule). Vardha: Kandid Prakashan.

Urban, Hugh B. 2001a. *Songs of Ecstasy: Tantric and Devotional Songs from Colonial Bengal*. New York: Oxford University Press.

———. 2001b. *The Economics of Ecstasy: Tantra, Secrecy and Power in Colonial Bengal*, New York: Oxford University Press.

van Buitenen, J.A. 1966. On the archaism of the Bhagawata Purana. In *Krishna: Myths, Rites and Attitudes* edited by Milton Singer. Chicago and London: The University of Chicago Press.

———., (trans), with Cornelia Dimmitt (ed.). 1978. *Classical Hindu Mythology: A Reader in the Sanskrit Puranas*. Philadelphia: Temple University Press.

van der Veer, Peter. 2001. *Imperial Encounters: Religion and Modernity in India and Britain.* New Jersey: Princeton University Press.

Vaudeville, Charlotte. 1993. *A Weaver Named Kabir: Selected Verses with a Detailed Biographical and Historical Introduction.* New Delhi: Oxford University Press.

———. 1987. Sant mat: Santism as the universal path to sanctity. In *The Sants: Studies in a Devotional Tradition in India* edited by Karine Schomer and W. H. McLeod, eds. New Delhi: Motilal Banarsidass.

Venkatachalapathy, A.R. 1995. Dravidian movement and Saivites: 1927–1944. *Economic and Political Weekly*, 8 April.

Viswanathan, Gauri. 1998. *Outside the Fold: Conversion, Modernity, and Belief.* New Delhi: Oxford University Press.

Visswanathan, E. Sa. 1983. *The Political Career of E. V. Ramasamy Naicker: A Study in the Politics of Tamilnadu* 1929–1949. Madras: Ravi and Vasant Publishers.

Wakankar, Milind. 2005. The anomaly of Kabir: Culture and canonicity in Indian modernity. In *Muslims, Dalits and the Fabrications of History*, Subaltern Studies Vol. 12, edited by Ajay Skaria, M.S.S. Pandian, Shail Mayaram. New Delhi: Permanent Black.

Weber, Max. 1904. *The Protestant Ethic and the Spirit of Capitalism.* In *Knowledge and Postmodernism in Historical Perspective* edited by Joyce Appleby et al. New York and London: Routledge.

White, David Gordon. 1996. *The Alchemical Body: The Siddha Tradition in Medieval India.* Chicago: University of Chicago Press.

———. ed., 2000. *Tantra in Practice.* Princeton: Princeton University Press.

Wink, Andre. 1991. *Al-Hind: The Making of the Indo-Islamic World.* Vol. 1. *Early Medieval India and the Expansion of Islam, 7th–11th Centuries.* Leiden: E.J. Brill.

Wolpert, Stanley. 1984. *Jinnah of Pakistan.* New Delhi: Oxford University Press.

Zelliot, Eleanor. 1995. Chokhamela: Piety and protest. In *Bhakti Religion in North India* edited by David Lorenzen. Albany: SUNY Press.

———. 1992. *From Untouchable to Dalit: Essays on the Ambedkar Movement.* New Delhi: Manohar.

———. 1969. Dr. Ambedkar and the mahar movement. Ph.D. diss. University of Pennsylvania.

———., and Rohini Mokashi-Punekar, eds. 2004. *Untouchable Saints: An Indian Phenomenon*. New Delhi: Manohar.

———., and V.L. Manjul, eds. 2002. *Sant Chokamela Vividh Darshan* (Various Glimpses of Sant Chokamela). Pune: Sugawa.

Journals and newspapers in Marathi

Bahishkrut Bharat (Mumbai, 1927–1929)

Din Bandhu (Pune)

Din Mitra (Ahmednagar)

Jagruti (Pune)

Janata (Mumbai)

Mooknayak (Mumbai)

Rashtravir (Belgaum)

Vijayi Maratha (Kolhapur)

Index